The Sitcoms of Norman Lear

The Sitcoms of Norman Lear

SEAN CAMPBELL

McFarland & Company, Inc., Publishers
Jefferson, North Carolina, and London

LIBRARY OF CONGRESS CATALOGUING-IN-PUBLICATION DATA

Campbell, Sean, 1989–
 The sitcoms of Norman Lear / Sean Campbell.
  p.   cm.
 Includes bibliographical references and index.

 ISBN-13: 978-0-7864-2763-5
 (softcover : 50# alkaline paper) ∞

 1. Comedy programs— United States— History and criticism.
 2. Lear, Norman — Criticism and interpretation.   I. Title.
 PN1992.8.C66C36   2007
 791.45'6 — dc22   2006030950

British Library cataloguing data are available

On the cover: *(insets on left, top to bottom)* Redd Foxx in *Sanford and Son,*
the casts of *One Day at a Time, All in the Family,* and *Good Times,* Bill Macy
in *Maude,* the cast of *The Jeffersons;* (right) Norman Lear

Manufactured in the United States of America

McFarland & Company, Inc., Publishers
 Box 611, Jefferson, North Carolina 28640
  www.mcfarlandpub.com

To all the people involved in the creation
of the sitcoms discussed,
especially those involved with this book:
Rue McClanahan
Bill Macy
Susan Harris
Franklin Cover
Marla Gibbs
Lou Richards
...and of course: Norman Lear

Acknowledgments

I'd like to thank the people I interviewed for this book for their cooperation. I learned so much from communicating with Rue McClanahan, Bill Macy, Susan Harris, Marla Gibbs, Lou Richards, and the late Franklin Cover, who helped me even though he was very sick. Thanks also to Bill Macy and Franklin Cover for donating pictures.

I'd like to thank three individuals for providing me with episodes of certain shows discussed in this book — Solomon Davis, Paul Bruker, and especially Dan Fingerman, who loaned me over 100 episodes of Norman Lear sitcoms, including the rarest ones.

Then there are three individuals who have served as surrogate fathers to me over the years, James Ferrara, Carlos Nodarse, and Richard Simpson.

Other people who helped along the way include Margaret O'Hagan, Jacqueline Dougherty, Kathy Marquet, Edward Loccke, Gloria Vaccarella, Daniel Kurz, Victor Lynch, Michael Labat, Barbara Lasher, Heather Lawler, Silvana Forne-Neves, Suzanne Halligan, Richard Weems, and Allison Hammonds. And I'd like to acknowledge all my friends, especially those who knew about the book since I started writing it in 2004: Ade, Aria, Bryan, Trina, and Yousef.

Thank you to my neighbors, the Sullivans, whom I consider to be family. Next are my cousins, Jason, Brian, Heather, Kathleen, and Andrea. My great grandmother Mary was the one who initially got me to watch these Norman Lear sitcoms — I remember watching *Sanford and Son* and *All in the Family* with her for the first time. My grandmother Sharon has supported me and my goals longer than anyone else I can remember. My grandfather Phil's principles are forever invoked inside of me. Then there is my aunt and uncle, Michele and Sal, and my grandfather Edward, and my godparents, the Beckers. A special thank you to the people I live with, my mother, my father, and my brother Brendan, who motivate me to persevere as an individual each day that I wake up. And finally, my unforgettable grandmother Tricia has had more of an impact on me than anyone else.

Table of Contents

Preface

As a young boy growing up, watching reruns of past television sitcoms such as the ones discussed in this book, I found television characters fascinating. They always had me laughing, but the thing that really attracted me to them was that I kept learning from their mistakes and their successes. Soon after, I realized that television must have had a major impact on the American public, because it had a major impact on me. I learned many important lessons from watching Norman Lear's sitcoms. From *Maude*, I learned that alcoholism is a disease; from *All in the Family*, I learned that there is nothing wrong with being gay; and from *Good Times*, I learned about the integrity of the poor. Early on, I made the conclusion that many others must have learned similar lessons.

The Sitcoms of Norman Lear focuses on Lear's illustrious career during the 1970s, and how the sitcoms he created in that span reflected the political and cultural agenda. It discusses how his shows provided solutions for certain national issues, and how they impacted the American people as individuals and as a nation. For example, many episodes became public service announcements acknowledging the need for blood donations, the importance of *safe* sex for teenagers, and the necessity of having cost-of-living escalation clauses in job contracts.

The first six chapters each talk about a specific show (*All in the Family*, *Sanford and Son*, *Maude*, *Good Times*, *The Jeffersons*, and *One Day at a Time*, respectively), while the seventh chapter discusses Norman Lear's final successes and failures as a television producer. Each chapter runs through its respective sitcom from start to finish. Episodes discussing the same issues are grouped and discussed in the same section.

A fair amount of analysis on Lear's work has already been published. But a sizable portion of the current analysis is critical, saying that Lear's shows had an adverse effect on America, by reinforcing stereotypes. I disagree with this perspective, so this piece looks at the same shows and discusses how America was influenced *positively*. I expand on the issues discussed in other books by considering the scope of Lear's influence. For example, I look at how *Sanford and Son*'s portrayal of senior citizens challenged stereotypes, how *One Day at a Time* expanded the parameters for sexy language in future television, and how *Mary Hartman, Mary Hartman* was used by psychiatrists to discuss issues with their patients.

Unlike many other books about television, this book contains statistics and quotes from newspaper pages outside the entertainment section. Many editorials are quoted, where people wrote about how they felt about the shows on the air. This book includes how the viewing public responded to the debut of *All in the Family*, Edith Bunker's narrow escape from being raped, Maude's abortion, and Tom and Helen Willis' mixed marriage.

I also interviewed some of the actors and writers from the shows: Bill Macy and Rue McClanahan of *Maude*, Susan Harris, who wrote the episode of *Maude* dealing with abortion, Franklin Cover and Marla Gibbs of *The Jeffersons*, and Lou Richards of *Gloria*. Their words are quoted in the text of the book, and are cited in the text and footnotes as a "personal interview." (If that terminology is used anywhere in a section, then everything that person says in that section is from a personal interview, not quoted from another published source.)

The final thing I would like to address is why an analysis of Norman Lear's sitcoms is important. The shows discussed in the book have been seen by millions of people, not only in America, but all over the world. Lear's shows have impacted the lives of many viewers, and even those not personally affected by his work have witnessed its influence — these shows paved the way for such groundbreaking series as *Will and Grace*, *Friends*, and *Commander in Chief*. And finally, the sitcoms of Norman Lear contain images of the way we would *not* want to live our lives, images of the way we actually live our lives, and images of the way we *want* to live our lives.

1

The Founding Family: Arrrrchie, Dingbat, Meathead, and Little Goil

In 1971, Norman Lear created the most notable figure in television — a gray-haired, blue-collar breadwinner in his late forties. This man had a quizzical face with chubby cheeks and wore a crisp white buttoned-down shirt with black pants — unless he was sporting his Disneyland shirt. Archie Bunker was a dyed-in-the-wool Brooklynite who believed in the days when "everybody pulled his weight" and "freaks were in a circus tent." The sophomoric, reactionary Archie Bunker represented the political perspectives of old-fashioned conservatives throughout America, who were collectively asking in consternation, "Why change? Why now? Why me?" In a decade filled with liberal protests and civil unrest, all of America, including the liberal demographic, turned to the Bunkers to enjoy a cornucopia of laughs that ultimately mocked their number one target — politics. At the same time, in mocking Archie Bunker, they mocked bigotry. By the mid–1970s, more than fifty million people gathered around their television sets each week to laugh *at* the malapropist Archie as he associated Asians with "chinkiepuncture," Italians with barbers, Jews with lawyers, female athletes with "hismones," and homosexuals with "four dollar bills." America loved watching Archie cite the Bible, accidentally join the Ku Klux Klan, or fear the apocalypse — his wife Edith's menopause.

But *All in the Family* was not a half-hour block of racial and political epithets in CBS's schedule. If it was, the show would have never made it past its initial season of thirteen weeks. Archie and his wife, Edith, had a daughter named Gloria. Her new husband Mike lived with them while Mike was going to college. Mike Stivic was a bleeding-heart liberal and therefore detested everything Archie Bunker ever uttered. Archie could not make a comment about the state of the world without Mike questioning how moral it was or how much sense it made. Archie's bigotry was never praised on *All in the Family*, as Mike (as well as daughter Gloria and spouse Edith) would not let Archie get away with his distorted views of life.

Archie and Mike disagreed on nearly everything — from the importance of war, to the status of the ecology and the economy, to the way to make a bed. The verbal fisticuffs that went on week after week, month after month, and year after year in the shell-shocked Bunker home made viewers laugh the most. Two grown men had convictions on the opposite sides of America's political continuum. And when these two adults argued over their creeds, they usually sounded like children.

Archie was usually shown to be the most puerile. But he possessed innate love for family. He yelled because he was trying to make his family better off, even though his advice was usually off the mark. As a child and as an adult, he believed his father was omniscient. "How can a man who loves you tell you anything that is wrong?" he once asked Mike.[1] Archie's prejudice was inherited. It was all he knew, because it was all his father knew. He also loved his "little goil," and he could not live without his wife Edith. And Archie cried when Mike told him he loved him as he left for a new life in California — with his little goil. Indeed, there was a sensitive side to Archie Bunker.

As they laughed and cried with the Bunkers, America heard the various messages that *All in the Family* proposed each week. Thousands of pins and bumper stickers reading "Archie Bunker for President" were sold. And who said it was only a TV show?

In the 1970s, *All in the Family* became much more than a sitcom. It became a mirror of society.

Before the Bunkers

In 1967, Norman Lear was watching television with the rest of America. Only he was watching British television — an industry light years ahead of the one he was a part of in Hollywood. The successful British sitcom *Till Death Us Do Part* was like nothing he had seen on television before. Instantly, Lear was inspired. The main character, Alf Garnett (Warren Mitchell), was a reactionary bigot, married to the stupefied Else (Dandy Nichols). The show's conflict originated between Alf and his live-in son-in-law, Mike (Anthony Booth). Mike was young and his opinions were far from Alf's. Mike was married to Alf and Else's daughter, Rita (Una Stubbs). *Till Death Us Do Part* became a staple in pop culture in Britain during the 1960s, mainly because the primary character, Alf, was a "lovable bigot." Even for naturally edgy British programming, *Till Death Us Do Part* still managed to push the envelope quite a bit.

Does the format sound familiar?

For Norman Lear, the scenario resembled his life. When Lear watched *Till Death Us Do Part*, it reminded Lear of his family; mainly his feuds with

Norman Lear basking in his fame on *The John Davidson Show*, ten years after *All in the Family*— the show that will forever be linked to his name — debuted.

his father. "We never agreed about anything; we fought about everything," Lear once said. "I'd tell him he was a bigot, he'd call me a goddamn bleedin'-heart liberal, and we were both right — but also wrong."[2] Lear thought to himself, "My father and I fought all those battles. My God, if I could only get this kind of thing on American television."[3]

Lear had not really been involved in television since the 1950s, when he and Richard Simmons were writers for *The Martin and Lewis Show*. He was successful while producing motion pictures in the 1960s, but since then, there had been a revolution in television. Sitcoms with bucolic settings ruled the network. The farm life was the major source of entertainment in the 1960s. For millions, it provided an arcadia from the tense Vietnam War, the tragic Kennedy assassinations, and for people like Archie Bunker, the zany counterculture. Lear was sick and tired of the interminable "perfect family" that, in the end, was anything but perfect. There were no echoes of everyday people in those characters. They seemed to live in a world where political and racial tensions were nonexistent. Their world was one full of chocolate chip cookies and family fishing trips. There were no Archie Bunkers on television; there were neither Norman Lears nor Mike Stivics. Lear sought for a television revolution — television shows that could promote discussion modeled after the trenchant opinions of the characters that viewers adulated. This, he hoped, would result in any director's dream — untouchable ratings. Lear was ready to take America on a rollercoaster ride — a quick turn from that bucolic simplicity depicted by shows such as *Green Acres* and *The Beverly Hillbillies*. The ride would screech right in front of the television sets tuned to these shows, right in the living room of a middle class American family.

Back in 1959, Lear and Bud Yorkin became partners in a company called Tandem Productions. In 1968, Lear and Yorkin pitched to ABC the idea for a show with a politically active setting filled with characters resembling Lear and his father. The network decided to pursue the idea. Lear and Yorkin wrote a pilot script titled *Those Were the Days*. The main character, Archie Justice, was living in the present, although he wished he were part of the previous generation. Lear offered the role to Mickey Rooney, but he declined, telling Lear, "If you go on the air with that, they're going to kill you dead in the streets."[4] However, Carroll O'Connor decided to take that chance. Not yet the recipient of a star on Sunset Boulevard, Irish American actor O'Connor was cast as Archie Justice. Lear reminisced in 2000, "I'll never forget the day that Carroll O'Connor walked into this office on Sunset Boulevard and sat down. I don't recall whether he rattled off a few lines or just slipped into the character or read a half a page. But he was Archie."[5] Lear originally sent the pilot script to O'Connor's home after seeing his performance in the film *What Did You Do in the War, Daddy?* "I saw O'Connor in a combination of bombast and sweetness. I needed both," said Lear in 1971.[6] Much of the credit for Archie Bunker's fame goes to O'Connor, who greatly assisted in the development of the character. Lear said, "Carroll O'Connor was the best writer for Archie we ever had."[7]

Next, Jean Stapleton was cast for the part of Archie's long-suffering wife, Edith. Stapleton, who became America's favorite mother, had been discovered in the Broadway play *Damn Yankees*. Lear recruited Stapleton because of her impeccable timing. "I have this thing about actors. I remember moments," recalled Lear in 1972. "She did this song in *Damn Yankees*. No, I didn't say to myself 'Now, this lady is *it*.' She read, then I knew."[8] Stapleton had confidence in *All in the Family* from the day she met Lear. She thought his show would be a hit. "I was optimistic from the beginning. I just thought it was so good and so true that it would have to be appreciated."[9] However, Stapleton was also surprised at what she was reading. "This on TV?" she wondered with amusement.[10]

Stapleton's television son-in-law was Robert (Tim McIntire), married to her daughter, Gloria (Kelly Jean Peters). Robert and Gloria were both liberals, much to Archie's disgust. This started wars based on politics, beginning in the pilot script. It was Archie and Edith's twenty-third wedding anniversary.

Robert and Gloria planned a quiet at-home celebration, that is, until politics totally ruined the tête-à-tête that they had hoped for.

With ABC's blessing, Tandem proceeded and taped the episode. However, Lear, Yorkin, and ABC were not satisfied with the performances of the supporting actors. McIntire and Peters lost their roles as Robert and Gloria. ABC funded a second pilot, keeping O'Connor and Stapleton in place in the starring roles. The plot remained the same, but with different supporting actors.

While all this was taking place, ABC tried to spin-off the popular *Rowan and Martin's Laugh-In*. But the product they aired, called *Turn-On*, was an absolute turn-off to all audiences. It was cancelled after one episode, and ABC lost both money and credibility. This contretemps greatly threatened the future of *Those Were the Days*. Greatly terrified of being responsible for subsequent flops, ABC could not gamble with this new controversial sitcom. After spending $250,000, the network withdrew from the project, fearing the potential to lose millions more.

Lear and Yorkin called it quits after ABC rejected *Those Were the Days*. But then, unexpectedly, the new head of programming at CBS, Robert Wood, was desperately looking for scripts just like *Those Were the Days*. Wood wanted to change the genre of programming on the network to something politically relevant; he wanted to diverge from the apolitical shows of the 1960s. He planned to designate certain time slots for shows that would attract a younger audience. It was a new decade, Wood wanted change, and he felt that Lear's proposed series was compatible to the network's needs. When Tandem Productions got a call from Wood, Lear contemplated proposing the idea to them. If he went with CBS, he would have to relinquish three movie opportunities. He went with them, despite his wife, Frances, pleading, "Don't do it, don't go back to television when this [the movies] is sitting here."[11] Lear then dug out the old script that was collecting dust in his office. Wood liked what he saw and wanted to finish what ABC had started. He decided to tape a third pilot, and was excited about what was going to happen for CBS. He declared in a press conference, "It's time to poke fun at ourselves."[12] Wood had to be quite assertive among his peers, especially long-time CBS chairman William S. Paley, whose chair was in the conservative spectrum, nowhere near Wood's. Paley censured the thought of such a show, but Wood told him, "You can sit on your front porch on a rocking chair, collecting your dividends on what you've created. A parade will be coming down the street and you may watch it from your rocking chair and get into the parade, so that when it goes by your house you won't just be watching it, you'll be leading it."[13] The parade he was referring to became the epic *All in the Family*. By this point, things were moving for Lear.

In response, Lear set out to find new supporting actors, and found Rob

The cast of *All in the Family* in 1971. (Top row, from left to right: Sally Struthers, Mike Evans, Rob Reiner. Bottom row, from left to right: Jean Stapleton, Carroll O'Connor.)

Reiner and Sally Struthers. Reiner and Struthers, who played Mike and Gloria Stivic, had known each other before they collided on the set of *All in the Family*— they had dated in the 1960s.[14] Rob Reiner knew from the start that he was part of something spectacular — but he was unsure of the show's future. "Never in my wildest dreams did I think it was going to go past thirteen weeks because it was, as we say in the parlance of stand-up comics, too hip for the room. And that was fine, too, because we just wanted to be part of something special and different and groundbreaking," Reiner told *TV Guide*.[15] Lear had known Reiner for some time. Lear was good pals with his father, Carl, who created *The Dick Van Dyke Show*. The younger Reiner had been exposed to show business since he was a kid.

Before getting the part, Sally Struthers was in the position of many Hollywood actors and actresses— unemployed. She was living in a small apartment, taking odd jobs to collect the rent money, which was $85 per month. "I was embarrassed every time I was in the unemployment office," she told *TV Guide* in 1974. "But I had no choice but to swallow my pride. Fortunately, I collected only ten weeks before my agent got me a job."[16] From then on, Struthers never had to look back. She recalled an interesting experience when she first met Lear while auditioning for the role of Gloria. "I went in and read for Norman Lear and I had bad laryngitis ... and he handed me a scene to do. A yelling scene. And I had to do this screaming scene with no voice. And Norman thought it was so funny with my yelling with no voice that he let me come back and do a second interview."[17]

Things were moving for Lear and CBS, partially due to perfect timing, and even a bit to the government's fallouts. Les Brown wrote in *Variety* in 1970, "ABC tested the pilot where there was still some disbelief in the national rift; CBS when the national anxiety over it became serious."[18]

Now the show had a talented ensemble cast, and a pilot episode. The show's name changed, as did the family's name. It was no longer called *Those Were the Days*, and the family was no longer the Justices. The show that was about to become arguably the most revolutionary form of entertainment in history was called *All in the Family*, and America's favorite family was the Bunker family. In August of 1970, when the show was finally destined to air, the premonition printed by *The Christian Science Monitor* became true. "American viewers have from now until next January to prepare themselves for the bold new program. That will be the night that will."[19]

January 12, 1971

It was the day that America changed forever. Everything that had ever been seen on television might as well have been washed down the drain, never to return. On that day, World War III was about to begin — or at least that was what CBS anticipated. Jeannie might as well have burst out of her bottle. Famine might as well have struck all of the rural sitcoms. The two beds in the Petries' bedroom (one for wife Laura, the other for husband Rob) might as well have merged. In 1960, television censors proscribed *The Jack Paar Show* from saying W.C., which stood for water closet, a British word for toilet.[20] Who would have expected by the end of the first season of this mysterious new show, America would hear the sound of a flushing toilet echoing throughout a house?

The night of the premiere, CBS opened extra phone lines just to hear the voices of disgruntled viewers and critics who seemed to never flush. At the network, nobody was more upset with what was about to happen than Lucille Ball, whose Lucy was America's favorite female character throughout the previous two decades. After the first episode, she told *Los Angeles Times* journalist Cecil Smith, "How awful. How could they put anything like this on the air, particularly at CBS, my station?"[21] But at 9:30 that night, the network was no longer Lucy's. It now belonged to Archie Bunker.

Norman Lear was a very busy man that January 12: He was arguing with the head censor of CBS, William Tankersley, and President Robert Wood. Throughout the months prior to the first airing of *All in the Family*, they had been dissenting over the content of the pilot script. They compromised and got rid of some of the sexual dialog, while keeping all of the political commentary. For example, Lear agreed to remove a scene where a jovial Mike came down the stairs while zipping his fly, after having sex with Gloria — on a Sunday morning. Tankersley felt that these instances alluded to sex too conspicuously for viewers to appreciate. Instead, he felt that viewers would censure the show from the first few minutes. Also, words that Archie was supposed to say, such as "smart-ass" and "God dammit," were axed from the pilot script.[22]

However, Lear balked at the idea of getting rid of words such as "spic." Lear told Wood, "If you don't want to do it, simply don't do it and forget the show."[23] Wood, intimidated, let Lear have his way. CBS Broadcast Group president Jack Schneider said, "Norman Lear fights, screams, and kicks and takes to crisis and takes to the public and the press any suggested change of even a comma in *All in the Family*."[24]

But on that day, Tankersley as well as everyone else at CBS, minus Lear, was still uncomfortable with the material that was about to be broadcast. He wanted the *second* episode to air that night; it was much less controversial, much less edgy. But Lear fought back, saying that the pilot introduced the principal characters better. Lear won.

Still nervous, CBS ran a warning before the pilot. Words appeared on the screen, as a sober voice read them. "The program you are about to see is *All in the Family*. It seeks to throw a humorous spotlight on our frailties, prejudices, and concerns. By making them a source of laughter, we hope to show — in a mature fashion — just how absurd they are."[25] This warning label aired before the first six episodes, and became the mission statement for the show that initiated an indelible reformation in television and society, *All in the Family*. For now, though, "There was a big disclaimer that basically said, 'Don't watch this show,'" said Rob Reiner.[26]

The key word in the warning was "absurd." By portraying America's "frailties, prejudices, and concerns" in a comedic light, Lear and the cast and crew of *All in the Family* hoped to make a major point. Moreover, they hoped some insight would flow into the ears of listeners. *All in the Family* became a social tactic — a catalyst to mollify the racial prejudices in America. *All in the Family* not only made people laugh, but it made an attempt to contribute to the improvement of society.

Carroll O'Connor was a large factor in *All in the Family*'s ability to influence. "I refused to do situation comedy," he said, "the imposition of wacky plots upon the characters. Situation comedy requires a goofball performances [*sic*]; it requires a suspension of common sense and a willingness to plunge merrily and confidently into the realm of the unreal. I maintained that we were satire. Satire is reality laced with ridicule. But the reality must never be eroded."[27]

The sources of ridicule were those who would not let Archie get away with his bigotry without an honest argument. Archie may have been lovable, but he was almost always proven wrong by the end of each episode. That was how *All in the Family* showed bigotry was "absurd." The situation was genuine, hence the "reality," yet when Archie was shown to be wrong, the "ridicule" was directed towards him.

The "satire" was successful. Neil Vidmar (associate professor of psychology at the University of Western Ontario) and Milton Rokeach (professor of sociology and psychology at Washington State University) teamed up to study how *All in the Family* influenced viewers' thoughts on bigotry. Results showed that "twenty per cent of those interviewed said that had gained insights as a consequence of seeing the show."[28] (This is the percentage of people influenced, rather than the percentage of people who were not bigots.) The notion of "lovable bigot" was also executed successfully. The study proved that "63.2 percent [of interviewees] *like* Archie more; only 12.4 percent *agree* with him more."[29] The fan mail the stars received was perhaps more powerful than the statistics. Jean Stapleton received a letter from a woman whose "most glorious moment came when her husband started swearing while doing some work in the yard. He suddenly stopped. 'Good grief,' he said, 'I sound just like that ass on TV.'"[30] That was the essence of *All in the Family*, something Lear wasted no time introducing.

Lear's new image for television began with a little hanky panky, when, in the first scene of the series, newlyweds Mike and Gloria had the stage. The setting was Archie and Edith's anniversary, and they were away at church. Mike and Gloria had the house to themselves, and decided to take advantage of the rare opportunity. As Mike carried Gloria upstairs to the bedroom, Archie and Edith returned home and interrupted the couple's plans. They only came home early because the priest overheard Archie swear about the speech from the front row. Archie felt the sermon was propaganda.

Out of that opening scene, the relationship between Mike and Gloria was the shocker, and for CBS executives, the nail biter. The first scene of this peculiar new sitcom featured some fondling, a short skirt, and a turned-on Baby Boomer. It was something completely different from anything ever witnessed on television. Right from the start, *All in the Family* had the ability to shock, but it also had the ability to inspire. This scene in 1971 was the beginning of a rollercoaster of sex mania in American entertainment throughout the 1970s. On a public and national scale, Lear was the first to introduce this concept into America's living rooms. Soon after, Marvin Gaye was demanding, "Let's get it on!" Ultimately, America began shaking its booty in the Lear-inspired sex age. While he did not write the lyrics for K.C. and the Sunshine Band's songs, he was the first to acknowledge on television that people had sex. However, sex was a minor topic on *All in the Family*. It was not long before viewers met the true plots behind this sitcom — politics and bigotry.

Soon after "the parents" came home and spoiled the newlyweds' fun, the querulous Mike and the irritable Archie got into their first of many spats throughout the 1970s, brawling about the breakdown of law and order in America. The pilot introduced the virulent relationship of Archie and Mike, when Mike started, "Guys like you are unwilling to give the black man, the Mexican-American, and all the other minorities their just and rightful hard-earned share of the American dream." But one thing about Archie was that he always had an answer for everything. Archie quickly came back, "If your spics and your spades want their rightful share of the American dream, let them get out there and hustle for it just like I done.... He's [minority's] got more [opportunity]. I didn't have no million people marchin' and protestin' to get me my job." Then Edith, who appeared to be the subservient housewife, chimed in, "No, his uncle got it for him."[31] In the pilot, Lear made it clear that the story was taking place in 1971. Since one of the major topics in the 1970s was unemployment, Lear decided to discuss it in the realm of satirical situation comedy.

Mike was concerned with the rising unemployment levels in the country — especially among minorities in the inner cities. In 1970, 4.9 percent of the people in the work force were jobless. In New York City, the number was 4.4 percent but 8.1 percent in areas where the majority of inhabitants were African-American or Hispanic, and the percentage was growing rapidly.[32] *All in the Family* always drew awareness to America's problems. Even if viewers never watched the news or read the front page of the papers, *All in the Family* gave them a distinct clue as to what was going on in America.

Meanwhile, viewers soon learned that Mike detested everything uttered by his father-in-law, especially when he referred to minorities as "spics and spades." But it worked both ways. Soon after, the ultra-conservative Archie bashed Mike, saying that minorities had more job opportunities because of the pressure liberals put on employers. Archie did not understand that it was ideas like his own, duplicated by millions of other voices, that caused the prejudice towards African-Americans, including prejudice in the workplace.

Later, Archie called Mike "the laziest white man I ever seen."[33] Word for word, that comment was exactly what Norman Lear was told by his father decades before. In the Bunker home, just as in the Lear home, it set off sparks. Mike tried to explain how Archie was "attacking a whole race" and "implying that the blacks [were] even lazier." While Mike explained morals, viewers were exposed to why Archie's statement was demeaning towards African-Americans. Mike would always put up a fight after Archie made an offensive comment.

Archie attempted to defend himself, replying, "I never said your black beauties was lazy. Just their systems is geared a little slower than the rest of us."[34] Yet again, Archie exhibited his prejudice by calling African-Americans "black beauties," and claiming their intelligence was less than the intelligence of Caucasians. Repeating himself, Mike tried to tell Archie, and prejudiced viewers, that his words were absurd. Edith put the finishing touches on the scene, acknowledging Archie's prejudice with despondence. "It's nicer than when he called them coons," she muttered, sipping her coffee.[35] Right there, she labeled Archie's bigotry as "not nice," which in terms of the mission of *All in the Family*, equaled "absurd."

After the Sunday-morning mayhem, Lionel Jefferson, an African-American friend of Mike and Gloria's, stopped by. When Lionel was written into the script, Lear had no idea how successful the character would be. Although there was a visible friendship between the two, Lionel was the one who patronized Archie, and the audience burst into convulsions every time he helped Archie put down "the blacks." Perhaps the interaction between Archie and Lionel most vividly demonstrated the wrongness of bigotry. Lionel, who caught onto Archie's bigotry years before, would lead Archie into agreeing with some stereotype regarding African-Americans. In the pilot, he got Archie to nod approvingly after saying he owned a purple-checkered suit, to wear around "my people." However, Lionel would look back at Mike and Gloria with a cross face, showing that he was leading Archie on. The audience saw the look, and immediately saw how Lionel truly felt about Archie's comments, getting a good laugh at the same time. In these cases, *All in the Family* made both Archie and bigotry look stupid.

Throughout the run of *All in the Family*, there was always some character who would respond to Archie's beliefs. Betty Garrett, who played Irene Lorenzo, Archie's neighbor and nemesis in seasons four through six, recalled in her autobiography, "Norman and the writers were very smart when it came to the terrible things Archie said. They never allowed him to say anything anti–Semitic, anti-black, or really vicious without a rebuttal. There was always someone around who made Archie look like a fool for saying such things and one of my purposes in the show was to have a zinger ready to put him down. And there was always some twist in the plot that made you see what a bigoted man Archie was."[36] But for now, that character was Lionel Jefferson. (By season four, both Lionel Jefferson and Irene Lorenzo would put Archie down for his derogatory comments, although Irene would usually censure his attitude towards women.)

Carroll O'Connor posing for a photograph with a cigar between his teeth, something Archie Bunker frequently did to unwind after a hard day's work on the loading dock.

Beginning in the first episode, Lionel got an ovation from the audience nearly every time he left the Bunker home. Also in the pilot, he and Mike tried to convince Archie that he (Archie) was Jewish, which brought out Archie's anti–Semitic beliefs. Invoking his parents' names, Archie gruffly shouted, "David and Sarah, two names right out of the Bible, which has got nothin' to do with the Jews."[37] (Two episodes later, he admitted that Jesus was Jewish, but he rationalized, "only on his mother's side."[38])

The *All in the Family* pilot introduced the older characters in relation to the time period they were living in. Not all of the characters wished to be living in 1971, still desperately trying to lead their lives the way they did decades before. *The Chicago Tribune* called Archie "one of the most indigenous American types. He is a funny, yet tragic figure."[39] Archie Bunker was locked up in the previous generation — giving off a vibe that he was the beer-drinking, tunnel-vision, war-buddy type. He did not appreciate what he felt were mutations happening in America. Archie was a blue-collar worker who had a strong conviction that the Baby Boomers did not have any work ethic. He would not appreciate the fact that, in 1970, about 33 percent of the line workers at the Big Three automobile manufacturers were under thirty years old.[40] But Archie was more in touch with 1971 than he thought, or even desired. He represented the average angered Protestant in the early 1970s — frustrated with the subject matter of the priest's sermons and the tithes the church requested.[41] Since age did not slow this man's mouth down, he was very vocal about his opinions.

Through the character of Archie Bunker, *All in the Family* was "explaining new attitudes in the country to old Americans."[42] Mike was the one who explained, and Archie was the one who covered his ears in a desperate attempt to stop the world from changing. David Marc, author of *Comic Visions*, wrote, "Archie maintains an abiding faith that traditional, institutional, authority is always to be trusted over individual organic desire."[43] But Lear hoped that other Archies, and those similar to his father, would not cover their ears all the way, and that they would become more tolerant towards change in the world.

Archie was also a chauvinist, and his wife Edith seemed subdued most of the time, like many typical housewives of the previous decades. However, there were many instances where it was apparent Edith wanted to crack out of that shell of 1930s subordination and become a part of the youth generation — best depicted by her warm relationships with Mike and Gloria. Aside from family, she was able to make friends with anyone she encountered because of her beautiful soul. As the women's movement began to escalate in popularity, it reached people like Edith, who attended women's meetings by the middle of the decade. And an occasional comment, such as the one about Archie's uncle finding him his job at the loading dock, could stultify Archie when he crossed the line into absurdity. She kept him from going too far.

In the final scene, Lear showed that lovable bigots do, in fact, have sensitivity chips somewhere deep inside their bodies. Lear fought so hard to air this episode first, because he wanted to include this tag scene. When Archie heard the words of the card that the kids bought for him to give to Edith, he began to get emotional. The same thing happened in the Lear home many years prior. "The sentiment on the card happens to be the poem I had written for my father to give to my mother on their fifteenth wedding anniversary. I wrote it and he cried when my mother read it. And Archie cried when Edith read it," said Lear.[44] And that concluded the first episode of *All in the Family* — an abrupt transition from whatever aired on January 11, 1971.

On the morning of the day that the pilot episode aired, critics were already tense about the premiere. Fred Ferretti of *The New York Times* denounced *All in the Family*'s racial epithets right from the start. "None of [Archie's epithets] is funny. They shock because one is not used to hearing them shouted from the television during prime-time family programs. They don't make one laugh so much as they force self-conscious, semi-amused gasps. They are not funny because they are there for their shock value, despite CBS's protestations that what is being presented are 'familiar stereotypes' with 'a humorous spotlight on their prejudices...' What is lacking is taste."[45]

Other critics disagreed with Ferretti. "*All in the Family* will shock and offend and start the most violent arguments you ever saw between those who think it's funny and those who don't," said Clarence Petersen of *The Chicago Tribune*. "*All in the Family* could become a very big hit, not only because it will be controversial but because the scripts are funny and the casting is brilliant."[46] Cecil Smith of *The Los Angeles Times* disagreed with Lucille Ball's reaction. "Another thing you have to give *All in the Family* — it's funny. Not gently funny, not sophisticated funny, not intellectual funny, not relevantly funny — but raw, rough, roaring, falling-down-in-the-aisles funny."[47]

On January 13, *The Washington Post*'s William C. Woods sided with Ferretti by not showing much support for Lear's pioneer show. "If most network shows— and certainly most situation comedies— manage to be cowardly through commission, this one tries to make good the lapse by filling 30 minutes with every racial epithet and prejudiced social stance available in the long catalogue of the ways we find for being cruel to each other."[48]

Few people tuned in to watch. The episode pulled a 15 percent share, meaning just 15 percent of the people with their television sets turned on was watching *All in the Family*.[49] Fred Ferretti was right about one thing. The day *All in the Family* premiered, he prognosticated, "It will be an interesting 13 weeks, for CBS as well as for the viewing public."[50]

From Rags to Riches

By February, *All in the Family* faced possible cancellation, unable to break into the top forty, after a month on the air. But cancellation for *All in the Family* was never really a serious threat because the show grabbed the attention of many critics, most of whom understood its intent. For example, Josh Gould of *The New York Times* commented, "Rarely has a series set so many reviewers and viewers dashing to their memo pads to record their feelings."[51]

However, some average citizens were appalled. One New Yorker was not enthralled with what she was seeing on Tuesday nights. Stephanie Harrington's editorial was published in *The New York Times*, challenging *All in the Family* by asking, "By making the expression of hostility more commonplace, do we really exorcise it? Or do we, in fact, make it more acceptable?"[52] Lear responded to Ms. Harrington's editorial by telling her the goal of *All in the Family* was to "hold a mirror up to our prejudices." He gave a personal example. "If I needed a blood transfusion and you asked me for my preference, a pint of blood from a black man, or one from a Caucasian, I would tell you it doesn't matter. I might even insist on taking the black man's blood. I know that all blood is the same ... but is that knowledge the true reason for my answer?... The truth is I am emancipated enough not to act out on the ingrained prejudices that to my sorrow exist within me. So, as I lay there during the transfusion, the black man's blood slowly entering me, in the quiet isolation of my mind the thought might flash and sputter — 'Norman, what if there is a difference'?"[53]

Lear also attacked the way Ms. Harrington viewed television programs. "To hear the words 'spic' and 'spade' four minutes into the show and think, however quickly, 'Oh, my! That kind of language won't exorcise hostility; it could make it more acceptable,' is to lose the show emotionally at the beginning and never pick it up again."[54]

Other viewers were just as harsh as Ms. Harrington. "*All in the Family* was the most repulsive show I have seen on TV," one angry viewer told *TV Guide* in February of 1971.[55]

The opinions of *The Charlotte Observer* more accurately represented how critics felt about the show, and how Lear wanted it to be perceived. "Enjoy the program for its acting and humor. And then, when laughing at Archie and the rest of the characters, it won't be so hard to laugh at ourselves."[56] *The Cincinnati Enquirer* agreed, calling *All in the Family* "a good natured look at every American, regardless of class, color, religion, or heritage."[57] Even Lear, who would scream at the prejudiced things his father would say, knew that in some way, he had to laugh at himself. Inside his mind, he knew he had a bit of his father in him — just like everyone has a bit of Archie in them. Soon, viewers were able to capture the essence of *All in the Family*. One proud viewer, Mark Anthony, told *TV Guide* in 1972, "Of course we laugh when Archie makes snide, bigoted remarks about other races, creeds, and religions, but we laugh *at* him, not with him."[58] Those words concisely summed up the "mission statement" of *All in the Family*.

Right from the start, Lear attempted to capture that essence. While the pilot episode was arguably the most audacious of the more than two hundred episodes that aired, the ones that followed in the first season did not fall very far from the original. He experimented with new subject matter in every episode, and always managed to make a significant point.

The second episode compared the contesting perspectives that America had of Richard Nixon, from a conservative bias and from a liberal bias. Archie and Mike both wrote letters to the White House, but while one was a letter of approbation, the other was critical, saying that Nixon did little to help environmental matters.[59] *All in the Family* discussed the topics that became the headlines of papers in 1971. Sitcoms in the past may have touched on or referenced politics, but never before had they devoted entire episodes to topical issues.

Another topic that was covering the first page of *The New York Times* in 1971 was a new national crisis—the shortage of blood donations. Blood supplies were so low that doctors were desperately resorting to commercial blood (blood sold by donors for profit). However, these donors were sometimes heroin addicts or positive for hepatitis. In September of 1970 it was reported that only 3 percent of people eligible to donate blood actually did the good deed.[60]

That was where *All in the Family* came in. In the fourth episode, the show attacked those who, like Archie Bunker, were reluctant to donate blood. *All in the Family* discussed the crisis on a national forum and elevated awareness about the dilemma at hand. In the end, Mike and Gloria convinced Archie to go down to the blood bank with them.[61] Blood banks hoped that many more would follow Archie. *All in the Family* provided an alternate source of advertising for blood banks—and a free one. The show put the idea of donating blood into the minds of those who had never considered it. The episode was so vital to America, because it had the potential to save lives. Through laughter, America became aware of the crisis at hand. And the same message came across every time the episode appeared in reruns.

In the next episode, Archie became the subject of ridicule, once again. Throughout the series, *All in the Family* strove to promote the equality of *all* minorities. By 1970, homosexuals represented 4 percent of the male population and 2 percent of the female population.[62] *All in the Family* tackled yet another topic previously considered taboo on television. Lear's episode showed how prejudice against the gay community was "absurd." Throughout the episode, he attempted to break the stereotypes about homosexuals. When Mike brought his friend over, a long-haired, high-voiced artiste wearing glasses, Archie immediately assumed he was gay. "[He's] as queer as a four dollar bill," Archie believed.[63] Yet Mike's friend was not gay at all. Later that day, Archie found out something he thought was horrific—one of his pals at the bar, who was a former professional football player, was gay. Archie could not believe what he was hearing, and Lear proved to audiences that homosexuals come in all shapes and sizes. Archie could not believe that a man with so much strength and muscle could like other men. This man was exactly the opposite of the people Archie automatically labeled as "gay."

Lear's discussion on homosexuality was far ahead of its time, as the majority of the country questioned homosexuality. Even by 1982, just 34 percent of the population believed that homosexuality was an "acceptable" lifestyle.[64] Even the medical world treated it like a disease, although most comfortable homosexuals found it offensive that homosexuals were paying money to change to heterosexual. In 1971, it was reported that 25–50 percent of homosexuals that went for psychiatric treatment to "become straight" were successful.[65] The month the episode was first broadcast, Congress proposed a bill prohibiting the discrimination against homosexuals in the workplace. Lear was also ahead of Washington. Nonetheless, months later, the bill was outvoted, seven to five.[66]

Previously, perhaps the farthest homosexuality ever went on television was that Paul Lynde, an openly gay entertainer, was the "center square" on *Hollywood Squares*. Now, Lear set the trend for homosexuals in future television, becoming the first to dissect the issue, or even acknowledge the existence of gay people. Americans knew that homosexuals existed, but they never expected to see them in their living rooms. Lear smoothed the transition for gay characters on television. Lear told *The New York Times* in 1972, "Richard Levinson [who co-wrote and produced *That Certain Summer*, a sensitive and moving exploration of the relationship between a homosexual father and his adolescent son] said that our show about homosexuality on *All in the Family* was a groundbreaker for everybody, that it was what allowed other people to explore the subject."[67] By the late 1970s, the sitcom *Soap* featured a gay regular, Jodie Dallas (Billy Crystal). Two decades later, *Will and Grace* premiered. The sitcom instantly became a hit, yet there was not one straight male character. *All in the Family* and *Will and Grace* shared striking similarities. Both had a small ensemble cast — four cast members; two in the leading roles, two in the supporting roles. And both shows can say that each of their four cast members has won an Emmy Award. As distorted as it may seem, without *All in the Family* paving the way, Jack McFarland (Sean Hayes) would never have sashayed around doing his one-man show, "Just Jack."

While quality episodes of *All in the Family* aired week after week, few people were watching them. By the end of March, the show had not been renewed for a second season. CBS was wondering what they were thinking by airing it in the first place. That March, Merv Griffin invited the cast of *All in the Family* on his CBS show. He recalled in his autobiography how CBS questioned him for it. "'Why are you putting them on? The show probably won't last the season.' It was a CBS show, and *still* we drew fire from the network."[68] Under the leadership of Lear, this cast stuck together when the ratings were nowhere near the ratings of hit sitcoms, and in the end, was rewarded for their patience. In the middle of April, viewers began tuning in and *All in the Family* held the fourteenth spot in the Nielsen ratings.

But *All in the Family* changed forever on May 9, 1971.

A major event took place in Hollywood that night — the Emmys, the most prestigious award ceremony in television. Norman Lear sat in the audience, as his show was a nominee for Outstanding Comedy Series. Then, host Johnny Carson announced the winner of the award. It was *All in the Family*! When Lear went up to the stage to accept the award, Carson jokingly congratulated him, acknowledging *All in the Family*'s war against bigotry. "I would like to congratulate Norman Lear. He's a great guy — for a Hebe."[69] Before the night was over, Lear won the award for Outstanding New Series, and Jean Stapleton won the award for Outstanding Continued Performance by an Actor in a Leading Role in a Comedy Series.

The Emmy Award was Lear's reward for six months of rough times. He could not have hoped for a better denouement. After the Emmys, *All in the Family* was the show everyone was raving about at the watercooler. Lear and the cast were walking on air that summer. After the Emmys, the hype for the second season became ubiquitous throughout the summer of 1971. One critic noted, "Cinderella had nothing on Archie Bunker. The move from dustbins to princess is as nothing compared with the step-up from television long-shot to frontrunner in the A.C. Nielsen ratings. Archie, TV's favorite bigot in the Columbia Broadcasting System's comedy series, *All in the Family,* has just done that."[70] The award win propelled *All in the Family* to prominence. That week, the televised Emmy Awards topped the Nielsen ratings — but *All in the Family* reruns were right behind them. The following week, Lear's sitcom would make its debut at the height of the Nielsen ratings — the most prestigious statistic in television for any show. ABC was astonished, because they knew *All in the Family* could have been theirs. Leonard Goldberg, head of programming at ABC, admitted, "It was one of those decisions that I guess when the history of television is written is kind of a landmark certainly for ABC in the late Sixties and early Seventies 'cause it would have turned the network around."[71]

Soon after, *All in the Family* was given the responsibility of carrying CBS, as president of the network Robert Wood began a massive summer network cleaning. Wood cancelled three rural sitcoms, *Green Acres, The Beverly Hillbillies,* and *Mayberry R.F.D.,* as well as two rural variety shows, *Hee Haw* and *The Jim Nabors Hour.* He also got rid of *The Jackie Gleason Show,* which had been around since the Fifties. *The Red Skelton Show* was waived after twenty seasons. Perhaps the biggest shocker was the cancellation of *The Ed Sullivan Show*, which had debuted twenty-three years earlier.

In the summer of 1971, America turned on CBS to see the reruns of the first thirteen episodes of *All in the Family*. Much of America was watching for the first time. *All in the Family* dominated the CBS lineup. However, Lear and CBS had a tough decision to make — what time to air *All in the Family* once new episodes began in September. They knew they wanted to move it from its original spot, 9:30 P.M. on Tuesdays. Originally, the plan was to see how the sitcom would fare on Mondays at 10:30 P.M. However, Lear was worried about the future of his show, since it would be competing against *Monday Night Football* and the *Monday Night Movie*. Lear and CBS decided to welcome America into 704 Hauser Street every Saturday night at eight o'clock. It was the perfect time slot. For the five years it aired there, *All in the Family* ranked number one in the Nielsen ratings in the season standings, all five years.

Meanwhile, Lear's sitcom formula was resonating with America, much to the surprise of everyone. Rob Reiner said in mid–1971, "When we went on the air four months ago, you couldn't get a bet down we'd last through spring. Even the cast wouldn't book the bet."[72] America wanted to know whose buttons Lear would push next. However, Lear wanted to stick to his simple algorithm, giving viewers political controversy that both shocked and fascinated, while making viewers laugh. In 1971, when asked about major changes to *All in the Family*, he responded, "I do expect to use the black neighbors more next year."[73]

That was one of Lear's smartest decisions in the 1970s. They would become very popular with viewers. By 1973, Mike Evans, who played Lionel Jefferson, was sharing *TV Guide* covers with Carroll O'Connor. As the Jeffersons appeared more regularly in the Bunker home, there were more racial disputes between the two patriarchs, leading to more laughs. By 1975, the Jeffersons got their own sitcom, which lasted even longer than *All in the Family*.

Because of *All in the Family*'s recent success, Lear didn't have to worry as much about censorship. One of the show's writers, Bernie West, said in 1974, "When you hear about other shows not being able to say this or that, it's nice to be with a show where we can be as free as we are."[74] Lear wrote the manuscripts for the first two episodes in the second season. The Jeffersons appeared in both episodes and Lionel Jefferson's deadpan delivery of racially risqué lines tickled America's funnybone. When Archie teases him about him jogging with Mike, Lionel counters, "If you were walkin' down the street at seven o'clock in the morning, and you saw this black guy, all by himself, running, in this neighborhood, what would you think?"[75] That particular episode garnered forty percent of the ratings and gauging by the show's increasing popularity, Lear's irreverence resonated with its audience.[76] And so the infatuation with Archie, Edith, Mike, Gloria, and the Jeffersons truly began. Carroll O'Connor told *TV Guide* in the fall of 1971, "I frankly thought the American public was too dour to laugh at itself. I was fooled. I'm gratified."[77]

When *All in the Family* began, Lear and the cast wanted the show to get inside the minds of viewers, and provoke thought, whether viewers liked it or not. Lear told O'Connor in 1968, "We may be thrown off the air, but while we're there we'll give them [the viewers] plenty to think about."[78] That was exactly what Lear and the cast accomplished. Entertainment great Jack Benny said to O'Connor several years later, "Your show is wonderful, it gives us all so much to think about."[79]

However, it was not all a cakewalk for Lear in late 1971. He was still being rebuked by disapproving viewers. Arguably his strongest criticism came six days before the season two premiere. On September 12, 1971, Laura Z. Hobson published a three-page grievance in *The New York Times* that vituperatively stated something rather unusual. It opened, "I have a most peculiar complaint about the bigotry in the hit TV comedy *All in the Family*. There's not enough of it."[80] Hobson said that bigots do not use words like *hebe* and *spade*, but only use words like *kike* and *nigger*. She was motivated to write this after Johnny Carson racially bantered with Lear at the Emmy Awards in May, and ultimately decided to publish the piece after she unsuccessfully spent her summer of 1971 trying to contact Lear to express her feelings.

Lear saw what she wrote in *The New York Times*. A month later, Lear published his rebuttal in *The Los Angeles Times*, taking time out of his busy schedule and the new taping season to ask Ms. Hobson some questions. "If kike and sheeny were all that bigots called Jews, why was I so enraged at age 8 that I tackled a kid twice my size because he called me 'a dirty Jew'? And at 11, why was I sent to the principal for fighting another kid who all but tore my heart out by calling me a 'Christ-killer'?"[81] However, neither Hobson nor Lear got the last laugh. Numerous letters to the editor were submitted, some siding with Hobson, others siding with Lear. Some criticized Lear for even responding.

In the second season, Lear was writing episodes about personal issues. First, Lear boldly tackled impotence — showing how various generations could look at a common sexual problem. Mike was the victim and, although a liberal, still felt bashful about the problem when Gloria discussed it with him or his doctor. However, audience members were falling off their seats laughing because the reactions of Archie and Edith towards impotence were identical to reactions of people they knew — or perhaps themselves. Edith began shaking and sweating when Gloria said the problem was sexual. Edith could not even say the word. The only advice Edith could offer was, "It's probably something that's going around." Meanwhile, Archie described the problem to his buddies at Kelsey's Bar as "stuck in neutral."[82]

Lear brought a very private issue into the public domain, providing awareness through situation comedy, and breaking the ice about it. The episode poked fun, perhaps ridicule, towards those, like Archie and Edith, who were not at all comfortable discussing the situation. It encouraged openness for those, like Mike, who were dealing with the problem. And at the same time, it was hard to keep from laughing.

But Lear went through quite a few aspirin before the episode was allowed to air. CBS censors were instantly worried about running an episode about impotence, especially with the show's move to eight o'clock. They felt some of their new audience might shut off *All in the Family* forever if they saw this episode. Eventually, censors deferred the decision to president Robert Wood, who held a three-hour meeting with Lear, trying to make him postpone the episode, at least until viewers became comfortable with *All in the Family* in the eight o'clock spot.

The meeting turned into a long argument, Lear threatening, as usual, to yank *All in the Family* from CBS if he did not get his way. Finally, as Lear left, Wood criticized Lear's *nouveau riche* status. "I bet if I was standing here with an attaché case with a million dollars in twenty-dollar bills, your mind might be changed."[83] The retort did not get inside Lear's head; he responded coyly, "That's a perfect last line. Sometime I will write it in exactly that way."[84] He walked out, ultimately having won the battle, since his demands were met.

By December, the majority of people watching television on Saturdays at eight o'clock tuned into *All in the Family*.[85] Before the end of 1971, *All in the Family* pulled an astounding 70 percent share in New York City.[86] For its outstanding success during its second season, *All in the Family* won seven Emmy Awards and a pair of Golden Globes. "Bunker-mania" had just begun, and much more was yet to come. *All in the Family* was appealing to two kinds of viewers, both conservatives and liberals. Still, in the 1971–72 season, America had not had its last, nor its loudest, laugh.

Sammy's Visit

In 1971, Sammy Davis, Jr., was one of the most popular figures in American culture, and a huge African-American icon. But when Davis had to perform a nightclub act at eight o'clock on Saturday night, he would move the act back thirty minutes for one reason — so that he could watch his white friends, the Bunkers, while getting ready in his dressing room.[87] Davis admired the metamorphosis of television that Lear and the cast and crew of *All in the Family* were responsible for.

Davis wanted to guest-star on *All in the Family*, and frequently tried to persuade Lear to allow him to appear. Although he wanted Davis to guest-star, Lear was worried that it would ruin the continuity of this newly golden show, which was still very fragile. In the end, Lear and Davis compromised. Davis would appear on *All in the Family*, portraying himself.

Davis was not guest-starring on *All in the Family* for the money or the publicity. They were not his priorities. He did it for his personal pleasure. Lear was pleased that Davis was that enthused about guest-starring, but had no idea about the ensuing euphoria.

Now, Lear had to develop a storyline. Lear began to set up the plot in previous episodes, giving Archie Bunker a side job — moonlighting, driving his friend Munson's cab. Then, Sammy's episode began when Archie came home excited, telling Edith, Mike, and Gloria that he had Sammy as a fare. Then, he got a call from Sammy, who had left a briefcase in the cab. Archie said Sammy could pick it up in person at Archie's house.

On February 19, 1972, America gave Sammy Davis, Jr., a standing ovation as he walked through the front door of the Bunker home. There stood some of America's finest superstars in the early 1970s. With the perfect opportunity at hand, Archie would soon display his bigoted self to the fullest — without even knowing it!

Archie had absolutely no idea he was being prejudiced. He felt he was having a nice, intelligent conversation with Sammy Davis, Jr. Archie seemed completely immune to the odd looks on Sammy's face, while he told Sammy how he was "a tribute to his race."[88] At the same time, he fed him Twinkies, because he felt that was what African-Americans ate. *All in the Family* never praised bigotry. There was always someone to censure Archie's behavior. This time it was Sammy Davis, Jr.

In this episode, *All in the Family* showed the root of prejudice — ignorance. Archie had no idea of the recklessness that he brought to the world, day after day. Donna McCrohan, author of *Archie, Edith, Mike, and Gloria: The Tumultuous History of* All in the Family, commented, "Archie believes that he's thought things through — that he's simply aware of the rules ordained by nature to make some people sluggish and other people cheats. Besides, to Archie a racist would only use negative labels — while he's the first to declare the sharpest lawyers are Jews."[89]

This episode directly focused on Archie's ignorance. Archie complained to Sammy that the kids always say he is prejudiced. Archie asked Sammy if he agreed. Sammy responded, "You prejudiced? Look, if you were prejudiced, Archie, when I came into your house, you would've called me a coon, or a nigger. But you didn't say that ... you said—colored."[90] In the midst of this classic episode, this line was a direct, blatant rebuttal to Laura Hobson's letter several months back, making the point that bigots use other words besides *nigger*. Archie's prejudice was piercing in this episode, yet as Sammy pointed out, he said "colored," which was almost as powerful, and suitable for network television, considering never before had a white man spewed the epithet *nigger* on the air.

Sammy then responded, "If you were prejudiced, you'd walk around thinking you were better than anybody else in the world. But I can honestly say, having spent these marvelous moments with you, you ain't better than anybody."[91] Archie was so ignorant—and apparently gullible—that he smiled, and shook Sammy's hand, feeling embraced by him.

The final subject in their conversation was African-Americans and Caucasians hugging and kissing on television. Sammy played along with Archie, saying he had a clause in his contract that forced it. Archie was appalled that Sammy was compelled to perform those actions.

When Munson arrived with Sammy's briefcase, Archie wanted to take a picture with Sammy. However, Sammy had a kind rebuttal to their "intellectual" conversation about interracial kissing. As the shutter clicked on the count of three, Sammy planted a kiss on the cheek of Archie and then left through the front door. Archie's face turned from very happy to completely stunned. Instantly, his entire face changed; his eyebrows slanting, mouth gaping, eyes twitching. It was almost as if Archie had a mini–heart attack. For a half-minute, Archie could not say a word, although the reaction from the audience hit the top of the Richter scale. All Archie could finally sputter out of his bigoted mouth was, "What the hell, he said it was in his contract."[92] Lear commented, "When Sammy kissed Archie, it might be as long a laugh as we've ever seen on television."[93] And in the history of *All in the Family*, the episode turned out to be the most powerful demonstration of how bigotry was "absurd."

All in the Family had more spontaneity than any other television show. There was no way to foreshadow the epic, landmark kiss. However, when Sammy's lips met Archie's fat cheek, it proved that Sammy got the best of Archie—and did not have to prove bigotry wrong by a screaming match. Archie's reaction took care of that. The way Sammy handled Archie's views on race was similar to how Edith handled them—by stupefying Archie in the end, but always with love, never damning Archie's character. At the end of each episode, Archie was still a lovable bigot.

The kiss between Archie and Sammy represented the separation of the nation that lingered nearly a decade after the Civil Rights Movement. The frozen face of Archie Bunker depicted the segregation that still greatly affected, and plagued, America in 1972. As Stephen Battaglio of *TV Guide* pointed out, "[The kiss] made us laugh, but it also made us think."[94]

That season, the director of this episode, and Lear's go-to guy throughout the 1970s, John Rich, won the Emmy Award for Outstanding Directorial Achievement in Comedy for this episode. In December 2004, *TV Guide* rated Archie's unforgettable encounter eighteenth out of the top hundred most memorable moments in television history. In the countdown ceremony, Larry W. Jones, president of TV Land, called it "the moment of the series."[95] Quincy Jones took the impact of the kiss a step further. He claimed it was a "hallmark for TV."[96]

The kiss was, by far, the pinnacle of *All in the Family*. Davis also considered it one of the pinnacles in his career. "I'm a late sleeper and not known for being prompt, but on this special occasion [the taping of the episode] I was 15 minutes early. It was a thrill which can only be compared to my first big break in show business," said Davis, proudly.[97]

Decades later, the kiss proved to be more than just the pinnacle, but a defining, revolutionary moment in television history. Cecil Smith was right; *All in the Family* would indeed be "falling down in the aisles funny."[98] People fell out of their seats laughing, yet then were unable to move a muscle because they were so shocked.

Elections, Watergate, Inflation, and Unemployment

The sweltering sun was beating down on Washington during the summer of 1972. It was election time once again. This summer, the show belonged to Senator George McGovern of South Dakota and President Richard Nixon. While Nixon was inside negotiating peace with Vietnam, McGovern was promising to remove troops from Vietnam immediately, and then beg the Communist government for the remaining prisoners of war. He felt his plan was superior to Nixon's, telling America that "we could finish off North Vietnam in an afternoon."[99] Meanwhile, the Nixon administration was just as critical of McGovern. "He has no record, no proven record. You're hard pressed to say anything he has done in the Senate, for instance, that's of any moment."[100] Aside from the war, McGovern was campaigning throughout the country, discussing his plans for the legalization of abortion and the decriminalization of marijuana.

By the end of the summer, Nixon's campaign had been much more successful than McGovern's, who was viewed by Republicans and some Democrats as an extreme leftist. And while Nixon had more than enough money to cover the costs of television and radio advertising, among other things, McGovern was in dire need of donations. By the end of August, despite getting money from the wealthy young, 90 percent of his donations were for less than $100.[101] Because of the lack of finances, McGovern was unable to campaign as extensively as Nixon.

As the fall began, the events of the summer angered Mike Stivic, who was now spending his afternoons at the McGovern headquarters. He was frustrated by what he and his wife felt were Nixon's broken promises—to stop war, to end inflation, and to decrease unemployment. When Mike inherited money from a deceased relative, he donated it to the McGovern campaign, just like many other young men who had inherited money. His donation of $200 fell into the 10 percent who donated more than $100 to the campaign. Mike felt he needed to help McGovern deliver his message. For *All in the Family,* it was a positive message for viewers to watch characters actively involved in politics; to see people going out to the voting booth. It was encouraging, in an era when the number of voters decreased dramatically. In the presidential elections before 1952, over 60 percent of citizens voted (except in 1948). Only half the nation participated in the 1976 presidential election.[102]

Archie was dead against McGovern from the start, feeling Nixon was the patriarch of America at the time. When he found out Mike was donating to the McGovern campaign, he demanded the money go to him as a fee for room and board.

Because of the vivid disparity in opinion between Archie and Mike, Archie would not let Mike eat the food he paid for until he was given the money, forcing Mike to obtain a part-time job to pay Archie. All of the mayhem and all of the conflict that occurred during the episode stemmed from the presidential election.[103]

Norman Lear did not favor either side during this episode. On the show, equal criticism was directed towards each candidate. When Mike and Gloria brought up Nixon's broken promises, Archie countered by mentioning McGovern's track record of indecisiveness.

Meanwhile, both Mike and Archie's favorites had faults that they did not know about. Nixon had committed a crime that developed into the Watergate scandal, and McGovern's chairman reportedly was cracking Polish jokes the night of McGovern's nomination.[104] (Mike was Polish, and felt Archie's Polish jokes were irksome, so Mike would not appreciate hearing these racial slurs on a national scale.) From the way much of the mainstream felt about McGovern, Archie augured the election results—Nixon won by a landslide. But Mike seemed to be correct about Nixon's level of honesty, as Nixon would resign in the biggest presidential scandal in America's history—Watergate.

To start off the fourth season of *All in the Family*, which discussed Watergate, Archie Bunker said something that had never been heard on prime-time television, but was frequently heard in the real world. When Lear tried to push this button the previous year, CBS would not let him. But now censors gave Lear a chance. In the season opener, Archie yelled, "God dammit!" The curse shocked the audience, who groaned very loudly, along with Edith. "Ever since Watergate, it's been G.D. this, G.D. that," she complained.[105] Archie failed to justify the word usage, claiming "God" is the most popular word in the Bible, and "damn" has to do with rivers. It was the first time any mass audience ever heard that malediction through the tube, but it would not be the last time Archie would ever say it. (Lear saved it for very emotional moments, such as when Archie yelled at a draft dodger at his dinner table.) In Lear's defense, his director John Rich said, "We do what people are talking about."[106]

Archie let go in the middle of a heated debate, when Mike began to tease Archie, saying, "Watergate, Watergate, Watergate, Watergate, Watergate, Watergate."[107] Of that debate, Marvin Kitman of *Newsday* wrote in 1973, "Bunker's and Stivic's analyses of President Nixon's actions in the Watergate affair, as far as I'm concerned, more than compensate for the removal of analysis by CBS elsewhere in its schedule."[108]

Across the country, people were also cursing about inflation. America began 1974 with one of the biggest inflation surges in history — a 14.5 percent climb from New Year's to the end of March.[109] Although the rate dropped slightly in April, America was still suffering its greatest financial predicament since the Great Depression four decades prior. While citizens pointed fingers at the government, the government did its best to reciprocate. Arthur F. Burns, Federal Reserve Board Chairman, blamed America for the intensity of the dilemma, claiming Americans were not holding their head up to "the menace of inflation."[110]

The biggest advantage for lower and middle-class Americans fighting the inflation epidemic was to have a cost of living escalation clause written into their contract, meaning their salary would rise in proportion to the cost of living. This clause was very beneficial to workers in the early 1970s, since the consumer price index rose by 53.2 percent from 1967 to 1974.[111] Midway through 1974, 5.4 million workers were protected under this clause; however, 85 million others were clamoring to have the clause written into their contract.[112]

Because of this controversy, strikes were rampant throughout America because workers were in pursuit of compensation for inflation — whether it be more money or the cost of living escalation clause, or both. For example, school years were postponed because teachers were on strike. But it was not just the white collar demographic that was upset. Kids had no method of transportation to school because bus drivers were on strike. Another blue-collar worker that was on strike went by the name of Archie Bunker.

Archie represented the group of workers who was complacent about their contracts and felt it was their duty to fulfill them. However, the majority who wanted better working conditions outnumbered them. Older people on the loading dock, like Archie and his pal Stretch Cunningham, felt at the time about those young protestors, "They don't want to work; they're a bunch of fairies."[113]

The strike scared the pants off of Archie, who was trying to support four people. He had come from an even tougher era, the Depression, where his father struggled for every cent, and did not ask for more than he got. His father was a tough man, which was where Archie got his tenacity. Obviously, they were both hard workers supporting a family they loved.

The strike also scared the apron right off of Edith — who dashed from the kitchen to work. Inflation, in combination with Archie's strike, forced the domesticated Edith to stop baking cakes and to stand behind the cash register at the Jeffersons' cleaning store. Edith was most aware of the financial woes in the Bunker home. She was the consumer of the family — the one who could not afford to buy the meat. She could only afford to buy pasta while paychecks were not coming into the home.

Archie kept to himself his feelings about Edith working, and also he held back his feelings about Edith working for his African-American foe. With Gloria already working for two years and Mike going to school and getting a tutoring job, Archie was the only one left in the house every morning.

And Archie would not vacuum the linoleum kitchen floors for long before his pride kicked in and he let it all out. The man who once called his son-in-law a "gigolo" for having his wife work while he went to school was now being supported by two women and the Meathead himself. His chauvinism also kicked in — he was not enthralled that Edith was working, although he did greatly appreciate her efforts. He knew his other alternative was food stamps.

Eventually, the workers at Archie's plant reached an agreement — a three-year contract with a 15 percent raise. But this four-part episode did not end on an entirely happy note. Although Archie felt victorious, he did not get the cost of living escalation clause written into his contract. The Bunkers' problems were better for now, but as Mike pointed out, the cost of living was projected to increase by 8 percent in the following year.[114] Another lesson from the Bunker family: Make sure to get the cost of living escalation clause. *All in the Family* was now giving financial tutelage to its viewers.

In America, inflation was not the only peril. Unemployment figures were at their highest in the post World War II era. By 1974, America had reached a recession. Stagflation — the combination of inflation with increased unemployment — was ubiquitous. At the end of the year, 6.5 percent, or 6 million Americans, were jobless.[115] By the end of 1975, the rate soared to 8.3 percent (7.7 million).[116]

The Labor Department defined three classes of the unemployed: those out of work; those so distraught from job hunting they stopped searching altogether (5.3 million by 1975); and those working part-time because they could not find a full-time job, but would accept one if offered (3.6 million).[117] By this definition, 16.6 million Americans were in trouble, and the unemployment rate was 17.9 percent.

From the Archie Bunker perspective, the unemployment picture became more troubling with the Equal Employment Opportunity Commission (EEOC) breathing down the necks of employers. There was already a paucity of job opportunities; from October to November of 1975, the number of jobs decreased by 160,000.[118] In order to stay in business, companies had to employ a certain number of women and minorities. Therefore, there were automatically fewer job opportunities for white males, who represented the majority of the nation. For example, in most cases, if a African-American man and a white man competed for a job, and the company needed to fill the "quota," the African-American man would get the job, whether or not he deserved it. The intent of the law was to ensure equality in selecting jobs, and many white males felt they were being robbed of potential employment opportunities. During the first six months of 1974, 335 complaints to the EEOC were filed by white males.[119] The year before, in what became known as *DeFinis v. Odergard*, a white male sued the University of Washington Law School because minorities with lower exam scores were accepted into the school, and he was not. (In the end, the plaintiff lost.)[120]

From the time when Mike Stivic first began paying attention to the country's affairs, he wanted to help minorities. He scoffed at Archie in the very first episode of *All in the Family* when Archie said, "I didn't have no million people marchin' and protestin' to get me my job."[121] But five years later, when Mike was competing for a job as a professor in Minnesota, he learned an important lesson about "reverse discrimination."

Mike was competing against an African-American friend for the job. The two men had equal credentials for the job. But the university needed to hire minorities to fill the "quota." Unfortunately for Mike, he was white. Mike was angered that he was at a disadvantage, and when he told the African-American friend how he felt, the friend asked if any white man ever felt guilty about taking a job from an African-American man due to race. Mike was speechless. It was one of those rare instances where Archie's words were true. Certainly the way Archie said it was incorrect, but his belief that the world is a bit crooked was shown to be quite correct.

Mike wound up losing the job to the African-American man, and wanted to practice what he had preached. But Mike knew he had been gypped by his own way of thinking. He finally let out the anger that was building inside, by shattering glass when he slammed the door. The door slam resembled the frustration that Americans, such as Mike, were facing. And the noise of glass shattering was the cry of those who were struggling to keep their heads above water.

Lear was often criticized that issues on his shows were indigestible for most viewers. However, these issues were right out of the newspapers. With indignation, Lear responded to criticisms: "I think it is arrogant of some television people to say that we overestimate the intelligence of audiences. I have sat with hundreds of network executives and most of them have no more intelligence than the average American."[122]

As the Bunkers faced common problems with America during the 1970s, they ruled America. Archie Bunker's face was the cornerstone of America's culture — it could be seen in any thrift store, on products such as coffee cups, T-shirts, and even presidential campaign advertisements. Bumper stickers and campaigns pins reading "Archie Bunker for President" featured his stocky face and gray hair adjacent to Richard Nixon. These pins were especially popular in both the 1972 and 1976 presidential elections. In fact, the lovably opinionated breadwinner and bigot received a vote at the Democratic nominating convention![123]

Betty Garrett (the Bunkers' neighbor throughout three of those five chart-topping seasons) recalled the universal popularity of *All in the Family* in her autobiography: "Rob [Reiner] was the only member of the cast who could go to lunch with me at the food stalls in the Farmers Market, where I loved to eat. Carroll, Jean, and Sally could not go because they would be mobbed. People would just gather around and literally prevent them from eating. But all Rob had to do was leave his toupee back in the studio and nobody knew who he was."[124]

By this time, it cost a minimum of $70,000 per minute for advertisers to run their commercials when *All in the Family* aired.[125] For advertisers, it was the hottest time to show off their products. Meanwhile, *All in the Family* was the paterfamilias of the shows in the Lear family, and arguably the paterfamilias of television.

But why was there a universal hysteria for the Bunkers? It was simply because people cared, because of the way that Lear allowed his viewers to relate with the characters. Over the years, the bond between America and this fictional family grew. But the reason people cared was not because the Bunkers were fictional, but because the Bunkers were, in fact, real.

Trouble in Queens

As *All in the Family* started out strong in the 1971–72 season, a vicious tug of war began between Carroll O'Connor, Norman Lear, and director John Rich. The three began to vie for power. Actually, it was more of a two-sided battle: O'Connor on one end of the rope, Rich and Lear on the other. In the middle was a huge, ugly pile of mud.

In that second season, O'Connor erupted during the taping of an episode where Archie was stuck in a stalled elevator with a pregnant Puerto Rican woman, who wound up having her baby right in front of Archie's bigoted eyes. O'Connor felt that the way the scene was written would destroy the episode, and perhaps the series. O'Connor said in the fall of 1979, "I yelled bloody murder.... Our director at the time was John Rich, a brilliant, valuable man and himself well-equipped with expressive lungs. John yelled that we had better settle down to do this goddamn thing; it was all we had and we had to shoot it day after tomorrow! I launched my script toward the ceiling and strolled off the set."[126] In the end, the three sat down and made some last-second adjustments to the script.

But who really was John Rich? Rich was the man who stood next to Lear during his long, arduous, and sometimes even monotonous days. The two men sat in front of monitors, playback machines, and scripts long after the actors left the studio. Rich was around Lear's age and experience, although he weighed a bit more and had a full head of hair. Rich would be the one to point out things to Lear, such as the facial reactions of Carroll O'Connor or Sally Struthers during filming. But Rich was more than an ordinary director nobody knew about. In the '60s he had worked on *The Dick Van Dyke Show*, one of the very few shows from the decade to contribute to the integration of television, featuring African-American guest stars on several occasions. However, the cast and crew felt Rich was more valuable than credentials. Rich could tell Jean Stapleton how to handle an emotional scene. He helped her develop certain characteristics of Edith Bunker. "A man of great taste and great knowledge of comedy," said Stapleton, "and a diplomat too."[127] Rich was the everyday director of the number one show in America, so it was a major issue when O'Connor defied his authority, even though O'Connor was one of the most adept actors in the business.

The next incident in this multi-part mess took place in December of 1973, during an elaborate dinner that was thrown on behalf of Norman Lear. All of the actors from his shows were there. But one man was missing. Not an ordinary man, but the man whose pudgy face could have been the logo of Tandem Productions. Where on Earth was Carroll O'Connor? The man who greeted America every Saturday night by singing "Those Were the Days" was singing Christmas carols at his son's school. To add to the excuse, he said, "Anyway, I can't stand those dinners."[128]

Things escalated from there. Soon, O'Connor's boiling point became much lower than it had been back in 1971. In one instance, O'Connor screamed at the top of his lungs, all because Rich asked him to repeat a line, not liking how the line came out. "Now let's get something understood right away," O'Connor began in his tirade. "If I make a change, I make it for a reason. If anybody up there in the booth wants to come down and play my part, OK. Meantime, I'm exercising my right of approval of the script."[129]

Next, O'Connor demanded a dressing room, with couches and a color TV. He was granted his wish. Soon after, Lear prevented O'Connor from appearing in beer commercials that would allow him to earn hundreds of thousands, in addition to his $25,000 per episode as Archie Bunker.[130]

This all happened in the middle of *All in the Family's* fourth season. The battle between the producers and O'Connor had not yet reached its climax, but temperatures were certainly rising. Lear was a competitive man who headed the number one show in the world. O'Connor was also highly competitive and was the main character of the most popular show in the world. Lear said of O'Connor in the summer of 1974, "Carroll is a marvelous person. He works harder than anybody I know — sometimes harder than he himself wishes. But, he can't help it. It's his nature. Whatever problems we have, we'll work out because essentially we want the same things."[131] Each day though, things became more bitter.

As the popularity of *All in the Family* grew, so did Carroll O'Connor's. However, his newfound fame brought many conflicts between him and the crew.

There were many times when O'Connor wanted to initiate a coup d'e-
tat, and overthrow Lear. Both men wanted the show to be at its best all the
time, but took very different routes to get there. Sometimes these different
ideologies resulted in long-lasting battles and tension-filled power struggles.
TV Guide commented about O'Connor in January of 1979, "Overnight he
became a self-professed expert in all phases of situation comedy production.
He was beset with that old and sometimes fatal feeling that he could write
better than his writers and direct better than his directors."[132]

O'Connor would always threaten to leave the show; not only did the
weekly schedule take its toll, but it irked him whenever a stranger stopped
him on the street to praise him for one of Archie's racist comments.[133] O'Connor, a liberal, was unhappy when Archie's satirical comments were completely
misunderstood. When strangers complimented him, it angered him even
more, making him feel that the show was not getting its message across. He
usually took his anger out on the scripts.

By the summer of 1974, O'Connor was very frustrated with his job. He
went on strike that summer, asking for more money and more input in the
scripts and in the show. O'Connor once said, "Show-biz contracts are never
honored. Show-biz contracts are never honorable. They are licenses to exploit,
which producers themselves expect to tear up in the event of a bonanza."[134]

The bonanza was already well underway. By fall, Lear had it up to his
neck with O'Connor's antics. Lear stormed into the office of Perry Lafferty,
who was the vice president of programming at CBS, and said, "Either Carroll O'Connor goes or I go."[135] Lafferty felt there was only one Archie Bunker,
who was irreplaceable. However, one of Lear's former writers, Frank Tarloff,
felt much differently, telling *TV Guide* in 1974, "By the third week, people
would accept a new Archie Bunker — and I think Norman has the guts and
the money to do it."[136] Would he?

Where would the show go if O'Connor was fired? Would Mike have to
quit college and find a job? Would Edith get a full-time job and become a
more liberated woman? Would Gloria's income become the primary source
of money for the family? Would the next door neighbors become series reg-
ulars? If Archie was no longer there, the racial tension, which was a major
asset of *All in the Family,* would disappear. Relationships would instantly disappear. No more arguments between Mike and Archie. Who would Edith tell
her long, convoluted stories to? Who would call Edith a dingbat?

In response to O'Connor's behavior, Lear and Rich nervously designed
a three-part script where Archie was killed in a plane crash.[137] Soon after Lear
wrote it, O'Connor acquiesced, and Lear made a substantial last-minute
modification. In the final script, Archie had too much to drink and got off at
the wrong stop, ending up in Buffalo.

The power struggle between the two men did not end. It lingered on through the seasons. However, by the time the show's run was over, Carroll O'Connor showed much contrition for his actions. "I regret nothing about my years on *All in the Family* except my own anger."[138] O'Connor felt this remorse for the rest of his life. Looking back a year before his death in 2001, O'Connor showed more pangs of regret for his volatile relationship with Lear in the 1970s. "Being an intellectual snob, I wasn't ready to give the little guys [the uneducated public] any credit. I had the power to really drive everybody crazy, including Norman, who had to give way a lot. He didn't like it that he had to give way. I had to fight all the way and very often got nasty. I got very nasty with him. I fault myself, I didn't have to get that nasty. And I made him dislike me. I made him dislike me and then, of course, I turned around and disliked him."[139] Lear said, "Carroll O'Connor, the actor, the producer, the intellect, I don't say those three things pejoratively. That O'Connor was fearful and misguided; I found most of the time."[140]

John Rich left *All in the Family* in 1974, and the set soon became more serene. When producer Paul Bogart took over as director, he began a friendship with O'Connor, and was liked by Lear. O'Connor did not have any complaints about Bogart, calling him "just about the best director in the business."[141] As a result, tensions eased between Lear and O'Connor as the series continued. "He and I began as warm, mutually respectful friends; we became antagonists, then in recent years we moved back to where we started," O'Connor said when *All in the Family* came to a close in 1979.[142] By that point, the two were in the friend zone. When Bogart came on board, the two remaining men dropped the tug-of-war rope and the entire cast became more of a team. Nobody actually ever fell in the mud. O'Connor said, "I finally discovered I wasn't the only guardian of reality. Jean, Rob, and Sally discovered effective voices once I lowered mine."[143]

However, O'Connor was not the only person who had problems with management during the course of *All in the Family*. In 1975, as the biggest disputes between O'Connor and Lear began to simmer down, Sally Struthers became unhappy with her contract: she wanted to get into movies, and she felt her contract was a hindrance. In 1975, she sued to get out of the contract, and because of this conflict, she did not appear in four consecutive episodes early in the sixth season.[144] Eventually things would work out (Struthers lost in arbitration), and after the problem was resolved, the cast members received large raises in salary, to try to prevent another conflict that had the potential to hurt *All in the Family*.

But the incident with Struthers was negligible compared to the big issue that haunted *All in the Family* and Norman Lear in 1975. In April of 1975, Lear's vacation in Paris was interrupted by a phone call from CBS president

Robert Wood. As Lear and wife Frances were preparing to go to dinner, Wood put a huge damper on Lear's vacation. Wood explained that the Federal Communications Commission had established "Family Hour." Actually, it was *two* hours; from 7 to 9 P.M., there was an embargo on excessive sex and violence on television, as well as excessive swearing. At the time, *All in the Family* sat right in the center of Family Hour, and the FCC was trying to force them out.

On the phone, Wood gave Lear two options: either soften the character of Archie Bunker (and his language), or move *All in the Family* out of its famous slot. Lear did not particularly want to pursue either option. "I just can't change Archie," Lear told Wood, his primary concern being *All in the Family*'s portrayal of reality. "He's a fifty-year-old man. Fifty-year-old men don't change like that."[145] As far as moving *All in the Family* to nine o'clock, Lear complained, "If you consider the channel selector a vote, they [the public] voted it the number one family show ... so you've got the public with you."[146] Lear was correct on that; 70 percent of the public was against stricter regulations on television content.[147] Geoffrey Cowan, one of the attorneys for Lear, wrote in his 1979 publication, *See No Evil: The Backstage Battle Over Sex and Violence on Television*, "What made the Family Hour so frightening was that it appeared to herald a return to the restraints of the pre–Lear era in comedy."[148] While Family Hour was in effect, shows like *Laverne and Shirley*, which Arthur Unger of *The Christian Science Monitor* called "mindless entertainment,"[149] ruled the air. Lear told Unger, "The networks will try to compete in those ways until and unless the public makes it known that that is not what it wants."[150] In the fall of 1975, Lear chose to begin the sixth season of *All in the Family* on Mondays at nine, rather than adjust Archie's character.

In October of 1975, the creative side of television responded. The Screen Actors Guild, the Directors Guild, and the Writers Guild of America, along with Lear and producers such as Grant Tinker and actors such as Carroll O'Connor and Mary Tyler Moore, challenged the FCC. They all vehemently felt that the Family Hour was a violation of their First Amendment Rights. Perhaps O'Connor was the most expressive about his feelings. He shouted to the press at a plaintiff's press conference, lambasting everyone, "What's at issue is the Congress moving in and interfering with the freedom of communication in this country, for whatever reason — maybe because of little pressure groups here and there in the Bible Belt, and the letters coming in. But instead of taking responsibility, of going back to their constituents and explaining the way this country should run, and explaining the freedom that we should have, Congressmen find it much easier just to put pressure on the FCC, and the FCC turns around and puts the pressure on the networks."[151]

After much testimony, Judge Warren J. Ferguson waived the Family Hour. The entire situation caused sparks to fly throughout the country. "I've gotten calls from schoolchildren who say they are talking about it in class as a First Amendment victory for freedom of speech,"[152] said Lear several days after he won his case.

But despite all the chaos behind the front door of 704 Hauser Street, members of the cast loved each other and loved Lear. Even O'Connor and Lear loved each other in some weird way, mainly because they understood that they both wanted to succeed. These two men handled their problems without hurting the show. The disputes over money and recognition did not affect the product that this entire team put together week after week, for nearly a decade — although it did come very close at times.

Edith, the Feminine Hero

Possibly the most distinguished and beloved female character in television history was Jean Stapleton's Edith Bunker. But why? On the outside, she seemed like an ordinary housewife. She was a lady with curly, reddish-brown hair running around yelling, "Here's your beer, Archie," in a somewhat shrill voice. Edith was not a fashion model — she wore old, threadbare dresses. She wore dresses as often as Archie wore his white shirt. In almost every scene, an apron covered the faded colors of those dresses. She was usually spotted chopping vegetables on the counter or making coffee by the stove. An analogy could be phrased, "Edith is to kitchen as prostitute is to bedroom." However, Edith would probably be bemused by the concept of prostitution. When it came to sex, she never spoke. Edith also had no intuition for politics, nor did she seem to understand what bigotry was. In one conversation, when asked her opinion on capital punishment, she replied, "As long as it ain't too severe."[153]

Yet Edith Bunker was loved by anybody who ever watched *All in the Family* — because of what she possessed internally. She could light up the room with her smile, ease tension with one of her harangues about cling peaches in heavy syrup, or show affection to people Archie hated, such as her relatives or gay liberators that came knocking on her door. Her political naiveté could even lighten up an argument between Archie and Mike. In fact, she was the one who made Archie appear respectable to the world and was the only who could tolerate the racism spewing out of Archie's mouth. David Marc wrote, "Edith transcends racism not by ideological decision, but rather through an innocent, unabashed, organic love of her fellow human beings."[154] Viewers appreciated Edith because she had everlasting patience. How else would she have tolerated Archie? Norman Lear told Jean Stapleton back in

1968 who exactly Edith Bunker was. "Edith is able *not* to listen to Archie. She puts her head in the sand, mentally blocking out his worst traits. And she's been doing it for years. How else would she survive?"[155] When Stapleton asked Lear how to "tune out" Archie, Lear said, "You pretend that you are the middle sister of the Andrews Sisters. You are singing 'Don't Sit Under the Apple Tree' or something, and that's all that is going through your head. It keeps you from hearing the things you don't want to hear."[156] Viewers wished they could possess Edith's intense patience in an era when things were not always perfect.

Edith exhibited a heart of gold towards everybody she encountered. But Edith also grew as a character, and as a woman, throughout *All in the Family*'s nine-year run. Most of the time, it seemed as if Edith accepted Archie's belief that, as a woman, she was inferior. She would run into the kitchen to get dinner on the table for a grumpy Archie, who demanded dinner as soon as he came home from work. Once, Archie even made Edith set the table as fast as possible while he timed her with his new watch. Seconds later, dialogue between Archie and Gloria was interrupted by a sprinting Edith, running around the table, placing all the plates down, and crossing the finish line by going back into the kitchen. "She loves it!" Archie told a rather puzzled Gloria.[157]

Then there were the times Archie had to try to understand Edith. Edith's first major backlash against Archie's self-imposed power came midway through the second season, when Edith began menopause. She walked into the kitchen yelling "Dammit!" at Archie, shocking the crowd because they never expected Edith to utter a curse. However, by the time she came back into the living room, she was marveling at the weather. The big moment of the episode came minutes later when Edith screamed "Stifle!" at Archie. That was the word that Archie always shouted at her, usually after she blindly told some neighbor the remark that Archie made about him or her. Edith did not stop there. "Stifle! Stifle! Stifle!" she cried in her frenzy. As she screamed, so did the audience. It was the first time they had seen Edith directly yell at Archie, but it would not be the last. At the end of that episode, Archie went to Edith's gynecologist, or as he said it, "groinocologist," and got some advice about how to tolerate Edith's erratic behavior.[158] It was considered one of the greatest episodes in the show's history. Burt Styler, who wrote the episode, won an Emmy award in 1972 for Outstanding Writing Achievement in a Comedy Series.

As the years went by, Edith became more liberated. When Irene and Frank Lorenzo moved in next door, Edith and Irene quickly became soul mates. The Lorenzos were a reversal of the traditional male and female roles. Irene (Betty Garrett) was the one who fixed the plumbing and heating, while

Frank (Vincent Gardenia) was the cook. While wearing a tool belt around her waist, Irene was an active participant in the women's liberation movement. Some of that rubbed off on Edith (along with Gloria's women's rights crusade). Edith began to attend women's meetings, much to Archie's dismay. In one episode, Edith asked Archie, "Is that all I am to you — a cook, a cleaning lady, a sexual object?"[159]

Soon, Edith began to speak up for herself. In the sixth season finale, Edith abandoned the housewife look altogether, trading in the discolored, tethered apron for a shiny, red suit jacket and pants. For a while, she had been stuck inside the house, since Archie would rather complain about Walter Cronkite than go out with Edith. On this night, she would have none of that. Archie accidentally told Edith that he sometimes goes to Kelsey's Bar to get away from her, which angered Edith a great deal. "See Archie, I've got to get away from you tonight," she told him, before she went to Kelsey's Bar and instantly became the life of the party — reveling in the center of the crowd, made up of Archie's friends.[160] It was nice, after six years, to see Edith finally enjoying herself.

To start off the following season, Archie had a very small fling with a waitress in a local diner. When Edith found out, she was very angry and dejected. Edith felt she had lost the only thing she could trust. Archie was also extremely mad at himself, for his disloyal and ultimately stupid actions. However, Edith had an epiphany during that experience. During their reconciliation, Edith told him who she learned to trust throughout the experience. "Me!" she replied with a smile.[161] At the same time, America smiled, and the audience gave her an ovation.

As the feminist movement progressed throughout the 1970s, Edith Bunker's independence grew. Edith became a liberated woman who led by example. She did not picket; she did not kick and scream. She may not have worked most of the time, but *All in the Family* proved that not all housewives were subdued by their husbands. Of Edith, Jean Stapleton said, "The image of Edith Bunker is good for the women's movement because Edith is a homemaker."[162]

As she grew, she also did things she enjoyed. By the midpoint of the decade, she was volunteering much of her time to the Sunshine Home (a nursing home), helping older folks. It fulfilled her desire to help others, the selfless gesture that gave her satisfaction.

Throughout the first six seasons of *All in the Family*, Edith became a fan favorite and an influence. Her innocent personality was one that people strive to emulate. Now, through the mini-affair, she had become more independent than she ever was before. She could finally trust herself 100 percent.

The development of Edith was not finished though. On October 16, 1977,

America truly realized how much they loved Edith, when Norman Lear gave the country a stroke. For the first time in television history, people saw a graphic approach towards rape. And it was not graphic because there was on-screen nudity — in fact, there was none. It was graphic because the poor victim was the matriarch of America.

By the eighth season, it was nearly seven full years after Edith, for the first time on television, got Archie a beer. Loyal viewers grew close to this real lady who was as sweet as pie. And they fell in love more and more each time she stood up to Archie. With the love came respect — and protection. "How could anything happen to my dear Edith Bunker?" asked America on that gloomy October night.

They watched the ensuing horror unravel when Edith gallivanted to the door, just like she had done many times before. This time she did not let in a gay liberator or Cousin Maude in. This time she let in a young, handsome man who flashed a police badge. The man looked like he could do no harm. Only his badge was not real. This man was about to commit the most evil crime on the face of this Earth. He was about to rape Edith Bunker. Lesson one from the episode: Do not judge a book by its cover.

The rapist, named Lambert, still acting as a police officer, began describing the profile of a sexual predator running around the neighborhood. He described his own characteristics—from the color of his hair to the stripes on his tie. The audience knew the hell they were going to witness. And they were sure when the molester locked the door with the chain. Lambert aggressively shoved a petrified Edith into her chair.

After the commercial, Lambert was sitting on top of Edith, stripping himself. It was at that point the sex was inevitable. But it was not sex — like all rape cases, it was an act of pure violence and malevolence. Now, viewers wanted to open their idiot boxes, jump into the Bunker living room, and break that idiot in half.

Edith tried to escape by going to the bathroom, but she decided to "wait until tomorrow" after Lambert followed her. He brought her back down the stairs by painfully grabbing her, pressing his body up against hers. Lambert threw her onto the couch and manacled her with his tie. At that point, the audience wanted to take that tie and hang him with it. They were silent — they could not believe the tragedy they were watching. It was not television. It was like they were witnessing their mother getting raped. Along with millions of viewers at home, they felt sick to their stomachs from the hypersecretion of adrenaline. America cried in synchronization on that night.

Then Archie came from next door to pick up a punchbowl. Lambert pulled out the gun that was exposed in his right pocket, and threatened to kill both Edith and Archie if she did not get rid of her husband. Eventually, Archie did leave. Then Edith smelled something burning in the kitchen. "Fire!" she cried.[163]

After all the amazing cakes Edith baked over the years, the cake she had been baking on this day was burned. Irony it was, indeed. In her final chance to escape, she spontaneously shoved the smoking cake in Lambert's face. The cake saved her life, and probably gave the rapist severe burns. Next, Edith opened the door, kneed the evil rapist in the crotch and slammed the door shut; as the noise from the studio audience instantly changed from mute to screams. Somewhere, hidden beneath all of Edith's warmth, there was an instinct for self-defense.

Edith sprinted through the dining room and into the living room — arms flailing in front of her, zipper down, bra showing, sweating and sobbing — and opened all the chains and ran out of the house, into Archie's arms next door. For the audience, despair instantly became great hope and relief. "Run! Run! Run! Run!" screamed the entire studio audience repeatedly at the top of their lungs, stomping their feet fiercely. Now tears of joy ran down the face of America. But the country's heart did not stop pounding until many minutes later. The producers, trying to move things along, began taping the next scene, but could not because the audience was still cheering for Edith. The dialogue could not be clearly heard. The audience was grateful that their mother was saved.

David Dukes, who played Lambert, recalled, "There was a moment when I did something, I tore her dress or something, to where it was clear that I am not going to be a funny rapist and the audience went 'Ahhhh.' And when 400 people do that it's a big sound, and it was like I just looked at Jean and it was like 'Jesus God, what's happening?' because the audience just hated me, hated me. And I had no idea what I was stepping into."[164]

The producers contributed to the drama of the scene by not stopping in between, at all. Dukes said, "Paul Bogart [the director] told us there would be no stops at the time of the taping. No time for repositions. We had to go straight through. If we gave the audience any time to settle and talk to each other, we'd lose the tension."[165]

The episode did not only show the physical aspect of rape. It portrayed the psychological tunnel that victims experience — paranoia that victims face after their life-changing, life-threatening horror. Once again, Lear showed the generation gap between the Bunkers and the Stivics — even through rape. Archie felt "rape" was a bad word, telling Mike never to say it loudly. Archie would only mouth it silently. At the same time, Mike and Gloria's first reaction was to call the police. However, that was the last thing Archie wanted. He read, and remembered from Gloria's rape case, that lawyers were famous for turning the case around, making the woman seem like she asked for it, although Edith was not wearing a short skirt and a tight shirt, nor did she ever. Her apron was not risqué— nowhere near risqué. *All in the Family* spoke to dispel the blame that defense lawyers were putting on female victims of rape.

But Edith did not like the idea either. "He's gonna kill me!" she sobbed, fearing retaliation more than what just happened.[166] And when she saw his clothes, she had the same reaction, running up the stairs, scared out of her mind, screaming, "He's gonna kill me!" in a sickly voice that America never heard Edith speak in.

But Edith's desire to keep the evidence inside was not due to the generation gap. The truth was that only 5–10 percent of rape victims ever reported what happened to them.[167] The vast majority of victims were afraid to once again face the man who hurt them. Like Edith, they tried to forget it —but of course they could not.

After heavy convincing from Gloria, the episode ended with another emotional moment: Edith (along with Archie) goes down to the police station to identify the man. Edith set an example for other millions of other female victims— to report rape cases. Donna McCrohan said, "Because Edith is Edith, the idea of reporting such indignities sickens her. But because Edith is Edith, she consents to go, rather than leaving her assailant free to endanger others."[168] And a great number of people were watching Edith deal with this situation. *All in the Family* was the fifth most watched show that year, its eighth season on the air.

Edith was truly a feminine hero. In the end, she was part of that 5–10 percent group and defended herself by identifying the rapist, after somehow escaping from the armed man. She gave America the hope they needed, even to escape rape. They could win the horrific battle, too. And many women probably wanted to say in return, "Thanks, Mom."

However, Lear faced a bundle of criticism for this episode. With indignation, he responded to critics, "How could we be reaching for sensationalism when we're taking something right out of our national life and dealing with it? Rape is the fastest growing crime in America. We worked on this script for over a year to get it right."[169]

Cecil Smith of *The Los Angeles Times* was amazed by the episode, saying, "Low comedy, high tragedy mesh skillfully in special edition of *All in the Family*," and calling the rape attempt "one of the most harrowing scenes of this or any season."[170] Yet, there were still angry viewers, who wrote back to Smith's column. One viewer wrote, "Rape is the most awful crime man can perpetrate against woman. There's nothing hilarious about it."[171]

Unfortunately, some crazy fans took their real infatuation with Edith too far, refusing to realize they could not actually jump into the television set without banging their heads on the glass screen, to a point where David Dukes received death threats. But he said in 1979, "That sitcom was more valuable than any show I've done Off-Broadway."[172] This scene was shown to many vice squads at the time, because it gave an accurate representation of rape[173], and, as David Dukes said, "conveyed the women's side of rape."[174]

That was just how real *All in the Family* was. Henry Fonda said in 1975, "*All in the Family* is one of the few shows that can blend the laugh and the tear."[175] And this episode was a paradigm of what Fonda said. The moment when the audience screamed at Edith, "Run!" was emblematic of why *All in the Family* was so successful and influential — because viewers cared about the genuine characters they interacted with, week after week, for nine years. As Norman Lear put it, *All in the Family* was a "celebration of life."[176]

The End of an Era

In the spring of 1978, *All in the Family* would complete its astounding run after eight seasons. In that eighth season *All in the Family* was still highly successful, being the fifth most watched show in America. Viewers tuned in to see Archie buying Kelsey's Bar, Edith getting the shock of her life, Archie revealing his abusive childhood to Mike, and Edith witnessing a murder on Christmas Day. Rob Reiner and Sally Struthers both announced that they were leaving the show to pursue other goals. Reiner had a deal with ABC; Struthers wanted to move on to movies. On the show, Lear decided that this was the perfect stopping place, and that Mike, Gloria, and their baby Joey would move to California.

In the final episode, Mike and Gloria, Archie and Edith renewed their wedding vows in the Bunker home, during the Stivics' final day in New York. However, the vows were overshadowed by the denouement of *All in the Family* — the painful parting of the Bunkers and Stivics. Gloria said goodbye to her parents, Grandma and Grandpa kissed Joey goodbye. Edith and Mike expressed their love for each other. Gloria and Joey went to the waiting taxi, marking the final sight of Sally Struthers on *All in the Family*. Then, arguably, the most touching scene of *All in the Family* happened. Archie and Mike said goodbye on the Bunkers' porch. Mike lovingly told Archie how he was like a father to him; he told him he loved him. Mike then dropped his baggage and put his arms around his "father" for the last eight years. Archie, who normally refused to express a sensitive side, hugged his "son" back. It seemed that all those years of bickering were worth it. Nine years earlier, Mike had walked into Archie's home wearing a tie-dyed T-shirt, which Archie had assumed to be a Halloween costume. Now, Mike headed off into the California sunshine with Archie's only daughter and only grandson. At the same time, Rob Reiner headed towards a highly productive directing career.

But now, Archie headed back into his home, pulled out a tissue, and sobbed. Edith came out of the kitchen, where she was doing the same thing. The two sat where they had sat for the last eight years, and many before that. Edith was crying, Archie stared upward, like he was asking the Lord for an explanation. The camera faded out, zooming out of the living room. The Norman Lear show that changed American television forever had just ended.

The cameras rolled after the taping as the cast said goodbye to the audience one last time, and exchanged tears, hugs, and kisses. Carroll O'Connor said that day, "It is the end of an era."[177]

Not yet.

In the 1977–78 season, CBS was still suffering from the blows of Family Hour, which had ended two years before. In that season, ABC picked up much speed in the ratings race, with hits such as *Happy Days* and its spin-off *Laverne and Shirley*. In the spring of 1977, ABC's *Three's Company* became an instant success; in the 1977–78 season, the show ranked third in the Nielsen ratings. The two shows seen by more people were *Laverne and Shirley* (#1) and *Happy Days* (#2).

Meanwhile, the success that CBS had before Family Hour was no longer there. *Maude* and *Good Times* had dropped out of the top thirty. *The Mary Tyler Moore Show* was off the air, along with its spin-off, *Phyllis*. Its other spin-off, *Rhoda*, was no longer a ratings contender and would be cancelled shortly into the 1978–79 season. And another Grant Tinker show, *The Bob Newhart Show*, ended in the spring of 1978. Finally, *The Sonny and Cher Comedy Hour* was never the same after the couple's divorce in 1974. CBS was concerned that *All in the Family's* departure would destroy the ratings. They spent 25 percent of their summer trying to bring *All in the Family* back for a ninth season.[178] Yet Norman Lear wanted nothing more to do with television.

After the final episode of *All in the Family,* Lear stepped down from the show. He was no longer at the studio. He did not even call to wish the cast good luck before the season's start.[179]

Lear picked Alan Horn to handle *All in the Family*, if CBS wanted to keep *All in the Family* alive. O'Connor and Stapleton agreed to return for another year, and *All in the Family* would be back. About the decision to keep the show on the air, Lear told *TV Guide* in 1979, "It was Alan's idea. I am out of the picture altogether. But it doesn't surprise me. If you asked me would the show tail off just because the kids were gone, I'd say no. Archie and Edith were always the guts of the show."[180] Horn said, "Already [*All in the Family* is] in the Smithsonian and as much a household word as baseball. So why throw it away?"[181] By this point, Archie Bunker's famous chair had made it to the Smithsonian, to be preserved just like the Declaration of Independence.

In the fall of 1978, viewers met a new character. The first cast change in the history of *All in the Family* was the addition of Danielle Brisebois; a nine-year old girl with much acting experience under her belt. She played Stephanie Mills, whose alcoholic father abandoned her, leaving her on the Bunkers' porch. Archie and Edith welcomed her into their home and took good care of her.

Midway through the ninth season, the Bunkers and Stephanie flew to California to join Mike, Gloria, and Joey for Christmas. However, Archie and Edith found an ugly surprise — the Stivics' marriage had ended. Gloria felt that Mike was more concerned with his job than her, and she soon began an affair. While the Bunkers were there, Mike and Gloria pretended to be together, until a fight escalated in the bedroom. It did not seem at all like the Mike and Gloria Americans knew for the last eight years — the two seemed like random people expressing their hostility towards one another. Gloria told Mike several times, "You're an ass!" while Mike bitterly commented that Gloria put on a few pounds since he moved out.[182] There seemed to be no hope for one of those kisses they routinely shared while living under Archie's roof.

Finally, on Christmas morning, Edith and Archie found out. Edith made both Mike and Gloria realize they still loved each other, making them consider saving their marriage. In the end, there was hope, as Mike and Gloria shared a brief kiss.

In the spring of 1979, with the future of Mike and Gloria still uncertain, *All in the Family* ended after 210 episodes. It finished in a tie for tenth in the Nielsen ratings, but more importantly Archie, Edith, and Stephanie had said goodbye.

Not yet.

Archie Bunker returned to the CBS lineup in the fall of 1979, but not with *All in the Family*. The show was now titled *Archie Bunker's Place*, a pseudo-spin-off of *All in the Family*. All three of the cast members from *All in the Family*'s final season were stars in the new sitcom. O'Connor was originally skeptical, but then, by the fall of 1979, wrote in *TV Guide*, "I have found reasons to be as confident as in any season of the past."[183]

There were several major changes, however. First, the primary setting was at Archie Bunker's Place, the bar he bought in the fall of 1977. Second, Jean Stapleton appeared less and less frequently, at her request, since she felt like she was becoming typecast as Edith. Stapleton only appeared in a handful of episodes. Third, O'Connor had producer status, controlling the show without any power struggle. By this point, with Lear out of the picture, the

Bunker legacy was his. He was even into casting, hiring his good friend Martin Balsam, the fourth major change from *All in the Family*. Balsam played Murray Klein, Archie's business partner, who happened to be Jewish. The character was created in an attempt to bring back some of the tension seen in earlier episodes of *All in the Family*. Balsam did not originally want to be a part of *Archie Bunker's Place*, until O'Connor raised his offer from $7,500 per episode to $32,500 per episode, which was the salary of superstars.[184]

Archie Bunker's Place would be back in the fall of 1980, but with a huge hole in America's heart. Jean Stapleton left, never to return. At the same time, Edith Bunker, America's mother, died that summer.

The season opened with Archie trying to cope with the loss of Edith. Only he tried to cope by forgetting. From Heaven, Edith was telling Archie that forgetting does not work — she learned that lesson when she tried to forget about the rapist. But Archie did not hear her. He even refused to take Stephanie to the cemetery. Finally, Archie let loose as he held one of Edith's slippers. He talked to Edith from above, tearfully telling her she should not have left without him saying "I love you" for the last time.

America cried with Archie. Writer Tom Shales of *The Washington Post* published an obituary for Edith. "Edith, Edith, Edith — how could you ever up and die on us?" he asked, later adding, "Shame on any eye that remains dry!"[185] Even Norman Lear was sad. Stapleton recalled discussing Edith's death with Lear over the phone, "[Norman] said it is just very difficult for me to let this happen. And so I said to him, 'Well you know Norman, she's only fiction.' And there was this dead silence on the phone and I thought that I had really offended him. But then he came back with this statement, 'To me she isn't,' which was very telling and very dear."[186]

The cast was also in mourning. Danielle Brisebois said, "In the show, we had to cry, and it came very naturally. It was an instant reaction — for everybody. After the show, Carroll came back to my dressing room and said that I'd done a really good job."[187]

Jean Stapleton found success after departing with the character of Edith. In her autobiography, Betty Garrett said about her former co-worker and dear friend, "Ever since playing Edith, she has had to strive to get beyond that image and since it was such an indelible character you can see how it would be hard for her. But Jean has a great deal of dignity about her and I think she has been quite successful in changing her image. People came to accept her as something other than a dingbat. She did an Eleanor Roosevelt that I thought was wonderful and a short operatic version of a Ruth Draper monologue called 'The Italian Lesson.'"[188]

Archie Bunker's Place did not lose many viewers after Jean Stapleton's exit; the show ranking thirteenth in the Nielsen race after its second season.

Despite that, there were several major cast changes before the start of season three. Martin Balsam decided to leave the show, missing his family who lived across the country in New York. By the time he left, Carroll O'Connor wished *Archie Bunker's Place* had gone farther with his character. O'Connor told *TV Guide* in 1981, "We went into the Murray Klein character without really knowing, but hoping something would emerge that would make him a dominant figure. It never did."[189] Executive producer Mort Lachman said, "Write the funniest speech for Murray, put both men [Murray and Archie] on camera, and the audience will still be watching Archie."[190]

When *All in the Family* began in 1971, Robert Wood wanted to air the show because it attracted a younger audience. Ten years later, with Wood out of the loop (he had resigned in the middle of the Family Hour crisis), CBS felt the show was not attracting that younger demographic. In response, they brought in youth. Denise Miller (previously starring in the *Barney Miller* spin-off, *Fish*) was cast as Archie's niece from Baltimore, Billie, who moved into the Bunker home. Miller could provide romantic heat to the show, something Danielle Brisebois was still too young for.

At the start of the third season, there was unity all around. "You couldn't kill it with a stick," said Lachman.[191] The show lived up to his belief, actually doing slightly better than the previous season (ranking twelfth). By the end of the year, Carroll O'Connor had played Archie Bunker for twelve years. A reporter asked, if it were possible, would he do it for another twelve. The man who frequently threatened to leave *All in the Family* responded, "If you give me a contract for another twelve years just as me I'll sign it right now."[192] At that point, O'Connor owned 50 percent of *Archie Bunker's Place*.[193] The *Chicago Tribune* called O'Connor "a TV institution."[194]

In the fall of 1982, Sally Struthers returned to network television. When she left *All in the Family* in the spring of 1978, she had hoped for more success. Instead, she got divorced, had a pilot show rejected, and was part of a failed Broadway play. "I guess I've done a lot of personal growing up in the last few years," Struthers told *The Los Angeles Times* in 1982.[195]

Now Struthers returned to television reprising her role as Gloria Stivic. Or Bunker? *Gloria* took place in New York at a veterinarian's office, with one major catch — Gloria had divorced Mike! Mike left Gloria and Joey for a commune, so Gloria and Joey (Christian Jacobs) packed up and moved near Archie. A 1982 *TV Guide* cover read, "Archie's Little Girl Is on Her Own — and Scared." But Gloria was very different — not the Gloria seen on *All in the Family* who pinched Archie and cried to everyone else. Struthers told *The Los Angeles Times* in 1982, "[Gloria's] a whole different character now ... the only thing familiar about it [playing Gloria] is that my name is still Gloria."[196] Archie's Little Girl and his grandson had changed considerably. Struthers looked very different since her tenure on *All in the Family* began. Her curls seen in 1971 were back — only accompanied by the long hair seen throughout the later seasons of the show. Obviously, Joey was no longer pint-sized, now played by Christian Jacobs, who bought youth and innocence to the show. He walked around with his long bangs and his cute smile — almost like he never witnessed the breakup between his parents.

Gloria, searching for a home and a job, found both after meeting Dr. Adams (Burgess Meredith). Meredith's Dr. Willard Adams was a lovable, yet serious veterinarian who was nearing retirement age, but loved caring for animals, and bought that zest to his office. He was a light-hearted guy who was very helpful to Gloria and Joey — especially since they had moved into a tornado of uncertainty. Gloria and Joey lived in Dr. Adams' home (the office was part of the house). Gloria earned a living while Dr. Adams trained her to become a veterinary assistant. For now though, she was cleaning the cages of animals. But like her father, she did what she had to do to support her child. Unlike her father though, on the first day of her new life she wanted to give up and move back with Archie, until Mike called. After an argument over the phone with him, she realized that moving back home would be taking the easy way out. So she went to work with Dr. Adams and two veterinary assistants, Maggie Lawrence (Jo deWinter) and Clark Uhley (Lou Richards). Maggie was the one with the repulsive personality, whose first words to Gloria were, "Who the hell are you?"[197] Clark was the silly one who hit on Gloria from time to time, but had a warm heart. Lou Richards enjoyed his time on *Gloria*. He said in a personal interview, "I had been a big fan of *All in the Family* in college. So it was kind of exciting to be working on a spin-off with Sally [Struthers]. Oh yeah, working with Burgess Meredith was pretty cool too. I'd been [acting] for quite some time now and the year I spent on *Gloria* was the most fun I ever had. I was getting paid to play this

Burgess Meredith in 1981.

silly character week after week. It was a blast." On working with Struthers, he said, "She was very generous on the set and we had a wonderful time."[198]

In the show, there were many references to Gloria's days in the Bunker home. In one case, Joey took care of a black male dog that was sexually attracted to other male dogs. Joey wanted to name the dog Archie. When he asked his mother if he could call Archie to spread the good news, Gloria began to laugh hysterically, telling him, "If you want to call your grandpa and tell him that you have a gay, black dog named Archie, sure!"[199]

Gloria would need two years of training before she was fully qualified to be a veterinary assistant. She never got there. Although the show was fairly successful, ranking in a tie for eighteenth in the Nielsen ratings (which beat out every single show on NBC except for *The A-Team*), it did not appear on CBS's schedule for the 1983–84 schedule. Said Richards, "I felt it coming in April of '83 when the network preempted us for most of the month. I felt something was up. Also, that was the year that the network thought 'the sitcom' was dead. However, in 1984, *The Cosby Show* pretty much put that theory to rest.... Even though I felt the cancellation was coming, it was still extremely disappointing."[200]

But that was not the biggest surprise. That September, *Archie Bunker's Place* began its fourth season, and ranked twenty-sixth at the end. O'Connor saw no end in sight. In September, O'Connor told *The Chicago Tribune*, "As long as we keep writing about real people and situations, we won't run out of material. It's when the writers start reaching for phony situations that limitations are placed on the series. We've been lucky so far."[201] However, that was not what people at CBS were saying. Lou Richards remembered, "I had heard rumblings that CBS wanted to get rid of the Archie Bunker saga."[202] By April, in addition to *Gloria*, there was talk about the cancellation of *Archie Bunker's Place*.

The schedule for the 1982–83 season was to be released on May 10. Norman Lear gathered O'Connor, Joe Gannon (executive producer), and Alan Horn in his office, and said to them, "Let's change their [CBS's] minds."[203]

The four of them proposed two ideas for major changes in the potential fifth season. Lear said at the meeting, "Everybody agrees Archie should have a wife. I say he should have a young one, much too young for him."[204] Another thought they presented to CBS several days later was, "We'd like to work Rob [Reiner] into seven or eight episodes. He and Carroll together gave us some of the best comedy we ever had."[205] However, on May 10, O'Connor received a phone call from Lear, who said, "Well, my friend, we lost."[206]

The show was cancelled without a proper goodbye. Lear told *TV Guide* in 1983, "All I can say is I think CBS behaved very badly."[207] Several years later, Danielle Brisebois said, "Instead of cleaning the bone before they [CBS] threw it out, they threw it out with a lot of meat still on it."[208] O'Connor looked at it through a positive light, telling *The New York Times,* "I feel like we're leaving on top."[209] Nevertheless, *Archie Bunker's Place* was over, and after thirteen years, so was Archie Bunker. America could not believe it. Haynes Johnson of *The Washington Post* wrote, "An America without Archie Bunker? Unthinkable."[210] Howard Rosenberg of *The Los Angeles Times* wrote to Archie. "Arch, you were always such an anomaly, a bigot who was lovable, a decent man who was prejudiced."[211]

Now, Carroll, it was the end of an era.

* * *

On *I Dream of Jeannie,* Barbara Eden could not show her belly button. In the fourth season premiere of *All in the Family,* Sally Struthers walked around the Bunker home in a two-piece bathing suit. Four years later, Suzanne Somers and Joyce DeWitt were doing the same on *Three's Company.* In the Nineties, *NYPD Blue* exposed all. Even though a police drama, the show still had *All in the Family* to thank for paving the way. In that same episode of *All in the Family,* Carroll O'Connor became the first to yell, "God dammit!" Shows like *thirtysomething, Will and Grace, Ellen,* and *Dawson's Creek* would have never come out of the closet if *All in the Family* did not twist the knob. America could finally flush the toilet without networks telling them that the noise was derogatory. On *Friends,* Chandler Bing could not perform sexually on the night he proposed to Monica. The producers of *Friends* could thank *All in the Family*'s portrayal of impotence, although Chandler probably would not want to. *All in the Family* may have left the air years ago, but in some form, America watches the revolutionary sitcom every time they turn on the television.

2

The Greatest Show in Watts

In 1999, *TV Guide* created a list of the fifty greatest television characters. Fred Sanford was ranked number thirty-six.[1] Yet he is also one of the most badly behaved lead characters in television history. When *Sanford and Son* was broadcast for the first time on NBC in January of 1972, Redd Foxx's Fred G. Sanford — that's S-A-N-F-O-R-D-period, as he liked to spell it — became the first African-American pop in American pop culture. Fred quickly became one of the most recognizable faces in comedy, featuring his curly gray hair and beard, which turned to white by the show's fifth season. His skin color was much lighter than the skin of his "dummy" son Lamont (Demond Wilson). He liked to drink, gamble, and watch the fights with pals Grady, Melvin, and Bubba. When he was not sipping "champiple" — or a mixture of champagne and Ripple — with them, he could be comedically unpleasant. Like Archie Bunker, he was a racist, associating Asians with squinted eyes, and Puerto Ricans with cockroaches — time after time after time. Fred also detested the face of his late wife's sister, Esther (LaWanda Page) — literally. He feared he would have to clean his mirrors after she left, in order to rid the glass of her image. He also was scared of getting electrocuted by her "5000 volts of ugly."[2] Nevertheless, America loved Fred Sanford.

Maybe it was his insouciance. Fred was hilariously lazy. While Lamont went out and worked hard all day long, Fred sat inside, watched television, and did some light reading. When Lamont came home and asked what he did, he said he "coordinated," excusing his idleness on account of "arthoritis."

Maybe it was his occasional sensitivity. Fred did indeed have a compassionate side. Once, Lamont went away for the week and bet Fred that he would make no money while he was away. But Fred rented Lamont's room to a single, pregnant woman — except, to Fred's anxiety, she had the baby a few days later! Fred was forced to take care of the pregnant girl, acting as the surrogate father of the baby for several days. When Lamont lost the bet, and the woman paid the rent, he gave all the money to her for the child.[3]

Or maybe it was his charm. Fred was the first black ladies' man on television. His age of sixty-five years did not stop him from dating women much younger than him. Eventually, he began a serious relationship with Donna, a nurse.

For six seasons, millions of viewers tuned in to watch Fred maneuver his women and his son, fail at his get-rich-quick schemes, and fail to work. And while *Sanford and Son* may have been the least politically involved out of the Lear sitcoms, it was certainly not the least successful.

Pop and Dummy at the Start

By 1972, it was about time for television to focus on senior citizens. About 15 percent of the American population had reached the big Six-O, but someone who never stepped away from their television set would have never known that.[4] During the 1960s, more and more elders began to fight for their rights. By September of 1970, a major campaign to demonstrate seniors' rights began across New York City.[5]

The development of the Gray Panthers, an organization advocating the liberation of elders and the fight against ageism, began in 1972. Maggie Kuhn, founder of the Gray Panthers, said, "[Older persons] constitute a great national resource, which has been largely unrecognized, undervalued, and unused. The experience, wisdom, and competence of older persons are greatly needed in every sector of society."[6] Something that vexed the Gray Panthers was the representation of their demographic on television. Kuhn told *TV Guide*, "Old age on television is seen as a disease — with death around the corner — or naptime. The strength of old age — the vitality and wisdom of those who have survived — is not portrayed."[7]

Norman Lear's timing could not have been better. In late 1971, he was not only concerned with the new hit *All in the Family*. Now, he and Bud Yorkin had huge aspirations. The next step on the road to more success originated in Britain, just like *All in the Family* did. Lear got the idea from the BBC series *Steptoe and Son*, which centered on an older man and his son in the junk business. Lear and Yorkin created *Sanford and Son,* a half-hour comedy show about a sixty-five-year-old man, Fred Sanford (Redd Foxx), and his thirty-two-year-old son, Lamont, struggling to keep their junk business alive, while struggling to tolerate each other. Entertainer Cleavon Little, who originally declined the role of Fred, referred Foxx to the producers. Demond Wilson was cast as Lamont Sanford. Lear thought of him after he guest-starred with Little on a 1971 episode of *All in the Family*, playing a robber. Fred represented the elder man the Gray Panthers hoped to see on the tube. Okay, so he may not have been the most intelligent man on the planet, but Fred Sanford was a multi-dimensional character. Although he may not have done all the physical, blue-collar work, he was still actively involved in the business he founded. He shared his "wisdom" and his knack for running a business. After all, he did win the award for Watts Businessman of the Year.

That was not the only catch to *Sanford and Son*. He and his son were also African-American! In 1973, *The Washington Post* reported that "blacks now constitute 23 million of America's total population, approaching 15 percent, the largest minority in the country."[8] Was it not about time they received their own show?

Because of the audacity and success of *All in the Family*, Lear was able to air a show like *Sanford and Son*. It turned out that Lear helped his own cause by changing the barriers for censorship on American television. "They would've stopped this show up front three years ago. If damn and hell won't make it," Redd Foxx said in 1972, "then sure as hell no blacks gonna make it."[9] Three years before was 1969. But because of the gateway Archie Bunker created, Lear could make *Sanford and Son* center on African-Americans. And because of the gateway, the barriers for what could be said on television changed. As early as the pilot episode, Lear allowed Fred to make remarks such as, "Ain't nothin' uglier on earth than a 90-year-old white woman."[10] Two episodes later, Fred told Lamont that he felt Lamont's fiancée's parents were "a bunch of jive niggers."[11]

All in the Family proved that controversy attracts discussion, which ultimately attracts a steadily increasing number of viewers. So in *Sanford and Son*, Lear made things controversial from the start, right down to the setting. Lear could have picked any location, but he put Fred and Lamont in Watts, the part of Los Angeles which was the site of the riots instigated by African-Americans in 1965.

But why did *Sanford and Son* appeal to such a wide range of viewers? Certainly, the success of *All in the Family* made people want to tune into another Lear sitcom. Advertisers were smart, too. NBC promoted *Sanford and Son* with the clever slogan, "America, you're in for a yock; Archie, you're in for a shock!"[12]

However, Fred Sanford was not a black version of Archie Bunker. Days before the pilot aired, Lear made that clear. "*Sanford* is not sensational like *All in the Family*," he said. "It deserves to be considered on its own merits."[13] Producer Aaron Ruben said, "The only similarity may be some kind of breakthrough, away from the safe antiseptic series where you're convinced the houses don't even have bathrooms."[14]

In fact, Fred Sanford was very different from Archie Bunker. Josh Ozersky called him "an old-time sitcom character embroidered with political consciousness."[15] Unlike Archie, Fred possessed finesse and acumen. He turned on the finesse when talking to women, and turned on the acumen when dealing with customers. Sometimes he was very spontaneous. In less than a second, he could develop an insult in his mind — such as a racial brickbat — and then spit it out. *Sanford and Son* was, in fact, much different from *All in the Family*, but early on, the majority of its laughs came from the racist beliefs of the show's main man. Just like Archie, Fred had his way for a while, but in the end, the joke was on him.

It also helped the fate of the show that Redd Foxx was a well-known figure, and his dozens of comedy records from the past fifteen years were treasured by millions of fans of all colors. However, the main reason Lear and Yorkin valued *Sanford and Son* like a diamond ring was that it was simple, yet simultaneously hilarious.

In the beginning though, Lear had trouble writing the scripts. It was simpler for him to write *All in the Family* episodes, because its principal character Archie Bunker resembled his father. In the initial concept, *Sanford and Sons'* characters were white. Then producer Aaron Ruben thought, "Who's in the junk business in this country? It's got to be an ethnic group — like blacks, Italians, or Jews."[16] Despite the producers all being white, they decided the show should have an all–African-American cast.

The producers were not fully familiar with what African-Americans said and did on a day-to-day basis. Eventually, Lear hired African-American writers for the show. While the show was still new, stars Foxx and Wilson made contributions to the scripts. However, even in the pilot script, Lamont said things that he would never utter again. For example, when he told his father how he was an art connoisseur, he said, "I reads all about this stuff."[17] Soon, the writers and cast would never settle for these stereotypes, which inferred that the lapses in grammar were African-American argot. Nobody on the set wanted *Sanford and Son* to evolve into another *Amos 'n' Andy*. Foxx said in 1972, "It's funny, Demond and I recognize things that just aren't right immediately, simultaneously. Some words are so obviously Negro to me — not black, but Negro. I wouldn't say it. I've ducked so many shows that are supposed to sound like the color of you."[18] Wilson commented in 1972, "For the first time it [*Sanford and Son*] won't let the blacks down, in terms of something like a *Julia*. It's honest. I'm not saying that all black people will be able to relate to it. But a lot of them will."[19] He also said, "Any situation Redd and I aren't comfortable with, we tell 'em. If anything, black militants might resent that we're showing this much of ourselves. I mean, we aren't caricatured. We aren't glamorized. We're poor but we're trying to get along, which is the way it is for most blacks. It's honest and I can say that 'cause I am from Harlem; I know."[20]

Sanford and Son was a midseason replacement in 1972, and critics had

Fred Sanford (Redd Foxx) "coordinating" the junkyard. The character of Fred Sanford appealed to two demographics — African-Americans and senior citizens.

high expectations from the start. In the series premiere (Friday, January 14, 1972, at eight o'clock), Lamont tried to auction off a porcelain antique to raise money for his own business, but his plans were ruined when Fred tried to raise the bid, outbidding the other bidders. Fred wound up winning the bid for Lamont's piece, but Lamont couldn't take $2,000 from his father. As a result, Lamont could not escape his father's junk business. The pilot episode was filled with many of the funny catch phrases that would become the vernacular of *Sanford and Son*, and on some level, America. Within six minutes of air time, Fred Sanford feigned a heart attack, and by the end of the episode, he complained about his "arth-or-itis," and asked his "big dummy" son, "How would you like one across the lip?"[21]

In the next episode, Fred celebrated his age and commenced a new era in his life — receiving Social Security. On his sixty-fifth birthday, the buoyant old man called to find out how much he would be getting, as the amount of Social Security given to seniors was on the rise. That night, Fred and Lamont went to celebrate his birthday, Fred wearing a new, expensive hat given to him by his son. Fred called the hat "the Social Security office hat."[22] The only time Kuhn's stereotype of elders was seen on *Sanford and Son* was when Fred would try to con Lamont into doing something, like giving him his birthday present. The Gray Panthers had nothing to be ashamed of. Through its characters and plots, *Sanford and Son* showed the American public that the equation, elder equals decrepit, is false.

After the first few episodes, the future looked bright for *Sanford and Son*. Like its brother, *All in the Family,* it thrived on pressure from critics and competition, and it became apparent that it would be on the air for a long time. In its first season, it ranked a stellar sixth in the Nielsen ratings, and would take off from there. For the next six years, Friday nights would belong to NBC. By early February of 1972, Lear had two shows— both of which ranked very high in the ratings. The following year, *All in the Family* attracted the most viewers, followed by *Sanford and Son.*

And both of the shows were important to the American public. *Sanford and Son* was the first show with an all–African-American cast — the first portrayal of African-Americans living with, loving, arguing with, supporting, and communicating with each other. It was the only image of African-American life that existed, and it was the pioneer for all African-American sitcoms to follow. Writer Gerard Jones attributed the *Sanford and Son* success to "its sociological bluntness. *Sanford* acknowledged that there are people locked out of the American consensus, living off its scraps (specifically, in this case, by reselling its goods as junk) ... millions could see themselves in Lamont, denied access to the affluent society."[23]

In Fred's case, *Sanford and Son* showed that bigots come in all colors.

Ten years before, African-Americans were forced to sit in the backs of buses. Now they were succeeding on network television. Jones said, "It was easier for blacks and whites just to accept the impermeability of the racial membrane for a while. Negrophobic whites could laugh at harmless Fred. Frustrated blacks (and browns and many poor whites) could enjoy a sad, sympathetic chuckle over Lamont."[24] Despite the laughs, it was nearly impossible for viewers to forget that the characters on *Sanford and Son* were African-American. That was a positive thing, because judging by the ratings, white viewers did not seem to mind that Fred and Lamont were African-American. Perhaps by introducing African-American characters into the homes of white viewers week after week, *Sanford and Son* helped to alleviate the racial tension present in America during the first half of the 1970s.

How'd You Like One Across the Lip?

If viewers had not caught the gist of *Sanford and Son*'s explosive racial punch lines, they did by the sixth episode, even if they were both blind and deaf. It was an episode where Fred staged a robbery after breaking one of Lamont's valuable antiques, and Fred hoped Lamont would not find out his own father was the one who destroyed it. When he went so far as to have the police investigate, and the police officer asked if the robber was colored, Fred responded with sincerity, "Yeah, white!"[25]

Fred was an assertive African-American who was sick and tired of being labeled as a criminal, just because African-Americans (only 12 percent of the population) committed the majority of the nation's crimes throughout the 1960s.[26] Fred Sanford, though, actually thought in terms opposite the statistics and the stereotype that originated from them. In this instance, he subconsciously vented his anger, trying to make a statement that white people commit crimes just as severe as the ones African-Americans commit. Fred had a deep-rooted anger toward people such as Archie Bunker, who blamed African-Americans for crime (and many other negative things in society).

But Fred was also a hypocrite, as seen in the second season of *Sanford and Son*. While he was angry at those who viewed African-Americans the way Archie Bunker did, he was busy viewing Puerto Ricans the same exact way. Meanwhile, *Sanford and Son* became the first show to have a Puerto Rican character recur throughout the series, and acknowledge his heritage.

Fred lived with the notion that all Puerto Ricans were criminals or pointy-toed-shoe–wearing community destroyers. "Before the Puerto Ricans moved into Harlem, it was a paradise!"[27] said Fred in his first meeting with this Puerto Rican.

Julio Fuentes was completely different from the version of Puerto Ricans

Fred envisioned. Portrayed by Gregory Sierra (who played the character with an accent that he did not normally have), Julio was a hard-working man trying to establish himself as a junkman in Watts.* Fred resented his presence, not only because he was of Puerto Rican origin, but also because he was competition — right next door. From the first episode, Fred tried to cook up ways to make Julio's junk business plummet, such as getting the housing authority after him. But Julio had previously restored the area, and received a positive citation. In the meantime, Fred attracted attention to the faults of his property, and was forced by the city to fix them. The scene showed that smart businessmen come in all colors, and it was beneficial for viewers to see a Hispanic citizen with integrity on the tube. By showing this, there was a definite chance of dispelling racial stereotypes and prejudices. Fred's theory that Puerto Ricans "run down every neighborhood they get into" was proved wrong by Julio's actions.[28] And while newspapers were filled with disputes regarding Puerto Rican oppression in the workplace, Julio portrayed a valuable, industrious Puerto Rican worker that any company would be lucky to have on the payroll.

Julio's character was the only representative of Puerto Ricans on television — at a time when they were coming into the country by the thousands. *The New York Times* wrote in 1973, "White middle-class New Yorkers are continuing to move out of the city. If present trends continue, the blacks and Puerto Ricans together would constitute a majority here in about 12 years [1985]." They also stated that the Puerto Rican proportion of total births in Manhattan during 1969 was 18 percent.[29] Julio was a spokesperson for all those Puerto Ricans, the same way Fred expressed his opinions as an African-American man — although Julio did it much more diplomatically, as he was not a character used for satire.

The first episode with Julio was the boldest and most provocative. Fred had no tolerance for Puerto Ricans. When he saw Julio's goat, he had one of his "heart attacks." The studio audience guided all viewers to see where Fred went wrong, by clapping loudly when Julio said, "I would rather live with a young goat who gives milk than an old goat who gives trouble."[30] While the audience may have laughed loudly at Fred's racist comment, they clapped with sincerity when Julio defended himself, setting an example for those watching at home to clap in respect.

However, most of the *Sanford and Son* episodes were apolitical, and centered more on common sitcom pratfalls than on *All in the Family*–style sit-

---

*Early on in his tenure on *Sanford and Son*, Sierra had a guest-spot on *All in the Family*. In a powerful episode showing the horrors of hate crimes, he was an advocate for Jewish equality — until he and his car were blown up by a bomb right in front of the Bunkers' eyes.

uations. Like *All in the Family* though, *Sanford and Son* hit the jackpot with an African-American superstar and a kiss. This time Lena Horne was the special guest star.

Horne, who was alluded to several times throughout the first year and a half of the show, became a guest-star playing herself (just as Sammy Davis, Jr., did on *All in the Family*) when Fred became her stalker. Wanting to spend time with Lena, Fred wooed her into his home — by telling her that his ill son, whose mother just died, wanted to see him. So Lena came to Fred's home right before a charity event to make "Little Lame Lamont's" day. Little did she know, "Little Lame Lamont" was not little, and Fred was the lame one. Lena was outraged, and became even more irate when she learned that Fred collected bets from his pals who did not believe Lena would show up. Saving himself, he improvised, and donated the bets to the charity, leaving Lena with one last thing for Fred — a kiss right on the lips! In response, Fred suffered one of his famous heart attacks.[31]

The episode featured none of the political friction that the Sammy Davis versus Archie Bunker match-up did. That was the major difference between the two sitcoms—*Sanford and Son* served a more comedic purpose, although never ignoring contemporary issues, while an overwhelming majority of *All in the Family*'s laughs reflected issues exposed in *The New York Times*. Both formulas seemed to work. In the 1972–73 season, *Sanford and Son* was the second-most watched show in America — only bested by *All in the Family*. Relationships on the set, however, were not nearly as perfect as the ratings.

Windows, Golf Carts, and Cocaine in Watts

Throughout his life, Redd Foxx was well known for causing controversy. He ran away from home when he was seven. Soon after, he became a juvenile delinquent. As he got older, he made money by telling dirty, bigoted jokes at Vegas nightclubs. Foxx took his tumultuous past of drugs, demands, and derogation, and moved it to the *Sanford and Son* set, where he was totally unafraid of stirring up rifts.

When *Sanford and Son* began, Foxx accomplished the dream he had always sought through his thirty-five years of toil. He was finally on television because of casting director Lear. Early on, Foxx had a lot of input in the writing as well as the acting (he improvised his way through scripts). But just as Fred Sanford bossed people around in his junkyard, Redd Foxx tried to gain control of the people on the set that held higher positions than him.

The rift between Foxx and the producers originated because Foxx felt *Sanford and Son* was not properly portraying African-Americans. He soon grew bitter at the white writers, as well as Lear and Yorkin. During a dinner in December of 1974 (the one that Carroll O'Connor did not attend), Lear made a speech, giving all the credit for the success of *Sanford and Son* to producer Aaron Ruben. A disgusted Foxx stood up, said loudly, "I'm going to the toilet!," did that, and did not return to his seat until the ceremony was over.[32] Betty Garrett (Irene Lorenzo from *All in the Family*) recalled in her autobiography, "Steve Allen [the emcee] was so incensed he followed Redd into the men's room and they got into a scuffle. Somebody said later that Steve actually hit him, he was so mad. Apparently, Redd was passing a few things around his table more potent than liquor."[33]

By the third season, Foxx and Yorkin seldom spoke to each other, even though they encountered each other nearly every day. If Foxx did not like something that was happening on the set, he would sometimes not show up for work, covering it up with excuses involving a mysterious illness.

Normally, two tapings of *Sanford and Son* would occur, with a ninety-minute intermission between the tapings, so that the producers and writers could make modifications for the next taping. During that time, sandwiches were served to the cast and crew. But soon, Foxx wanted more than sandwiches. He wanted a five-course meal of soul food served by waiters in uniforms that he picked personally. Yorkin and producer Aaron Ruben were afraid that he would not show up for work, so they gave Foxx the soul food he wanted. Yorkin said, "What could I do? When Redd is displeased, he develops some kind of illness and doesn't show up for work. So I okayed the five courses of soul food and the waiters and all the rest."[34]

The fastidious Foxx decided to go to war with the producers of *Sanford and Son* until he was the highest paid actor on the small screen.

Foxx, still angry about the material on *Sanford and Son*, told reporters in 1974,

"I found myself arguing because we had agreed that if something was distasteful to me I could delete it from the script. They would say they didn't think something was offensive to black people."[35] He once stormed out of a room of writers (and Lear) after being asked why he thought something was offensive to blacks. His response was, "I've been black longer than anybody here!"[36]

Money was the next issue on his laundry list of complaints. Foxx wanted to be the highest paid man in television, or as he once put it, "whatever Carroll O'Connor gets, plus a dollar."[37] At the time, Foxx was making about $10,000 per episode. But now he wanted a lot more. An eruption was imminent.

Before he even brought up the thought of money, he told Lear and Yorkin that his dressing room was inadequate because it lacked a window. NBC's response was that every entertainer had the same type of dressing room. He believed he needed a large room to compensate for the bad schedule that he was put through. Foxx said about the first dressing room he was granted, "That little bitty dressing room I had; there wasn't enough room in there for six people."[38]

Foxx left for a week. As the day-to-day head of *Sanford and Son*, Bud Yorkin was responsible for making him return to work. "We rented the entire convention room," said Yorkin, "at a hotel called The Sportsmen's Lodge, miles away from the studio. It had plenty of nice big windows and it was plenty expensive. Redd spent just one week there. He told us he couldn't stand all the people looking in at him through those windows and he wanted to go back to the NBC rehearsal hall without windows."[39] Foxx's antics made Yorkin contemplate whether he wanted to stay in television. "I woke up and said to myself, 'Is this the kind of life I want to lead?' *I'm* the one who has to deal with these idiotic demands."[40]

In addition to wanting the window — or not — he also wanted a golf cart for traveling through the NBC studios. Meanwhile, Foxx told Lear that, three years later, he was still adjusting to his new bedtime. "I came from a job where I had freedom," said Foxx in 1974. "I worked 90 minutes a night, and I was through until the next night. Now I have to convert and try to learn to sleep at night when I've been up at night all my life. I'll be sitting at home in the evening, and 11 o'clock comes, I get nervous. I want me a drink of Scotch, because all my life, around eleven, I had already had a couple."[41]

Foxx had many Scotches throughout his life, and was, in fact, addicted to alcohol. He also acquired an addiction to cocaine over the years he had been hanging out at nightclubs. He brought both to the *Sanford and Son* set, and as a result, the working atmosphere was far from amicable. Demond Wilson enjoyed getting high with Foxx. At the time, Foxx claimed he suffered from nervous problems, while Wilson had paranoia. Reportedly, while enraged and high, Wilson chased Norman Lear down an NBC corridor with a pistol.[42]

Foxx was unhappy with his income, because 72 cents out of every dollar went to the government, and Foxx was a big spender.[43] He owned 7 percent of the show, but wanted 25 percent. He wanted $25,000 per episode and $5,000 for reruns.[44]

NBC was not ready to offer Foxx this much. In response, the sly Foxx contrived a plan to get his money, while jeopardizing the show if he did not get his way. It started with six weeks left in the taping season, when Foxx called in sick, reporting nervous problems. He did not show up the next week either, causing anxiety in Learville. He reportedly went to Mexico for a few days to relax, and then checked into a hospital for nervous problems. But still, in the back of their minds, Lear and Yorkin questioned the validity of these claims of nervous problems.

They had no idea when the main star of their main show would be back, if ever. This called for some hasty revision to their scripts. As the clock ticked, episodes were revamped, and Fred's friend Grady (played by Whitman Mayo) filled in for Fred while he was away in St. Louis. Some of the highest-ranked episodes of *Sanford and Son* were Foxx-less. Fan mail was pouring in to Lear's office, saying they liked the switch from Foxx to Mayo. This begat new thoughts in the back of Lear and Yorkin's heads about a Foxx-less show. Meanwhile, NBC executives wondered if there would be a fourth season.

Then, thunder struck when NBC found out that Foxx taped a guest-spot on *The Merv Griffin Show*, implying that his health was not as bad as they thought. Then, Foxx talked to reporters using a vituperative tone when referring to Lear and Yorkin, the writers of *Sanford and Son*, and NBC. NBC offered Foxx a $50,000 bonus to return to the show to finish out the year. Foxx told *Ebony* about the bonus, "If I have to work under those conditions, the money ain't worth being dead for."[45]

After Foxx taped the spot and after he verbally denounced *Sanford and Son*, the indignant Lear took Foxx to court for breach of contract. Tandem won; Foxx could not work anywhere else without Tandem's permission.[46] Meanwhile, Tandem was suing both Foxx and Wilson for not showing up to work. They dropped the charges against Wilson once he began to appear, but insisted on suing the still M.I.A. Foxx for $10 million.[47]

Foxx still had not shown up by the end of taping for the third season. There would be a fourth season, and Mayo would be the star until a deal was reached. But it was a good thing for the welfare of the show that Foxx came back — because audiences wouldn't follow Grady's life forever. At the end of the fourth season, they tried to spin his character off into *Grady*, but this show flopped and was cancelled after twelve episodes. America would, however, enjoy Grady making guest appearances throughout the later years of *Sanford and Son*. Three episodes into the fourth season, NBC capitulated, granting Foxx everything he wanted—from the money to the golf cart. He returned to work, and the lawsuit was dropped.

Once Foxx returned, Lear's partner from day one, Bud Yorkin, decided to leave Tandem Productions. He had founded the company and worked with Lear since 1959. At the time, he was more involved in *Sanford and Son* than Lear (because Lear had his plate full with *All in the Family* and *Maude*). It was not because of his tumultuous history with Foxx. He did not have any problems with Lear. His departure was amicable — he wanted to pursue his true dream, films. "There's nothing wrong with our relationship," said Yorkin when he left in September 1974. "I've decided doing both films and TV is too strenuous for me."[48] With Yorkin gone, Lear hired two new executive producers for *Sanford and Son*. Saul Turteltaub and Bernie Orenstein directed the show until its end in 1977.

Despite this season from hell, *Sanford and Son* ranked third in the Nielsen ratings. With everyone back to work, Orenstein and Turteltaub became the executive producers in charge of leading the cast in the right direction.

Sanford Arms

Things changed around the set of *Sanford and Son*. Gone were the days of the live studio audience; now canned laughter was heard every time Fred Sanford insulted someone. Now, though, Fred directed much of his enmity towards the world at his sister-in-law Aunt Esther, the loud-mouthed woman who lingered around Fred's environment over twenty years after the death of her sister, his wife.

The show moved away from the racial encounters seen so frequently throughout the first couple of seasons. Julio moved out towards the end of the fourth season (since Gregory Sierra went to work on *Barney Miller*); however, the show still was able to maintain the level of calamity. LaWanda Page's portrayal of Aunt Esther was a rather vociferous one. Esther was a very defensive character who always put up a fight against the offensive Fred Sanford, leading to shouting matches and more. Esther often used her purse as a weapon to hit Fred after he would freely hurl insult after insult. These instances had become a purely comedic routine that appeared in many episodes throughout the final few years of *Sanford and Son*.

Sanford and Son had lost much of its political edge; yet it found a new way to portray African-Americans in a positive light. In the fifth season, Fred and Lamont acquired the land that Julio had left behind when he moved away, and decided to do something productive with it. Of course, the racial agenda on *Sanford and Son* never faded completely. Regarding renovation costs, Fred commented, "$300 worth of chili stain remover. And then $19.98 for a pair of them pointy-toed shoes ... to kill all them cockroaches in the corner."[49]

Fred and Lamont put their heads together and renovated the area next door, forming "The Sanford Arms." They rented it out to several different tenants at a time, making themselves the first African-American landlords on television. At the same time, they increased their income while still running the junk business they had managed for so long.

Despite the jokes and the raucous humor, *Sanford and Son* portrayed characters that were willing to be serious when it was necessary. These were important role models for African-Americans, and certainly they were also relatable ones. They were not some rich moguls living the dream life — they were struggling just like many of the African-Americans watching. *Sanford and Son* showed the characters making progress in their financial status. "If they can do it, why can't I?" was the message in front of millions of viewers.

Things went well in Watts throughout the fourth and fifth seasons, as *Sanford and Son* ranked second and seventh in the Nielsen ratings, respectively. However, things took a turn back in the sixth season. The show dropped to twenty-seventh place in the Nielsen ratings. But that was not the most major issue. Just like it did three years before, the issue was one that Redd Foxx sat right in the middle of.

Foxx became uneasy with the work yet again, and was ready to move on. He fell right into the hands of ABC, who was lining up big name stars. ABC was climbing back into the networks race, after being shut down by shows such as *All in the Family* and *Sanford and Son* in the early 1970s. Meanwhile, Demond Wilson was unhappy with his contract, wanting more money. Rather than giving Wilson what he wanted and continuing the show without Foxx, NBC ended *Sanford and Son* in the spring of 1977 after six seasons. Foxx revealed in 1983, "I'd had enough of *them*, not the show."[50]

Meanwhile, the network tried to create a show out of the recurring characters of *Sanford and Son*. However, *Sanford Arms* was a complete failure, ranking one hundredth in the Nielsen ratings, and was cancelled after four episodes.[51]

Over at ABC, Foxx was busy trying to create a life on television without the aid of Norman Lear. In the fall of 1977, he starred in his own variety series, *The Redd Foxx Comedy Hour*, which consisted of his standup act, an occasional song or two, his perspective on African-American history, and many guests. However, the show did not fare much better than *Sanford Arms*, being cancelled in January of the following year, not even lasting a full season. That marked failure number one for Redd Foxx on television without Norman Lear.

Foxx returned to NBC once Lear had stepped down from television (which happened in 1978), appearing in a spin-off of *Sanford and Son. Sanford* debuted in 1980, and focused on Fred running his junk business with two other men while Lamont was away (Demond Wilson did not appear on the show). Although the show lasted only a season and a half, it was Foxx's most successful television show during his post–*Sanford and Son* years. However, it still marked failure number two for Redd Foxx on television without Norman Lear.

Five years later, Foxx tried once again on television with *The Redd Foxx Show*. Perhaps Arthur Unger of *The Christian Science Monitor* summarized it perfectly, calling it a "premiere of the old Foxx trying still another show. In this one he plays a cantankerous widower, insulting everybody in sight. So what else is new?"[52]

Nothing was new. The show debuted as the forty-sixth most watched show that week, and was off the air in three months.[53] That was failure number three for Redd Foxx on television without Norman Lear.

When the puzzle pieces of Redd Foxx's career after the spring of 1977 are put together, the picture that forms shows the power that Norman Lear had in Hollywood. He had the ability to take great talent, such as Foxx, and turn it into a winning product on television time and time again. Work with Lear, and a winning product will be put on the table.

Sanford and Son proved to be one of Lear's greatest winning products, not only because it was the first all African-American show on television, but also because millions of people tuned in each week. Most importantly, by using laughter as a tool for integration, viewers of all backgrounds forgot the color of the Sanfords and considered them one of their own — even though Fred Sanford probably would not have liked to be part of an all-white or all–Puerto Rican family.

3

Lady Godiva

Beatrice Arthur's Maude Findlay could take on any character in television. Maude was a unique character — a distinguished female figure on and off the screen. She was one-of-a-kind in many ways. Maude was much more abrasive than Mary Richards or Rhoda Morgenstern. She was married, but much older than Jeannie — and she lived in a wealthy home rather than a bottle. Unlike those who came before her, Maude Findlay had the potential to dominate anybody who came in her path — whether a man or woman. On some level, she enjoyed it with a deep passion.

Right from the first time American viewers set eyes on her, they fell in love with her spontaneity. The moment this first occurred was when Maude stood at the Bunkers' door, smiling, saying, "Maudeeee is here!" after Archie sent her a not-so-nice telegram to stay "the hell away" from his home.[1] She could adroitly mock anything or anyone, and certainly did over the years, beginning with America's favorite middle-aged man, Archie Bunker.

A *New York Times* article in the fall of 1972 was titled "She Gave Archie His First Comeuppance,"[2] but it was certainly not the last scolding she handed out. By the time Maude left the air in 1978 she had criticized hundreds of people, making millions of viewers cry laughing. "You're fat!" she told Archie during her first appearance.[3] In their next meeting, she asked, "Still fighting mental health?" Moments before, she gave a repairman (who hadn't fixed anything) three dollars for doing absolutely nothing, even though he demanded fifteen, closing the door in his face when he complained.[4] When Maude was spun-off into the eponymous *Maude*, Ms. Findlay kept spitting out America's favorite lines. Once, husband Walter demanded dinner, so the feminist handed him a frozen TV dinner and made one quick retort. "Walter, if you think that's a frozen chicken, wait till ya see what you find in bed tonight."[5]

But Maude had some flaws herself. She had divorced three men prior to Walter, and patronized her maid to the point where the maid almost quit after her first week. It seemed as if she cried in every other episode, whether it was about a fight with Walter, a new job, or an abortion. On some level, just about everything was covered on *Maude*. It kept the show genuine, leaving viewers on their toes, biting their nails, waiting to find out what crazy event would happen next. And they were desperately curious for six seasons and 141 action-packed episodes. At the same time, by discussing controversial issues, *Maude* forced its fans to examine issues that they may have previously been embarrassed to think about, perhaps helping them in their journeys of life.

Edith Bunker's Cousin

Although the television show *Maude* did not air until 1972, Norman Lear found the "Maude" of the show eighteen years earlier. Back in 1954, Lear sat in the audience of an off-Broadway production called *Shoestring Revue*. As he watched, he spotted a tall, bold actress who quickly caught his eye. Two decades later, he would introduce Beatrice Arthur, now a household name, to television.

For *TV Guide*, Lear went down memory lane in 1972, recalling the first time he saw Arthur perform, and he saw her address serious feelings through laughter, something she would do all the time on *Maude*. "I'll never forget her [Arthur] singing a torch song called 'Garbage.' She sang it while leaning up against a street lamp, with a single spotlight on her. The idea was 'Garbage, he treated me like garbage,' and every time Bea sang the word *garbage*, the house rocked with laughter and I was afraid they'd have to send out for coffee and doughnuts from the Red Cross for the survivors."[6] At the time, Arthur was not a Hollywood actress, and her résumé was filled with off–Broadway credits.

Five years after Arthur embedded herself in Lear's mind, he hired her for a spot on *The George Gobel Show*. Five weeks later, the show was cancelled.[7]

Twelve years after her spot on *The George Gobel Show*, *All in the Family* was strolling in its second season. Arthur's husband, Gene Saks, was a film producer and had to fly from New York to Hollywood to shoot a new movie. Arthur stayed behind, until she received a long-distance phone call from Lear. He wanted her to fly out to Los Angeles to be a guest star on *All in the Family*. She declined: "I'm terrified of flying, and I'm absolutely content to just sit home with the kids and relax."[8] Lear kept on insisting. "Don't bug me!" Arthur told him.[9] But she began to miss her husband, and decided to be brave and fly out to the West Coast to visit him. Arthur told *TV Guide* about overcoming her fear of flying. "If you have enough vodka and you start early enough in the morning, particularly if it's an 8 o'clock flight, then it's OK."[10]

And that was what she did. Bea Arthur got off her plane and went to see her husband. A few days later, she received another call from Lear. He had heard that she was in town, and persuaded her to stay in the area for a few weeks. Meanwhile, he would write her into an episode. She accepted the one-time role of Cousin Maude with hesitation. After seeing the script, she could not quite figure out who the character of Maude was. Lear classified Maude as a "Roosevelt liberal who has her feet firmly planted in the '40s."[11]

By the time of the taping, she figured it out. On the set of *All in the Family*, Archie, Mike, and Gloria were all sick, forcing Edith to stay on her feet, catering to all three. Edith asked her cousin Maude to come help, although Archie felt that seeing and hearing the loud-mouthed lady would only make him sicker. Maude came, despite a telegram from Archie to stay the hell away.[12]

Maude instantly became a fan favorite quicker than she could come up with a rhetorical comment. She scolded a sleeping Archie, simply making fun of him. "Now you can come to the table and eat, or you can lie there and feed off your own fat. And if you choose the latter you can probably lie there for months,"[13] she told him. Later that day, as the two debated the influence of Franklin Delano Roosevelt on the country, Maude being an advocate, she finished the argument by telling Archie, "You're fat!"[14]

"Who is that girl?" executives wondered, with their jaw down to the ground in amusement.[15] That taping day, Norman Lear said to Bud Yorkin, "This woman is a show."[16] CBS agreed.

So Lear began to develop an idea for a show called *Maude*, along with Rod Parker, who would become executive producer of the series. In 1974, Parker said of Lear, "The man's brilliant. He's sometimes intrusive, but like in a marriage, you argue yet you still love each other. Norman's willing to admit he's wrong and he's also willing to admit he's right."[17] However, Lear got some help from his wife, Frances, in further developing the character of Maude Findlay. The character had to be strong enough to last seasons, which was more of a hurdle than developing a character for one episode. She had to be dynamic. She had to be a star. And Bea Arthur was the one person who could deliver that. She loved her work. "I'm exhausted all the time, but I feel that *Maude* is a heaven — like doing a beautifully written one-act play every week on very topical subjects."[18] When the show ended, Arthur called it the six happiest years of her life.[19]

Lear based the character of Maude on his wife Frances, who was actively involved in the feminist movement. Frances came from a broken home where she was sexually abused by her foster father, but she did not let this ruin her life, becoming a well-known advocate in the women's rights movement until her death in 1996.[20] (She and Norman divorced in 1988, after twenty-eight years of marriage.) The quality that Frances and Maude shared was that they took the initiative. Maude was actively involved in politics, promoted equal rights, and later became a Congresswoman, while Frances worked to begin companies promoting the five-hour work day for mothers in industry, and the advancement of women to high-level executive jobs.[21] Later, Frances founded *Lear's Magazine*, a magazine for women. About *Maude*, Frances said, "A great deal of *Maude* comes from my consciousness being raised by the movement, and from Norman's consciousness being raised by mine."[22] With these characteristics, as well as some shrewdness, Lear created the inimitable Maude Findlay. "Maude was working on her fourth marriage, was twice as smart as Mike Stivic, and three times as caustic as Archie," said Josh Ozersky in his book, *Archie Bunker's America*.[23]

That was exactly what Maude became, and more. Rod Parker gave the credit to Bea Arthur. "This lady's perfect timing and fantastic talent is just unbelievable. If she loves a line of dialogue or a bit of business and she wants to take a big laugh and make it into a big scream, she'll challenge the audience by holding off until the last possible second. Then when she finally does it, they'll go bananas. That takes a lot of courage and gives the writer a bonus."[24] Usually she would take a long pause and then rebuke her husband. "God'll get ya for that!" became her trademark line, although she had many other sayings that she would use just once. She once told her husband, "There's a thin line between love and hate, and you're erasing it."[25]

The next step for Lear was to find a husband for Maude, someone she could bark those words at. He went back to Broadway, where he remembered actor Bill Macy, who, just like Bea Arthur, had little television experience. Lear remembered Macy from the production *Oh! Calcutta!* and cast him in the part of Walter Findlay. Oddly enough, Lear's first impression of Macy was in the nude — Macy exposed all in some of the scenes from *Oh! Calcutta!* Macy brought his comfort with nudity to Hollywood. Occasionally, Macy would joke around on the set of *Maude* during scenes where he was only wearing a limited amount of coverage (boxers or a towel, for example). He would drop whatever he was wearing and expose all![26] Once, he did this with a child actor on the set. Child actors had to be supervised by social workers, and the social worker filed a complaint after seeing Macy in the nude![27] But Lear and members of the cast and crew loved to have Bill Macy aboard. Lear described his disposition as "light and innocent."[28]

Bea Arthur and Bill Macy did not know each other before they worked together, although they were vaguely familiar with each other's work. They soon became friends, carpooling to the studio each morning. Lear admired their chemistry. Comparing them to a double-play duo in baseball, he commented, "They're able, as few teams are, to anticipate and add bits without throwing the ball into the stands. All their comedy is controlled."[29]

Macy recalled times when Lear would motivate the cast, feeling they

Bill Macy (left) and Norman Lear (right) have a little fun together at a Hollywood wedding in 1976. (Photograph provided by Bill Macy.)

were not acting to their highest potential. In a personal interview, he said, "He would interrupt the taping after telling the director to do so, and he would gather the cast behind the set and say, 'Ladies and gentlemen, I want you to hit the Second Balcony!' We knew he wanted that passion and conviction to reach the audience, not only in the studio but at home as well."[30]

By this point, *Maude* was scheduled to air in the fall of 1972. That March, the Bunkers visited the Findlays for one final wrangle between Archie and Maude—foreshadowing what was to come in the fall.

Still, the casting was not complete. With all his shows, Lear preferred to cast experienced off–Broadway actors and actresses, even if they had limited television experience. He felt they had made adaptations long ago to survive the rigorous and sometimes humdrum routine week after week, proving they were versatile, and also proving they loved their jobs. Also, Lear ran tapings like one-act plays. "I love a theatrical experience," said Lear in 1973.[31] Like *All in the Family*, episodes were taped in front of a live audience, meaning the laughs heard during each episode were a revved-up audience, not the canned laughter that had dominated previous television.

Perhaps Lear's most interesting casting experience was with an off–Broadway performer, although CBS, not Lear, recruited the actress. They saw Esther Rolle in an off–Broadway performance, liked what they saw, and soon invited her for an audition as Maude's African-American maid, Florida Evans. In a 1974 *TV Guide* interview, Rolle remembered arriving at the audition as "the only black among a sea of white young actresses auditioning for Maude's daughter: one fly in a bowl of milk.... As a black, I had to prove myself. I was uptight."[32] Lear

Bill Macy in 1972. (Photograph provided by Bill Macy.)

viewed one minute of her audition and offered her the part.[33] But Rolle originally declined the role of a maid in *Maude*, because she felt the character would be offensive to African-Americans. In fact, when she began her acting career, her father made her promise she would never play the role of a maid. She admitted to telling Lear back in 1972, "No! I don't want to be no Hollywood maid. They don't want a *black* woman. They want something they cooked up in their heads."[34] At the same time, Rolle was part of a Broadway hit — her dream. "To me Broadway was the rainbow's end," she told *The Chicago Tribune* in 1974. "But Norman was very insistent and wouldn't let me say no."[35] Finally, Lear convinced her that the character would hold her head up to the motor-mouthed Maude, and she would not be inferior. Rolle accepted, as long as she could make sure Lear stuck to his promise.

Still, Rolle was very nervous at her first rehearsal. "The first time I saw her I was a little in awe," said Arthur. She was so sedate and terribly dignified. I didn't think she'd ever loosen up, but she did after the first day."[36] Rolle did. "I loved my role as Florida. Like Maude she is a strong woman and [though] they are always fighting, they are fond of each other. Both have big mouths but are real softies underneath."[37]

Rue McClanahan said, "Esther Rolle was easy to work with. She didn't particularly like playing comedy; she was a serious stage actress, but was good-natured about doing our wild and wooly Norman Lear series."[38] McClanahan played Vivian Cavender, Maude's best friend. She was cast after an outstanding guest appearance on *All in the Family* during the fall of 1972 (the episode won an Emmy Award), and became a recurring star during the first two seasons, officially joining the cast full-time in the fall of 1974.

Vivian's love interest on the show was a cast member from the beginning. Conrad Bain portrayed Dr. Arthur Harmon, a corny conservative who lived next door to the Findlays. He served as Walter's friend and Maude's foe — and by the time McClanahan joined the cast full-time, Vivian's wife. He was also a nomad in the acting world — starting in Canada — before getting his big break on *Maude*. Lear saw him in two plays, *Scuba Duba* and *Steambath*, and picked him for the role. "I knew he had the range and the intelligence as an actor. We talked for an hour and I knew the cameras would

Maude (Bea Arthur, left) and Vivian (Rue McClanahan, right) attending a funeral in one episode. Maude and Vivian were best friends, even though Maude often tried to persuade Vivian to become more of a feminist.

capture the humanity and the humor of the man. Most actors are subjective, always counting their lines, only seeing themselves. Bain is objective — he sees the vehicle as a whole and his part within it. He's very talented, very warm and funny."[39] Arthur was a bit more concise in describing Bain's acting ability. "Look, it's very simple — Conrad Bain happens to be a damned good actor!"[40] she told *TV Guide* in 1974. As soon as *Maude* ended in 1978, Bain went on to star in his own show. On *Diff'rent Strokes*, he played a wealthy white man who adopted two African-American boys from Harlem.

Adrienne Barbeau was a young, sexy model who played Maude's daughter from a previous marriage (Maude had had three husbands before marrying Walter). In the *All in the Family* episode with the Bunkers and Findlays, Carol was seen, but played by a different actress (Marcia Rodd). On *Maude*, Carol was a feminist, although not as radical as her mother. She was frequently seen with new boyfriends, and lived with Maude while raising her pre-adolescent son from a previous marriage, Philip (Brian Morrison).

That rounded out the cast, a cast that instantly meshed together. Lear's Broadway casting method proved to work yet again. Arthur told *The New York Times* in 1978, "I really believe that we had spectacular writers and a spectacular director and a brilliant theater-trained cast.... I worked with Conrad Bain, who plays Dr. Harmon, off-Broadway 25 years ago. It was like having a great repertory company."[41]

As of September 12, 1972, *Maude* became a show of its own, never looking back at the Bunkers— never even mentioning their Queens relations. They also lived in the suburbs, but in a much more affluent area. However, *Maude* reflected *All in the Family* in one way. It was just as cutting-edge — right from the first episode of the first season. Arthur said in 1978, "The first year it seemed to me that every single week we were doing some controversial subject."[42]

Psychos from the Start

The image of the American home rotated 180 degrees on September 12, 1972. That was the night that *Maude* debuted on CBS. The contemporary home seen in the opening sequence of *Maude* was not a tiny and crowded home like 704 Hauser Street. Instead, it was a large home located in the New York suburbs and surrounded by manicured shrubbery. Inside, the background strayed from bland to bright. The walls changed from the hackneyed wallpaper that the Bunkers stared at while they argued, to the effervescent turquoise wallpaper that insulated the cacophony from the Findlays' shouting matches. Abstract paintings hung from these walls, representing the liberal beliefs of the household. Between the spacious living room and dining room, there was a small bar with half-empty vodka bottles, a change from Archie's beer that rested on the side table adjacent to his chair. From the bright yellow tablecloths in the dining room to the flowers that decorated the house, the entire home was just slightly effeminate, like *Maude*. The wardrobes on the actors and actresses quickly broke the dress code from previous television. Maude wore a light blue blouse, in contrast to her cousin Edith's apron. Her husband, Walter, wore a neutral pink. Maude's daughter, Carol, wore a bright blue dress exposing her figure, a figure that led Adrienne Barbeau to a successful modeling career outside of her tenure on *Maude*. The color television set may have arrived in the previous decade, but it was not put to use until the premiere of *Maude*.

That night, colors were not the only thing that rotated 180 degrees. Lear and his avant-garde writers decided to open their series provocatively. In response to criticism for *Maude*, Lear said, "Do we really want to go back to the shows that lasted 30 minutes and centered on whether the father could get a window unstuck? Do we want to go back to the smarty children and the father who can't get anything right?"[43]

In the pilot, Carol came home wearing sunglasses to disguise tears. When Maude realized Carol was crying, Carol revealed that she had been out seeing a psychiatrist. Previously on television, the most ever heard about psychiatry was when conservative Archie Bunker said, "Anybody that goes to see a psychiatrist ought to have his head examined."[44] Normally, Maude, the liberal, appreciated psychiatric therapy, but not when it related to her daughter. "But Carol, you were always such a happy child," she told her daughter. "I was a model mother."[45] Carol told Maude that she had memory lapses from her childhood, not being able to recall any events. Soon, Maude began to cry, a fight between Maude and Carol ensued, and Carol threatened to move out.

By this point in the script, Lear had set up the plot. Now it was time to get some huge laughs. The next morning, Maude stormed into the psychiatrist's office and used her domineering disposition to her favor. She sat next to the fragile woman who had an appointment at that time for three consecutive years, and demanded she give her the time slot. But Maude did it kindly, or at least that was what she made herself believe. "I want you to want me to have this hour, but not because you think I'll do you great bodily harm. I wouldn't hurt a fly."[46] Maude's intimidating height of 5 foot 9½ inches, all "hard, crusty exterior"[47] as Carol called it, in combination with her deep, husky voice, made the poor, trembling woman run out of the door. As the woman was about to cry out of fear, the studio audience cried out of laughter.

Maude advanced into the office, accusing the psychiatrist of making her daughter move out. Soon though, Maude began dissecting her own life — her three failed marriages and her neurotic mother. About her total of four marriages, she lightly commented, "Life is trial and error, doctor."[48] In the final segment, Maude went home wearing sunglasses, covering her own tears.

The pilot episode of *Maude* discussed a very bizarre topic for most. Rue McClanahan, in a personal interview, said, "Psychological therapy was still considered weird by the mainstream people in the 1970s. We folks in show biz who had been in therapy, who were in therapy, who were getting more centered and emotionally healthy by seeing therapists realized that it was as natural to seek such help as it was to seek a dentist for a toothache."[49]

The episode of *Maude* made three points that were important for viewers to understand. First, eccentrics and pariahs of society were not the only people that sought professional help of this sort. Viewers saw Carol and realized she was not a crazy woman, but a beautiful, healthy, and independent woman. By exposing psychiatric therapy to a wide, diverse audience, they would be able to see that it was, in fact, as simple as "seeking a dentist for a toothache." *Maude* could change the way viewers looked at the issue, and show that psychiatric therapy was a feasible option for every single one of them.

Second, *Maude* criticized the fear that many people had with psychiatric therapy; this episode helped to assuage that fear, through the character of Maude, who was worried why the psychiatrist was taking notes when she was talking. "I've seen enough movies to know that when a psychiatrist picks up a pencil, he is not leaving a note for the milkman."[50] *Maude* began to erase stereotypes about psychiatry, and like its parent show, *All in the Family*, strove for reality.

Third, *Maude* gave viewers the courage to seek help if they felt it necessary, without fretting about the stigma. The episode had the ability to influence people's lives for the better, because it told them to help themselves. *Maude* helped erase that stigma, having an impact on the way viewers saw methods of self-improvement. No show about a father fixing a window had that ability.

From the start, there was hope for this progeny of *All in the Family*. Critics backed up the show with support. Even before the show aired, John J. O'Connor of *The New York Times* predicted the show would be a hit for two reasons. One was that Norman Lear handcrafted it. The other was that it starred Bea Arthur.[51] *The Christian Science Monitor* called it "the latest brainchild of Norman *All in the Family* Lear."[52] Indeed, *Maude* was an instant hit, never having to worry about early cancellation. Because viewers were tuning in, they were obviously receiving the messages that *Maude* was putting forth. That allowed Lear to challenge his audience even more as the series progressed. (The largest challenge came eight episodes after the pilot in November of 1972.)

Lawrence Laurent of *The Washington Post* laughed at the realism in *Maude*. "All it really means is that the content of television is now only a few hundred light years behind motion pictures and a thousand light years behind the theatre. At this rate, TV will catch up to what is actually happening in America about the same year that we colonize the planet Uranus."[53] However, by the next month, Laurent may have been eating his words, because Uranus was much, much closer to colonization than he ever imagined.

The Birth of Controversy

Norman Lear was working on making his third television show since 1971 a successful one. *Maude* was doing just fine — eleventh in the Nielsen ratings after the first eight episodes. That was much better than the first few episodes of *All in the Family* fared back in 1971. But that was not good enough for Lear, the perfectionist.

So he called upon Susan Harris, as well as Austin and Irma Kalish, for assistance. Harris had written some of those *All in the Family* episodes treasured by millions over that summer. Lear wanted Harris to help him make a statement in the late fall, a bit over a year later. So Lear played script supervisor while Harris wrote a two-part episode about abortion.

Harris recalled in a personal interview, "[The writing process] was pretty much standard — a story meeting, then first draft, notes, second draft."[54] The episode focused on Maude's best friend Vivian (who at this point had never been seen on the show), who became pregnant at an age when she was sure she would never be breastfeeding again, and was forced to make the emotional decision of whether to give birth or abort the baby. The episode also talked about whether or not Vivian's husband (who would not be shown) should sever his vas deferens in order to prevent the situation from happening again.

Lear knew that the script would open a few eyes. However, something did not seem quite right to him. He was very proud of the job Harris had done on the script. Harris remembered Lear telling her, "This is too good; we have to give the story to Maude." In response, Harris said, "That involved a big rewrite and the rest is history."[55]

Indeed it was.

CBS had a coronary when they found out what Lear was up to. Just the idea that Maude, a pre-menopausal 47-year-old woman, was pregnant, was racy enough for most CBS affiliates. CBS could not believe the episode would center on the show's main character. Lear told *The New York Times* in 1972, "I realized the only way to engage the audience's interest was to let Maude get pregnant."[56]

CBS refused to see it that way. Even though the show was on the brink of the top ten plateau, Lear threatened to remove it from the air if CBS did not allow him to make the adjustments he requested. CBS was used to that — he threatened to take his show away from CBS when the network refused to air the impotence episode of *All in the Family*—but they were not used to winning. And the tides would not change here. Although CBS was wary when it came to the subject matter of their shows, they could not cancel an eleventh ranked show, which was the highlight of the Tuesday night lineup, and seemed to be the first of many successful years for the network. Lear won the battle, which ended only several hours before the episode was broadcast. He won because he did not feel that he was taking a chance by threatening them. "It isn't that I wouldn't have taken a chance if I thought it was a chance, but I think people — even in their anger — enjoy being involved, enjoy having their emotions stirred."[57] Once again, Lear's form of threatening the networks was a routine situation. In a personal interview, Rue McClanahan said of Lear's audacity, "[He] went head-to-head with the network many tape nights, the network threatening to pull the show from airing if certain things weren't deleted. Norman refused to budge, and many times it was eight o'clock, time to tape, before we got the go-ahead. Norman Lear was so courageous— so ahead of his time."[58]

Nobody could argue that Lear was ahead of his time — abortion had not yet been legalized on a national level. Lear was broadcasting a *Maude* episode about abortion, taking place in New York. In some areas where viewers lived, abortion laws were much narrower. The issue certainly had social significance — it was one of the major issues that influenced voters in the 1972 election, which took place only two weeks before the episode aired.

The controversy occurred because the nation was very confused about what would happen if abortion was legalized. There was definitely a "market," so to speak, for abortions. One gynecologist anonymously told *The Chicago Tribune*, "When I began private practice, women quickly made it evident to me that I could make a fortune, more money than I ever dreamed of, by forgetting my Hippocratic Oath and becoming an abortionist."[59] These anti-abortionists worried that abortions would become the new trend — and could replace older birth control techniques. However, there were pro-abortion advocates, like Carol on *Maude*, who looked at the issue as a feminist one, stating that "We're free. We finally have the right to decide what we can do with our own bodies."[60]

On November 14, 1972, Lear finally got the cue from conservative CBS to shock America in what would become arguably the most famous and controversial abortion procedure in the history of America.

It all started when Maude postponed a game of bridge with her announcement. Maude, a grandmother, was pregnant. "That means that I live in a house where an uncle is about to inherit his nephew's potty seat," cried Maude.[61] When Carol first proposed the idea of not having the baby, Maude did not even think of abortion, still living a generation back when it was an evil word. "What'll I do? Trade it in for a volleyball on *Let's Make a Deal*?" Maude asked sarcastically.[62]

But the abortion episode was not all about jokes. It was about the grueling decision that Maude had to make. Susan Harris said, "[Lear] was my favorite producer to work with as he was the only one doing television that was finally addressing reality. His comedy was also character-based and not joke-based and that's what I liked to write most."[63] The episode showed that unwanted pregnancies did occur. One of Walter's lines compared this episode to previous entertainment discussing unwanted pregnancies. "This is the place in the movie where they say they're kidding," he said with hope.[64] But since Lear wrote and aired reality, Maude was really pregnant.

While anti-abortion proponents were worried about the substitution of abortion for contraceptives, *Maude* made sure to still promote the viability of birth control. When Vivian (who did appear in the episode, although not as the pregnant woman) asked, "Weren't you using the pill?" Maude responded, "No, it gives me migraines." Carol responded with contempt, "What did you do, Mother, cross your fingers?"[65]

Two CBS affiliates refused to air that first portion of the two-parter. WCIA-TV in Champaign, Illinois and WMBD-TV in Peoria made history, as it was the first time any affiliate had ever refused to broadcast an episode of a recurring series.[66] Before the second half aired, the National Organization for Women filed a class-action law suit against the Champaign affiliate for refusing to air the episode. The station manager James Fielding said, "We don't think abortion is a proper subject for treatment in a frivolous way in a comedy program."[67] The National Organization for Women lost, and the episodes never aired. Fielding reported that by midday on November 22, the station had received 390 letters supporting the cancellation and 82 against it. Through the phone, they received 410 phone calls protesting the cancellation in the first two days after the episode was supposed to air, but only 70 angry people had called after that.[68]

Meanwhile, WCBS-TV in New York set up extra phone lines. It was a good thing, too. They received 383 phone calls, but a mere 10 were calls of approbation.[69] After the episode aired, CBS received 7,000 letters of protest.[70] Lear loved it. "I enjoy stirring feelings, even negative feelings, because I think that is what theater is about. It's marvelous to know you have engaged the feelings of millions of people."[71]

The second portion of the episode discussed less common forms of birth control — vasectomies. Vasectomies were becoming more and more frequent — between 1967 and 1969, the number of men who were sterilized increased by 400 percent, from 50,000 operations to 200,000 operations.[72] *The Chicago Tribune* quoted the American Medical Association, who said that vasectomies have become a status symbol with "a certain air of fashion and even faddism."[73] While Maude was grappling with the decision whether to have an abortion, Walter was grappling with the decision on whether to get a vasectomy. The episode made sure that Walter was partially held responsible for the pregnancy. Walter talked to a man who had gotten the operation, and he said it was "the best thing I ever did," because he did not have to worry about his wife getting pregnant. He called it a "simple" operation, and said it "took all the worry out of being close."[74] While Walter did not have the vasectomy, he still vowed to take full responsibility if Maude decided to have the baby.

Meanwhile, Maude struggled to make that decision. Carol tried to convince her that the procedure was "like going to the dentist."[75] That line infuriated many people, including one person who wrote to *The New York Times*. She ranted, "Only a plastic moron like Maude's daughter could equate the removal of a decayed tooth with the removal of a new life. Real people don't think abortion is funny when they are faced with making this sad decision; only cheap gag writers are amused."[76] However, *Maude* described the *procedure* as simple — it did not describe the thought process as simple. It showed Maude agonizing over the decision for weeks — and most of that time she was planning on having the baby. She felt "guilty for even thinking about [abortion]."[77] Only in the final moments of the show did Maude and Walter truly decide they should not have the baby, and nothing was holding them back from making that decision.

Throughout the episode, *Maude* educated the older generation, mocking their myths and beliefs and replacing them with the newest revelations in medical science. The episode laughed at Walter and Arthur, who came from a time when they were told to line the toilet seat with paper, or flush the toilet with their foot, in order to prevent diseases. One article called that "the lasting effects of distorted psycho-sexual development."[78] At the same time, Maude came from a period when abortion was totally immoral and under no circumstances acceptable. It was not that *Maude* was fervently pro-abortion, like it was for women's rights. Bluntly putting it, one of the primary messages throughout the two-part episode was that people must be open to change, even if it goes against what they were originally taught.

After the episode, though, some people never noticed those messages and soon the papers were filled with anti–*Maude* crusades. One disgusted viewer wrote, "How could they beam a program such as *Maude* into the American living room.... What a show for 8 P.M.! And to think they are taking *Bonanza* off the air [which left in January 1973, one month after this complaint was written] in favor of this trash."[79] One Catholic priest, Reverend Brian T. Joyce, in Oakland, California, said that CBS "betrayed" its audience by airing *Maude* and her abortion. The show, he said, "trampled insensitively" on Catholic beliefs.[80]

However, there were the people who thought Maude's abortion was appropriate subject matter for television, even if they were not pro-choice. *The Los Angeles Times* journalist Cecil Smith wrote in response to the *Bonanza* fan above, "Whether you agree with Maude's decision (and I'm not sure I do), it is a subject which I believe television has every right to discuss even within the limitations of popular programming."[81] Bea Arthur told *TV Guide*, "Most of my mail came from very bright, genuinely concerned people. They weren't nutsies writing to harass me. As a result, all I've arrived at is a state of complete confusion. If I were presented the same script now, I really don't know what I'd do. It would give me pause."[82]

Journalist Jane Rosenzweig of *The American Prospect* summarized the situation perfectly: "A half-hour comedy had become a battleground over America's values. [T]he controversy suggests people had come to see television as playing a significant role in the shaping of our social morality."[83] The episode even influenced how the actors looked at the issue. Arthur told *The New York Times* in 1978, "The abortion thing, for instance, never entered my mind. Tackling 'in depth'—put in depth in quotes—subjects that might have only been lightly discussed previously has changed me — I now think more about these matters."[84]

But the war was not even close to over. The abortion episode came up again in the summer of 1973, once *Roe v. Wade* had been passed, legalizing abortion in all fifty states. This time, CBS aired reruns of the abortion episodes that originally ran back in November. This time there was even a bigger outcry—17,000 letters of protest were received this time, ten thousand more than when the episodes originally aired.[85]

But Lear's plan worked — the show's ratings skyrocketed. During the week ending October 29, 1972, *Maude* was twelfth in the Nielsen ratings.[86] By the week ending December 3, the show held the seventh spot.[87] The week of the original airing of the abortion episode, *Maude* was the fourth most watched television program.[88] Perhaps the most mind-blowing statistic was that 65 million people saw one of the four half-hour segments of Maude's abortion and Walter's vasectomy decision.[89] By this point, CBS could not have been regretting airing the episode like they once were.

Lear was on a roll, and did not feel like stopping with abortion. To many, it seemed as if he could do anything. *New York Times* journalist Aljean

Harmetz said, "The honorable vulgarity of *All in the Family* has opened the door to Maude's abortion. If we're lucky, it's a door that will never shut properly again."[90] And Lear did his best to keep the door open, finding controversy for the character of Walter Findlay.

The Stress of Life

John Carmody of *The Washington Post* worded it fittingly, saying this ageless peril existed "almost as long as our tenure on Earth."[91] As the years went by and times changed, the peril kept growing, endangering more and more lives. By 1973, *The Chicago Tribune* reported that there were nine million alcoholics living in America, and an estimated 100,000 new people were succumbing to booze each year.[92] Fortunately, at the same time, professional help for alcoholics was becoming increasingly popular and accepted, and as a result, more effective. The number of alcoholic treatment centers in Illinois, for instance, increased 162.5 percent from 1973 to 1974.[93] The "bum" stereotype was slowly fading out of America's consciousness, as many began to recognize alcoholism as an illness. Pauline Buxton, executive director of a California alcohol treatment center, told *The Los Angeles Times* in 1973, "Ignorance is the greatest stumbling block in the curbing of alcoholism. We hope to remove the stigma from the word alcoholism and arrive at a point where alcoholism will be thought of and treated as any other major health problem."[94]

That was when *Maude* stepped up to the plate. Norman Lear spent much of his time in the summer of 1973 studying alcoholism. While progress had been made, *Maude* and Lear decided to make their contribution towards raising awareness, devoting two Tuesday nights in September of 1973 to the issue. "But on situation comedy?" some wondered, just like they had wondered about previous material Lear covered on his shows. Lear answered that question in *The Washington Post* in 1973: "I don't feel saddled by the phrase 'situation comedy.' We're in the business of drama; we produce a half-hour drama each week that that leans towards comedy."[95] Lear wanted to accurately demonstrate the horrors of the *disease*, even if it meant defying the standard boundaries of situation comedy.

To open the second season of *Maude*, Lear wrote a two-part episode where Walter, Maude, and Arthur realized their self-imposed "social drinker" status was taking its toll. When they decided to quit together, Walter broke the promise within twenty-four hours, spiking his Shirley Temple, even after making a $100 bet with his best friend Arthur to see who could abstain from alcohol the longest. When Maude found out, she rationalized, telling herself she could drink since Walter was drinking.

The first message that *Maude* promoted was the many dangers of drinking, and for the first time in prime-time network television, a show depicted the total aberration that arises when one has too much to drink. It would not be purely comedic, like when, in 1972, Edith Bunker had too much to drink on her birthday. It even poked criticism at those who had previously mocked alcoholics, and those who used alcohol without much thought. When Walter tried to reason with Arthur that Dean Martin gets paid for his buzz, Arthur replied, "Show business people making fun of drinking is part of the problem."[96] Lear and *Maude* were ready to turn the page on these portrayals, and show viewers that alcoholism was a very serious disease in America. The line discouraged this sort of portrayal of alcoholism in future television. Simultaneously, what *Maude* would do for viewers was censure the use of alcohol to get a "buzz," show that the entertainment industry in the past was not always a source of role models, and stress the fact that alcohol could ruin lives. The episode was a wake-up call for viewers, all of whom comprised a diverse background of alcohol experience. Since tens of millions of Americans were watching, the messages expounded by *Maude* were absorbed by alcoholics, heavy drinkers, those in denial of their drinking problems (Walter could be classified in all of the above), wives and relatives of the previously mentioned, children and teenagers who would soon encounter alcohol, children and teenagers who had witnessed their parents' excessive encounters with alcohol, and those who had abstained from alcohol throughout their entire lives.

Lear and the writers were faced with the challenge of making sure their story could be understood by all those demographics. First, *Maude* focused on the short-term effects, and through the genuine acting of Bea Arthur and Bill Macy, would establish the symptoms of drunkenness before moving onto anything more serious. By doing this, *Maude* would establish the groundwork of the illness, getting all of the various demographics on the same page.

Now, symptoms were no longer words read in newspaper articles and medical journals. Now they were exhibited by some of America's favorite characters. Arthur demonstrated the change of speech; she talked in a low, monotone voice, a shift from her loud nature. Then she added, slurring, "How can you be sho soor?" she asked Walter.[97] (She meant "so sure.") Meanwhile, Maude and Walter's actions were completely controlled by the alcohol flowing through their blood streams. In the middle of it sat their grandson Philip's birthday cake, which they decided to decorate as a surprise to Carol. She was certainly in for a surprise! Maude went into the kitchen and got the whipped cream, but because of her lack of coordination, her unsteady hands, more ended up on Walter's shirt rather than the cake. Then, Walter put the finishing touches, writing "Happy Birthday" on the cake. The only thing wrong was that he spelled it "Hippy." Finally, he took a large candle that could light a room, and planted it into the center of the cake. Why not traditional birthday candles, one for each year? Because of Walter's lack of judgment, induced by alcohol. Had he been sober, he would have most likely stuck with tradition. In these ten or so minutes, *Maude* gave a quick lesson on the effects that alcohol has on the body: change in speech, loss of coordination and balance, and bad judgment.

Now that *Maude* established the symptoms, it could move into discussing the long-term effects of alcohol: addictions. *Maude* had already discussed part of the issue, when Walter could not go a whole day without alcohol. The audience knew that Walter was hooked. But Walter was in total denial. That night, when Maude talked to Walter about having too much to drink on a daily basis, Walter yelled, "I'm not a cripple."[98] *Maude* wanted people to be more open about the illness. Rather than hide the problem, they should come out and realize they have an illness — the clichéd, yet vital first step to treating any addiction.

The episode educated all of the types of people watching — even those who had never picked up a bottle. Through entertainment, *Maude* clearly told everyone who tuned in exactly what alcoholism was, and how to detect it. It also pleaded with viewers that a person can still be a victim of alcoholism even if that person states that he or she is not.

When Maude pleaded with Walter, he retaliated with violence — hitting her in the face, giving her a black eye. Still, looking at the big picture, Maude may have saved Walter's life. Walter felt remorseful, crying immediately after he hit her, and then the next morning when he saw her black eye, he yelled, "I hate myself."[99]

The second part of the episode focused more on the disease of alcoholism. While Walter promised Maude he would quit, Maude soon learned that cold turkey quitting is extremely difficult. When Walter found out that something was awry down at work, he used it as an excuse to drink. So Walter broke his promise, downed a martini, and went off to save the day. He tried to drown his sorrows in alcohol, which only led to more problems. When Walter went to work, Maude spoke to a recovered alcoholic who advised Walter to seek professional help. At first he resisted, but in the end, he went for help to improve his life.

Maude also acknowledged those affected by the disease. *The Washington Post* said in 1973 that at least fifteen people are affected by an alcoholic's drinking problem.[100] *Maude* showed how Walter's drinking affected his wife, but also Carol, who wanted to move out so her son, Philip, would not have to grow up under the roof of an alcoholic. It also affected all the people he worked with, such as the person Walter screamed at over the phone. Of course, it affected his best friend Arthur, as well as Florida, the maid. *Maude* viewed alcoholism peripherally, not only acknowledging the problem drinker, but also acknowledging those whose lives were influenced by him or her. By doing this, it gave those people the attention they needed. Finally, someone said something about the conditions they lived in. Someone actually cared.

The episode was one big public service announcement, filled with billboard phrases, such as the fact that alcohol is the number one drug problem in the country. The most clear and obvious message from the show was why not to drink alcohol.

But *Maude* went further than that. It presented alcoholism as a serious issue, not a funny joke. The recovered alcoholic told Maude and America, "Alcoholism can't be cured overnight ... alcohol is an illness—a prolonged illness."[101] Out of all of the issues ever discussed on *Maude*, Bill Macy felt chemical dependency was the most influential because, he said in a personal interview, "We did not look down on our audience. We respected them." He felt the comedy was used effectively to get through to people. "Laughter was the oil," he said.[102] *Maude* treated alcoholics as people — not as drunks, bums, or transients.

The outwardly jolly Walter Findlay (Bill Macy) was sometimes implacable after having a few drinks out of stress. (Photograph provided by Bill Macy.)

Pauline Buxton said that ignorance was the worst thing for helping alcoholism, and by respecting the issue as a disease, *Maude* helped to break the trend that alcoholism and addiction are dirty words. *Maude*'s portrayal of alcoholism completely strayed from the bum stereotype still known to some. Statistics in May of 1974 showed that 95 percent of this demographic were employed, and Walter represented the 45 percent of alcoholics who were professional and managerial personnel.[103] Walter was a healthy, handsome man, not someone lying in the gutter in the streets of New York City. Because viewers cared about Walter, they wanted to see him improve. Walter was a role model when he went to seek professional help, proving that there was hope. After all, in 1973, *The Chicago Tribune* reported that "the percentage of cure in alcoholism ranges from 50 to 75 percent."[104] Walter Findlay became one of them.

But two seasons later, *Maude* showed that alcoholism can still linger inside a victim. Walter had not had any problems for two years, until he and Maude separated, and began to see other people. Even though the separation had nothing to do with Walter's old drinking habits, Walter became so depressed that he used the situation as an excuse to drink. He hoped that by drinking, Maude would see how miserable he was and return to him. But best buddy Arthur sat him down and respectfully, yet assertively straightened him out, how his relapse in drinking was inexcusable. In the end, Walter stopped. Afterwards, Maude and Walter resolved their original problem and lived happily ever after.

Almost.

A year later, Walter succumbed to, as Bill Macy put it, "the stress of life"[105] yet again. This time, he suffered from a nervous breakdown and over-dosed on pills after his business went bankrupt.

But Walter always got back up, even after some of his biggest falls. Macy called his character a "survivor."[106] During these falls, one beneficial thing happened. Walter taught the American public about the dangers of alcohol and drugs, and the true meaning of addiction.

Maude, *the Feminist Liberal*

By listening to the opening theme song of *Maude,* a person who had never seen the show would think that the character of Maude Findlay was an omnipotent heroine. The lyrics put her in the same category as classic heroes such as Joan of Arc, "a sister who really cooked," and Isadora, "the first bra burner." It seemed as if Maude was a born leader who was destined to have her name in the encyclopedia. But during the actual show, viewers quickly learned that Lady Findlay was just as confused as the rest of America. Norman Lear told *The Washington Post* in 1973 that Maude proved the "liberal in her own enlightened way can be just as doctrinaire on one side as Archie Bunker is on his side."[107]

In the third episode of *Maude,* Maude wanted to hire a maid. However, since Maude's idea of Equal Rights was twisted, she judged applicants on their racial background, rather than ability and experience. The more oppression their race suffered from, the better chance they had at "earning" the job. It was as if Maude was seeking personal catharsis for past discrimination towards minorities in America. It was as if Maude felt she had to be the spokesperson for the Equal Opportunity Employment Commission. Daughter Carol worded it perfectly. "A black maid says hello. You say you're sorry."[108] However, when she hired African-American Florida Evans, Maude would be quickly straightened out.

As soon as Florida walked into the Findlay home, she knew something was not quite right. When Maude insisted that Florida call her by her first name, and that her home was no place for titles like "Ma'am," Florida still asked to be called Mrs. Evans, much to Maude's confusion. Maude automatically assumed that Florida was oppressed because of her color. She began to patronize Florida, even marveling at the origin of her name. Within five minutes, Maude told Florida that it was also her home, and she was part of the family. Florida replied, "I got a family" and "I got a home." Maude, not realizing that Florida led a normal life, just living by her distorted liberalism, replied, "You bet you have," and "You can say that again," respectively.[109]

When Florida went to work the following week, Maude sabotaged her work hours for a lesson on African-Americans in the ghetto, while *she* served her *maid* martinis. Maude did not realize Florida knew all about African-Americans in the ghetto, considering she lived there for years. At the end of the week, Florida quit because she could not get any work done. All Florida wanted to do was clean Maude's house, get paid, and get home to tend to her own family. Florida was not only a domestic, but also a dignified professional who was proud of her job, and treated her duties seriously. In the end, Florida stayed after having a long talk with Maude. In the conversation, Florida, the employee, laid down the ground rules.

Immediately, Florida represented a smart, assertive African-American female with integrity. Donald Bogle, author of *Prime Time Blues: African Americans on Network Television*, wrote, "Florida preferred to be a traditional maid *except* when it came to expressing her views. Weekly, she did so, and it was funny to see an African-American woman so readily and knowingly matching wits with her employer."[110] Neither Florida Evans nor Esther Rolle would succumb to Maude's domineering presence. If Florida thought something was wrong, she would be sure to say so. If Rolle thought something was wrong, she would be vocal about it towards Lear and the writers. Florida may have been a domestic worker, but from a social standpoint, she refused to be a servant.

On television, Florida Evans presented a positive African-American image, because she was realistic. Florida was not decorated with unreal characteristics—she did not walk around badmouthing everyone she ran into, just to get laughs. Rather than hitting someone with her purse, Florida explained her side of the story calmly. As a result, people could listen. And they did. Florida was a true role model for all those women cleaning up in white kitchens. Rolle made sure of that. "I've always been unhappy about the role of domestics. The black woman in America doesn't need to go to drama school to be a maid. The old actresses who played the black maid stereotypes are not villains—it's the ones who hired them. We've been stereotyped and unrecognized for so long," she said.[111] Rolle was very proud of her work on *Maude.* "I've had some rewarding things happen as a result of that role [Florida] and my standing up to Maude," said Rolle in 1974. "The typical Hollywood maid has always been such a lie. So many black people have always resented being spoken to in certain ways and now they come up to me and say, 'Hey, I could have sworn I wrote the lines you said last night. It's just the way I felt the other day.'"[112]

As Florida resonated more and more with viewers, more stories were written for the character. Soon, her home life was seen on *Maude.* Her husband Henry (John Amos) appeared occasionally, often showing displeasure because his wife had to work. He felt guilty because his wife could not sit home like Maude did. Henry had no idea as to what the feminist movement was; he had no idea that working gave Florida pleasure. As a poor man trying to feed his family, he had the misguided notion that it was his duty to provide his wife with the luxury of sitting on her couch. In addition, he had "male pride," and did not like his wife earning an income to help put the food on the table and pay the bills. *Maude* sought to educate the many men who, like Henry Evans, had misguided notions about the feminist movement, and why their wives wanted to leave the house.

However, Florida would have none of that. In one situation, Henry demanded that Florida quit because he earned a job driving a cab, in addition to his regular job as a fireman. Because he did not want Florida to work as a maid, he ignored the fact that it might be too stressful for him to perform both jobs. He told Walter, "All I'm trying to do is get the same things for my wife that your wife has."[113] However, when he refused to be the husband of a African-American maid, Florida reminded him of the wonderful women that supported him while working as maids, such as his mother. As a liberated African-American woman, one proud of being a domestic, she told James, "There are a lot of women, Henry, on both sides of my family who worked all their lives in white kitchens so their kids could get some of the things they should have. You want to be proud of something, Henry? You be proud of them, 'cause they was all black women. And I tell you there ain't ever been a better woman than that."[114] Through Florida Evans, *Maude* exemplified the strength of the African-American woman, and Florida never became, as Esther Rolle phrased it in her first conversation with Norman Lear, the "Hollywood maid." In fact, she helped to obliterate the stereotype.

The African-American woman was not the only type of woman portrayed on *Maude*. Maude showed three other demographics of women: Carol (Maude's daughter), Maude (herself), and Vivian (Maude's best friend).

Carol represented the complacent, liberated woman. Her sense of independence seemed to be innate, almost like it had been inherited from her ultra-feminist mother Maude. Out of the three white women regularly seen on *Maude*, Carol was the most comfortable with her feminism — she felt self-sufficient, yet did not feel the need to join protest marches to let the world know.

Carol's definition of independence included feeling indifferent about how others felt. She minded her own business. Carol, a very attractive woman, was simply worried about her active sex life and her child. (She had acquired custody of Philip from a previous marriage.) Carol led by example, and although never mentioned on the show, one could assume she was a believer in the Golden Rule, which said, "Do unto others as you would have them do unto you." Men treated Carol as an equal, because Carol treated men as equals. Carol, a much tranquilized version of Maude, was ahead of her time. If the world was full of people like her, the feminist movement would not be necessary, because the relationship between men and women would be a much more equal one. While Maude was the most outspoken figure for women on *Maude*, Carol, not Maude, was the epitome of the feminist movement.

On the other hand, Maude was the loud liberal — who would go through any trouble — who would give anyone a headache — to share her beliefs with her world. Maude did not care what others thought–including her three former husbands. Maude was not shy about using the word "divorce"— Maude frequently referred to her three previous husbands, and on top of that, Carol and Vivian were also divorced. Maude freely spoke of her previous marriages with humor. She once told a friend, "I hit three lemons before I hit the jackpot."[115]

The great thing about the character of Maude was that she put herself in a position to share those beliefs. Unlike Archie Bunker, she spoke from a pedestal. Maude set an example for women to get involved in politics and government: to take advantage of the democracy dearly treasured in America. Carol may have been the epitome of the feminist movement, but Maude was the most powerful influence on the show, because she led with her mouth. Not only was she a working woman (a real estate agent), representing the 205 percent increase in working wives from 1947 to 1975, but she also was actively involved in politics— often campaigning or protesting.[116] On several occasions, she, a woman, held parties at her home for prominent males running for government positions.

Since Maude was quite vociferous, it was not too difficult to make everybody hear what she had to say. Maude did not change her personality depending on who she was talking to. She did not mind giving backtalk to men, abandoning the entire system of male dominance that ruled the Earth for so long. Laconic comebacks were her prized possession. She could tell her husband, "Walter, go sit in the corner,"[117] or she could tell her conservative neighbor, Arthur, "I hate everything you stand for."[118] And it would not take any energy out of her. Maude was the first woman on television to verbally hold her head up to any man, time and time again. In a personal interview, Rue McClanahan said of Maude's character, "Maude threatened most men, men who couldn't take a strong female."[119] Even her husband knew that he was not the boss of the house—and he was fine with that.

There were several times that Walter tried to challenge Maude's rule, though. In one case, Lear and the writers of *Maude* combined an extremely liberal issue—the decriminalization of marijuana—with the issue of "the rights of an individual" within a marriage.[120] The writers discussed two contemporary topics in one episode. The issue of laws against marijuana possession was a major topic of discussion, especially in the state of California, where there was debate over the bill called Proposition 19, which would mitigate the penalty for marijuana use. On November 2, 1972, just more than a month before the episode aired, *The Los Angeles Times* published two articles on the same day. One presented why people were against this bill—because marijuana was a gateway drug. The article argued, "The proportion of chronic marijuana users progressing to heroin increased from 9 percent in 1970 to 30 percent in 1971."[121] The other article supported Proposition 19, which focused more on the discipline of sellers, not users. It said, "Most people don't want their sons and daughters arrested for being at the wrong party at the wrong time, but still want to see police action against sellers ... of the total number of marijuana arrests in California, better than 80 percent are for mere possession."[122]

Meanwhile, Maude sought the decriminalization of marijuana, after a 19-year-old boy was arrested for possessing a quarter of a pound of marijuana and faced three to seven years in the slammer. The episode began when Maude and her friends were searching for weed so they could deliberately get arrested for possession of marijuana. However, when Maude got her hands on the drug, Walter took it right out of them. Walter said, "I'm not going to give you my permission," feeling that Maude could get severely punished by the law.[123] When Maude quickly yelled at him for even mentioning the word "permission," Walter responded, "The rights of an individual stop when it affects the marriage."[124] Maude came back with one of her feminist comments, "Walter, I am me, and I was me long before I became Mrs. You. You don't own me."[125] So Walter again tried to make his point, and succeeded this time. He called a young, sexy girl from his store and asked her out, telling

Maude, "I'm doing this strictly as an individual, so it shouldn't affect our marriage."[126] Maude then proceeded to rip the phone jack out of the wall.

But Maude got her way, as she always did. She went to the police station with oregano, and tried to tell the police officer that it was marijuana. The Italian police officer knew the difference, but said to Maude, "If I ever got into any trouble, I'd want you on my side."[127]

As the seasons went by, Maude did not stop fighting for her rights. A survey conducted in 1974 showed that two-thirds of women felt they were victims of discrimination based on sex.[128] Had the fictional Maude been asked, she would have been included in that category. In a five-part fourth season premiere, Maude campaigned in the primary elections for state senator, taking her involvement with politics to the highest level. She felt it was the best thing that ever happened to her—until Walter vehemently denied her the opportunity, saying he could not be part of a marriage where he only saw his wife on the weekends (Maude would have to live in Albany five days of the week). But Maude was tired of being treated like a second-class citizen due to gender; she was tired of being discriminated against, ever since the last of her parents' savings went to her brother's education, rather than hers. Therefore, jeopardizing her fourth marriage, she accepted the nomination, and Walter moved out. "I can't control the feeling that life holds something more for me, that I can be something more," she told Walter after the separation.[129] On screen, Bea Arthur brought determination to Maude's character. "I don't care," she told Walter and Carol, when they questioned her decision. "This is something that I have to do for me, so damnit—I'll take you all on."[130] In that line, Maude encapsulated the goal of the women's liberation movement: freedom. Weeks after the separation, Walter allowed Maude to run, and their marriage resumed. At the same time, *Maude* showed women in government, a pattern that was growing in the 1970s. The number of women candidates for state legislature positions increased 300 percent between 1972 and 1974.[131]

(Surprisingly, Bea Arthur did not understand the women's movement. She told *TV Guide* in 1976, "I've never felt that being a wife and mother is not enough. I've never felt secondary to my husband."[132])

Episodes of *Maude* were filled with women's liberation vernacular, such as "free to do and to be whatever we [women] want."[133] *Maude* also conveyed the tenets of the feminist movement through the character of Vivian, who was confused while caught in between her chauvinist husband Arthur and her feminist best friend Maude. She wanted to be happy, yet she wanted Arthur to be happy. Maude constantly tried to convince her that her *own* welfare should be her *primary* concern. By doing this, she convinced the audience of the same thing, encouraging them to worry about themselves before anyone else. Rue McClanahan commented on her character, "Vivian was the safe little feminine wife, oversexed and dumb, very lovable."[134] There were many times when Vivian would prefer to clean the house for husband Arthur rather than attend a women's meeting with Maude. Because of Maude's trenchant beliefs, Walter knew that he could not forbid Maude from attending women's meetings. Arthur felt he could.

In one episode, Vivian enjoyed spending her day at a Congress of Women meeting, until she and Arthur got into a fight about it. When Vivian cursed at him, Arthur felt that Vivian should not be allowed to swear. Later on, an enthused, turned-on Vivian tried to sexually entice Arthur, until he said it was "not a woman's prerogative," "unfeminine," and "a man's job."[135] Vivian stormed to Maude's house, where she decided to put women's liberation behind her and go back to her old ways. But Maude told her, and those faithful viewers "in transition," not to give up, and to complete the process of becoming independent. Rue McClanahan said on Vivian's importance to *Maude* and to the public, "She was used as a foil for Maude. Maude tried to enlighten and educate her (and the audience as well), and in a painless-to-watch way."[136]

Through these three women, *Maude* was able to debate various contemporary issues—a major one being plastic surgery. Maude Findlay and Vivian Cavender were aging gradually—more wrinkles and more frustrating hormones. They were dealing with their own sort of stress of life, different from Walter's. Their problem was growing older—they felt that their looks had faded. For their "psychological good,"[137] they decided to do something about it.

Maude discussed the issue of plastic surgery through the feminist lens, when Vivian came home with a facelift. She was much more self-confident about her appearance, feeling more aesthetically pleasing. After a recent divorce (this all happened before Vivian began to date Arthur), she gained back the self-esteem she had before the split. Vivian took advantage of her "freedom" as a woman—something that the women's movement strove for. The women's movement would have been proud of Vivian. Still, the idea of plastic surgery–surgically changing one's physical appearance—was very controversial. Rue McClanahan said, "We were still crawling out of our 1950s shells." McClanahan also wishes that a show with the daring nature of *Maude* would air at the current time. "And looking at our country now, I think we are being *stuffed* back into them."[138]

Carol, the comfortable woman, saw nothing wrong with facelifts. Maude, normally the most outspoken of all three on such feminist liberal issues, was against it. Her initial response when seeing Vivian was, "My God, you had a facelift!"[139] Maude felt that Vivian capitulated to "sexist propaganda," but Carol insisted that, "Part of the feminist movement is the freedom to do your own thing ... there is no stigma anymore if you want to change the way you look to make you feel better."[140] After much discussion, Vivian and Carol did change Maude's mind. They did a very good job of convincing Maude; *she* went out and had a facelift! Week after week, *Maude*'s women — the no-nonsense maid, the role model, the spokeswoman, and the coming-of-age housewife — discussed, agreed on, and argued about issues in an attempt to reach the public. Not only was *Maude* highly popular, ranking in the top ten each of its first four seasons, it also succeeded in reaching its viewers. Ultimately, *Maude* was able to present feminist issues in unique ways that may not have been absorbed by viewers beforehand. *Maude*'s arguments were persuasive, having an impact on viewers, telling them to get involved in the feminist movement, and get involved immediately. It had the potential to give viewers, especially women, the confidence they needed to follow their dreams, because Maude was doing just that. Maude never exhibited a lack of confidence, nor any diffidence, and never gave up until she was satisfied, and these qualities were passed through the television screen and into the minds and hearts of those watching.

For some viewers, *Maude* was much more than a sitcom, and the stars received the ultimate compliments. McClanahan said, "I still hear from women now about how our emphasizing certain female issues gave them heart and courage to make the fight for reform, themselves."[141] Twenty years before, journalist Cecil Smith said that through "raucous humor," *Maude* was "the statue of women's lib."[142] Meanwhile, Maude Findlay was not finished with her campaign. Now she was ready to tackle the highest level of all — the national government.

Maude in Washington

The ratings for *Maude*'s fifth season (1977–78) had a significant drop-off from the previous year. The show was no longer in the top ten — even missing the top thirty that year. However, CBS would have appreciated that statistic had they been able to anticipate the 1977–78 season's ratings— 78th.[143] Arthur blamed much of the drop-off in viewers on CBS, who switched *Maude*'s time slot several times in a short period. She said, "I don't think interest in *Maude* has lessened. We were just buffeted around by CBS until my own kids didn't know what night the show was on."[144]

Everyone was ready to improve those ratings in season seven, and they planned to accomplish this via major changes. So they decided to introduce these changes at the end of the sixth season.

Maude Findlay was fully prepared to go where no woman on television never dreamed nor dared to go, and few women in the real world actually went. Now with the moral backing of her husband, Maude decided to run for the United States Congress. It was a huge decision, and had she won the election, major things would change in her life. Her biggest change was that she would have to move to the nation's capital full-time. For Lear and his entire crew, this would also mean significant changes. Gone would be the bucolic simplicity of Tuckahoe — and gone would be some of the supporting characters that had been an integral part of *Maude* for six years.

During those six years, much in the feminist movement had changed. Even before *Maude* debuted, the number of women running for Congressional positions was increasing significantly — 69 women ran for Congress in 1972, compared to only 42 in the previous election.[145] But people predicted that this number would increase dramatically throughout the 1970s. In 1972, Katie Herring, candidate coordinator for the national women's political caucus, told *The Los Angeles Times*, "There won't be vast numbers of women in Congress for six to eight years, simply because people don't run for Congress right off. They begin on state and local levels first."[146]

That was exactly what Maude Findlay had done throughout those six years that Herring referred to. She did it on television, while encouraging those women watching to do the same. Perhaps Maude took the uncertainty out of the minds of those who wanted to run. Maude started out on the local level, and then slowly progressed to higher political echelons. In 1976, she missed being a part of the state government by a mere one vote. And now, she was ready to tackle Washington, after making her voice heard.

But America never got to see Maude Findlay battle men and the world in Washington. In fact, they never even got to see a seventh season of *Maude*. It was because, despite all the changes, if Lear wanted to continue *Maude*, they would have to do it without Bea Arthur, who announced that she was leaving the series. And that would be a major hurdle, since she was the star of the show, and all the proposed changes revolved around her. "We've accomplished what we set out to accomplish. We brought good theatre to television," she said. "I may be kidding myself, but I think we gave quality shows to television ... six years is a long time for anything. That long in a part can be very rewarding; you can grow in it, but after a while it has to stop. I don't think *Maude* was a challenge to me anymore."[147] Arthur had been hinting about this for several months, so Lear and the writers figured that even if the show never continued, this would serve as a proper finale. *Maude* ended as one of the most popular and arguably the most controversial series of the 1970s, spanning six seasons and 141 action-packed, compelling episodes that made an indelible mark on the landscape of television, and in the lives of millions of viewers who watched week after week. *Maude* began a trend of assertive females in the white-collar, upper middle class world of television.

Six years after the end of *Maude*, Clair Huxtable (Phylicia Rashad) became the first female lawyer on television on *The Cosby Show*. She had a heart of gold, but could be just as pushy as Maude when she was in the courtroom.

As a result of the female-centered *Maude*, more television shows began to focus entirely on women and their problems. The same year that *The Cosby Show* aired, *Maude* co-stars Bea Arthur and Rue McClanahan teamed up to star in *The Golden Girls*, along with Estelle Getty and Betty White. *The Golden Girls* had a small ensemble cast, and the show centered on four middle-aged female characters who shared a home together in the Florida suburbs. While the show did not tackle controversial issues, it portrayed these women in all aspects—from their active sex lives to their grandchildren. Finally, Americans were able to see women simply interacting with each other and their surroundings. Although never seen before on television, women had been doing this for a long, long time.

Twenty years after the premiere of *The Golden Girls*, a television show called *Desperate Housewives* surfaced. This hit comedy depicted the lives of several women in their forties. These women were all neighbors and each one dealt with their own brigade of life-changing events.

Maude seemed to set a trend in American television. Because the sitcom succeeded in introducing females and their problems to television, the all-female ensemble cast soon became a hot thing for writers and a moneymaker for networks, as seen by NBC's *The Golden Girls* and ABC's *Desperate Housewives*.

Maude helped out its own network, CBS, also. One decade after the final episode of *Maude*, another sitcom, *Murphy Brown*, began airing on CBS. It centered on another female who was not afraid to say what she felt. Murphy Brown (Candice Bergen) was just as picky as Maude—firing secretaries like Maude divorced husbands. Over the sitcom's ten-year run, Murphy went through ninety-three secretaries. But *Murphy Brown* tackled one issue that *Maude* viewed for the first time many years before. Murphy, like Walter, had to seek professional help for alcohol and drug dependencies. Then, *Murphy Brown* caused just as much controversy as *Maude* once did when Murphy decided to raise a child that she had after a fling with her already divorced husband. Although both he and her new boyfriend wanted to help raise the baby, she turned them both down and raised him alone. Like Maude's decision on what to do with her baby, Murphy's decision did not go over well with everyone in the public. Even presidential candidate Dan Quayle bashed Murphy's decision in one of his campaign speeches when he discussed American family values. He denounced the show, saying, "It doesn't help matters when prime-time TV has Murphy Brown, a character who supposedly epitomizes today's intelligent, highly paid professional woman, mocking the importance of fathers by bearing a child alone and calling it just another lifestyle choice."[148]

If *Maude* had never been able to tackle such controversial issues relating to its time period, *Murphy Brown* may never have been able to stage such a national debate. That year, *Murphy Brown* won the Emmy Award for Outstanding Comedy Series. In the thank you speech, one of the many people the creators could have thanked was Norman Lear, because he made it much easier for them to ever get on that stage.

However, the most profound reflection of *Maude* in television since 1978 came in 2005, twenty-seven years after Maude became a United States Congresswoman. *Commander in Chief*, despite being a drama, took it one step further — possibly where *Maude* could have gone had Bea Arthur stayed on the show, and had the ratings improved. When the President of the United States died after a rupture in one of his blood vessels, his vice president Mackenzie Allen (Geena Davis) became the first female president of the United States.

Commander in Chief and *Maude*, although separated by three decades and many different relevant issues, share striking similarities. Both shows focused on a female character who has risen to a high political echelon with a similar burden — being a woman. Skeptics who felt women were incapable of holding high positions surrounded both president Allen and Maude. On *Maude*, when Maude ran for New York Senate, even her own family told her not to. On *Commander in Chief*, president Allen's daughter told her not to accept the job as President. So did the President, who was lying on his deathbed. Yet in both cases, the women did what their hearts told them to do, and the shows provided positive motivations for all women to pursue their true goals, further instilling the notion that women are capable of anything. Without the advancements that *Maude* made, a woman in the wonderful world of television would never have been able to become president. Perhaps it is time that all the actresses currently in starring television roles join together on one stage, hold hands, and say thank you to *Maude* for making the success they have achieved much easier to achieve.

4

Scratchin' and Survivin'

Good Times' James Evans possessed a certain integrity that the wealthy could only appreciate — but never fully understand or experience. He spent his entire life — right up until the day he died in a tragic car accident — searching for odd jobs yielding meager wages. He sacrificed himself day after day, day in and day out. He scratched and survived. And he did not do it for himself. He did it for his wife and three children, whom he truly loved.

On the outside, James was a proud, tough, adamant man. He would defend any of his children, either with his words or with his muscles. Once, when a roast from the local market got the family ill, he went to the manager fuming, calling the market a "ptomaine tabernacle."[1] And when gangsters mistook J.J. for a compulsive gambler who never paid off debts, he used his physical strength to save his son.

James always seemed mercurial. But that was because many times he was caught in a grumpy mood from working a very long shift, making wages that his family could hardly survive on. And he knew there was very little he could do. When Michael suggested sending letters of grievance to Washington, James told him why that was impossible. "They [the government] stopped us from doing that by raising the price of stamps."[2] While the audience laughed, James was certainly not trying to tell a joke. On top of the financial woes, he had to worry about his children's grades, the men his daughter was dating, and the people his boys were hanging around. A lapse in supervision in any of those areas could change his children's lives forever — and not in a positive way. However, he must have done something right — his kids turned out to be great adults by the end of the series' run. Even J.J., who was considered a negative role model by many critics, was not so bad.

On the inside, James was the family hero. He had been scratching and surviving since he was in the sixth grade, when he quit school to help support his family. He was forced to become the man of the house at such a young age because his father fled from the pressure, and never returned. Running away was the last thing James would do. He loved that family more than anything in the world, and they loved him back. Supporting them and loving them made all the hardships seem worthwhile. His family certainly did not live an easy life. There was only one person they could depend on. And he always did his best to deliver. When he did deliver, there was nothing but "good times."

Florida Moves On

Back in 1971, Mike Evans, who played Lionel Jefferson on *All in the Family*, along with his friend Eric Monte, a longtime resident of a Chicago ghetto, began to develop an African-American sitcom. Evans told *The Los Angeles Times* in 1975, "Norman Lear told me CBS was looking for a show about a black family. I asked if I could try to come up with one and Norman said fine. I went to this friend of mine, a dedicated writer named Eric Monte, and we created this family — the mother's name was Mattie then, the father John, the kids, J.J., Thelma, and Michael, after me."[3] However, Lear saw the family and decided to get rid of a major member — the father, John.

By early 1973, rumors began that Lear wanted to spin-off the character of Florida Evans (played by Esther Rolle) on *Maude*. According to *The New York Times,* the proposed series was originally supposed to be a daytime drama, and would become "the first series about a real ghetto family."[4] The plan to show a single mother struggling to raise her family was still intact. However, Rolle was concerned with the impact the message of the show would have on its viewers, and would only agree to do the show if it included a strong father figure. Looking back, Rolle said, "I told [the producers and Lear] I couldn't compound the lie that black fathers don't care about their children. I was proud of the family life I was able to introduce to television."[5] Rolle was an African-American woman who had been outspoken all her life. For example, she was intensely involved with the NAACP. She was willing to give up her job in order to make sure that African-American families would be accurately depicted. Lear listened to, and was influenced by the things Rolle believed in. Rolle believed, and convinced Lear to believe, that since the members of this fictional family were supposed to be role models for people stuck in the same boat, their lives had to be realistically portrayed in a positive light.

November 8, 1973, was Esther Rolle's birthday. On that day, Lear told her she would have her own show. In response, Rolle broke down in tears. After she finished crying, the next step was casting the supporting roles for Florida's new sitcom. First, John Amos reprised his role as Henry Evans on *Maude* (although his character's name was no longer Henry, but now James). About working with Amos, Rolle said, "On and off stage we just *like* each other."[6]

Now, Lear needed children for Florida and James. He cast the youngest one first. Ralph Carter, courtesy of the Broadway play *Raisin*, played Michael Evans. Michael may have been the youngest, but certainly was the most politically conscious, second only to his father, who experienced it first hand as he stood in mobbed unemployment lines. Next, Jimmie Walker, a novice actor, got the role of J.J., the smooth-talking, bean-pole shaped "artiste." Cecil Smith described him perfectly: "He's a kind of black pogo stick with great rolling eyes and a mouthful of gleaming teeth . . ."[7] Walker had spent his childhood just where J.J. had — in the projects. He recalled his days hanging out in the South Bronx. "There were like 20 guys I hung out with on the street. Five of 'em were dead before they were old enough to vote. The rest of 'em? If they aren't in the slam, or 'away for a rest' someplace else, they're still on the street, hustlin'. And drinkin', smokin', shootin', snortin', sniffin'. Sure, I did all those things."[8] But in the end, Walker said farewell to the streets and began a career as a comedian. When he was discovered by producer Allan Mannings, the part of J.J. became his. He did *Good Times* during the day, and stand-up comedy at night.

Walker was not the original choice for J.J. Mike Evans was. He said in 1975, "I was expected to play the oldest boy: J.J. When I was growing up, I was J.J. That was me at 17. Only Jimmie Walker plays J.J. as tall and skinny and funny looking, while I was short and fat and funny looking."[9]

BernNadette Stanis was cast as Thelma Evans, the middle child, sixteen years old. Stanis seemed to have it all — sexiness, intelligence, and affability. Ralph Carter said about his television sister, "BernNadette Stanis came to us not only as a professional dancer, but also as a budding actress. She began to flower even more the longer she worked with us as a complete ensemble unit."[10] A special bond quickly formed between Rolle and Stanis. By the fifth episode, Rolle complained to Lear about her television daughter's role. "In the first five shows there wasn't much about me or my daughter. They were about men. My daughter is not to be a sponge to soak up men's problems. We have young black writers. I asked for young black *women* writers."[11]

Multi-faceted actress Ja'net DuBois portrayed neighbor and dear friend Willona Woods. Lear discovered her in the play *Hot L Baltimore* and offered her the part. He liked her so much he did not even have her audition. DuBois completed the cast.

On Tuesday, February 5, 1974, America saw the tearful farewell between Florida and Maude, but three days later, Florida would be back. That Friday, Florida and her never-before-seen family returned to prime-time, scratching and surviving in urban Chicago.

The day before *Good Times* aired, *The Christian Science Monitor* said, "Producer Norman Lear breeds television shows like racehorses. His latest —

Good Times—has great lineage: *All in the Family*, and *Maude*. In this case, those bloodlines really tell and CBS's new show premiering tomorrow at 8:30 p.m. Eastern Time looks like another champion for Bud Yorkin-Norman Lear Tandem Productions."[12]

Before the first episode even aired, the talk was all about spin-offs, since Lear's *Good Times* appeared to be the first spin-off of a spin-off. As *The New York Times* phrased it, *Good Times* was a third-generation series.[13] The journey started in a Queens neighborhood and ended in the Chicago projects. But Lear did not believe that *Good Times* was a true spin-off. "I got the idea for this show 2½ years ago, before there ever was a *Maude*, from Michael Evans," Lear told reporters in 1974. "We'd never seen a black family on the tube and it sounded like a good idea. It's taken two years to develop it; we went through 30 drafts of the story for the first episode."[14] The idea for *Good Times* had undergone many script and character changes before Florida Evans ever arrived in Tuckahoe. As the show evolved and continued season after season, Lear was appalled by anyone who called *Good Times* a spin-off. By the third season, he went around Hollywood telling people he would "throw up" if he heard it called that one more time.[15]

Since the show quickly appealed to people–of both colors—America wanted to know if there would be any more spin-offs of *Good Times*—if *All in the Family* would have a great-grandchild. Even before the pilot aired, *The Christian Science Monitor* asked, "Do I see any more spin-offs in the future, Mr. Lear?"[16]

The Birth of the Evans Family

Perhaps the biggest breakthrough during the debut of *Good Times* was not a catchphrase, not a hairstyle that made the nation run to the nearest salon, not even the color of the Evans family. Perhaps it had to do with the fact that the Evans family had more than one parent. The simple two-parent family taken for granted in today's sitcom era was a major change of pace in early African-American sitcoms. Esther Rolle said in February of 1974, "To my way of thinking, it's a television first. The black family — a mother, a father, and three children — is shown as a complete family unit, and this has never been done before."[17] *Good Times* showed the importance of two parental figures for children residing in the ghetto. During the course of the series' run, *Good Times* showed gang leaders who did not have fathers, as well as a pregnant girl whose parents were alcoholics. *Good Times* depicted that strong, positive, parental figures were one of the few protections that a teenage boy had from becoming an addict or impregnator, or that a teenage girl had from getting drunk, letting a boy get lucky, but them both becoming very *unlucky* nine months later. Sometimes these kinds of parents were more effective than contraception. James Evans was one of them. As J. Fred MacDonald, author of *Blacks and White TV* put it, James was "as quick with a hug for actions he approved as he was with a belt for those he condemned."[18] Unfortunately though, "in 1974 only 56 per cent of all black children under 18 lived with both parents, down from 71 percent in 1965 ... between 1960 and 1970 the percentage of single-parent families among blacks increased at a rate five times that for whites."[19]

The representation of African-Americans on previous television — shows such as *Amos 'n' Andy* and *Julia*— angered Rolle. It angered her to the point where she refused to do a show that had a family with only a mother. When Lear originally wanted to do a show with that scenario, Rolle gave him an ultimatum. Either that idea went, or she went. If she went, the show went. Lear gave Rolle the television husband she had sought.

Rolle refused to be a part of a show such as *Julia*, which centered on a young widower raising her child. On *Julia*, Rolle told *The Christian Science Monitor*'s Arthur Unger, "Who could have such a beautiful home, dress so well, never have a hair out of place and still be a struggling breadwinner without a husband in the home? I hope we will do a little better than that."[20] Several months later, *That's My Mama*, which also portrayed a single mother raising her children, premiered. Geoffrey Cowan wrote in 1979, "The stereotype [of the single mother] was one that infuriated blacks of all political persuasions, and it was one that concerned them because of their belief that black youths tended to follow the role models provided for them on television."[21] Rolle echoed that statement five years earlier. "The black matriarchy is a myth that has no more validity than any other racial stereotype," she said.[22] In 1975, *The Los Angeles Times* provided one theory as to why images on television were extremely important for poor African-American youths. "While some children spend weekends in the mountains learning to ski and exploring and appreciating the wonders and exhilaration of nature, other youngsters, particularly the housing-project dwellers, are physically and financially trapped — captive audiences of the tube."[23] In 1977, *The Washington Post* said, "By the time the average American youngster graduates from high school he was spent more hours watching the television screen than he has spent in school, or in any other activity except sleeping."[24]

Rolle knew that African-American children would be watching by the millions, and she wanted to make sure that they saw the truth about African-American culture. "I will be able to explain to black kids that black families have fathers, too. These kids wonder about that when they watch TV. They never see black families with problems like who should wash the dishes. Real people."[25]

At the start, everything about *Good Times* was real, from the characters' traits to what they wore. During *Julia*, Diahann Carroll (who played Julia) "sashay[ed] around in $2,000 originals," according to *The New York Times*.[26] In *Good Times*, father James owned one suit that he wore for job interviews and a small assortment of shirts otherwise. The only one who looked like she came out of a boutique was neighbor Willona, and that was because she worked at one.

And the set looked like it had been picked up out of the ghetto, carefully put in a box marked FRAGILE, and shipped to Hollywood. The set was in dire need of a paint job. Paint certainly would have covered up the graffiti in the hallway. Matriarch Florida was not sitting on the newest, finest couch like she did at former employer Maude's. But in order for *Good Times* to portray ghetto life realistically, how could she? If graffiti covered the buildings in the ghetto, why paint over it?

In the first episode, *Good Times* showed some of the nightmares that haunted families who were not exactly financially fit. In 1973, one-third of the African-American race was "living in officially defined poverty," so it was simple for many to relate to.[27] In this pilot, James received a government job paying $4.25 per hour, money that he had never come close to earning before. But something was too good to be true. It turned out that the government job was only for people in a certain age range, and James was too old by several years. Frustrated because he wanted a better life for his family, he let some of his steam out of the job interviewer and the government. "Government rules can't be broken," said the interviewer. James responded coldly, "Unless you runnin' the government."[28] While the audience and the viewers at home laughed, some of their pain was alleviated. It was as if James had taken the words right out of their mouths. After James said that line, viewers—even if they were not part of an oppressed minority group—could root for the Evans family because they were stuck in the same boat. Rolle said, "I think that if viewers close their eyes, they will be able to identify with our [the Evans family's] problems which are human ones, even [though] we are black. Poor people everywhere have the same problems, whether they're white, blue, black, green or yellow."[29]

Viewers learned after the first episode that James, the father figure, was the hero of the Evans family. In the first episode, it was as if *Good Times* was making up for lost time. There had never been a complete African-American family on television, and now the Evans family was singing "For He's a Jolly Good Fellow" when they thought James landed the job. Florida and the kids always supported him — whether or not he got the job, whether or not he could buy them much, materially. They knew that he was trying hard. In one later episode, Michael wrote a composition about how his father was a hero, even though he was not a celebrity.

James felt the same way about his family. James did not have the Hollywood life, no Mercedes in his driveway — no car, not even a driveway. But despite being frequently laid-off, James would be the first to admit that his situation was better than most. He had a loving family who cheered him because he never fell short of working those arduous shifts to feed his family. And he loved them, too.

In 1974, an article ran in *The New York Times* with a photo of a dishwasher and a caption that stated, "Typical of workers in American cities who are not able to earn enough to support their families but who are not included in the standard index of the nation's employment health."[30] The article referred to a four-person family. In the third episode of *Good Times*, James found himself trying to support a five-person family while working as a dishwasher. At the same time, the Evans family received an eviction notice from the landlord. Because of the economy, James found himself working long and hard, yet having little to show for it. When Florida asked James why he only came home with six dollars after his long night shift at a restaurant, he responded, "They paid me a lot more. But after they got finished takin' out the federal withholding, the state withholding, the unemployment compensation, the state disability insurance, then this extra goodie they slipped on me at the last minute, a two-dollar charge for gettin' my dishwashing uniform cleaned ... if I'd worked a few more hours, I'd end up owin' them ten bucks."[31] But as television always seems to go, James got the money and the Evans family lived happily ever after.

Until the next episode. That was when James found out one of his long-time friends, Sam (Roscoe Lee Browne), was a scam artist in the name of God. He used religion to make money. Sam wanted James to join his scam, where he would earn $100 per day. But James declined, feeling honesty was more important than money. He needed to teach his children to be honest. He needed to be a positive role model. In this episode, he was also a positive role model for people, especially children, living in the ghetto. *Good Times* showed the public to always be wary because people will do dishonest things when desperate for money. But most importantly, James Evans preached the importance of honesty. Several episodes later, Florida was approached at a supermarket to be in a commercial, and she almost became involved in another scam. She was going to receive $5,000 to participate in a commercial advertising a health tonic called Vita-brite. But when Michael decided to taste it, Florida learned that it contained 18 percent alcohol by volume, and dubbed it "Vita-booze."[32] As a positive role model for her children and as someone with integrity, she gladly declined the opportunity, and the potential five grand.

These episodes demonstrated to the public that there are good people living in bad places. Many saw that African-Americans were connected to crimes; in the 1960s, African-Americans committed the majority of the crimes in America.[33] However, *Good Times* showed that there are honest African-American people. Showing that was a major contribution towards the exorcism of the racial bigotry that stemmed from stereotypes.

In one episode, *Good Times* gave a detailed description of the sometimes unsanitary living conditions in the ghetto. The Evans family had to walk seventeen flights of stairs because the elevator was broken. They were forced to waste food when the refrigerator broke down. Ironically, the heat was also broken. The water was not running. And finally, the Evans family walked those seventeen flights to realize the laundry machines in the basement were not working.

Good Times publicized an issue that had been overlooked. Perhaps the show was putting pressure on housing authorities, or maybe even the government. Jokester J.J. commented, "Pretty soon we gotta go to the bathroom at the gas station. We're only gonna be able to go on odd-numbered days."[34] But *Good Times* was definitely attracting attention to the unhealthy living conditions of the poor. And it also censured those who were not doing anything about it. When "militant midget" Michael drew attention by writing a complaint letter to the newspaper, one of the housing authorities dropped by the Evans home. But when asked how long it would take to fully renovate the apartment, he replied, "Thirteen, fourteen months tops," and walked out, receiving boos from the audience.[35]

The penultimate episode of the first season was about the physiological stress that wears down people like James Evans, who, as the script put it, are constantly dealing with "the stress and frustration of ghetto life."[36] Between temporary lay-offs and rising costs, James rarely had a minute to relax. In addition to that, he did not have the healthiest diet. The episode of *Good Times* was filled with public service announcements, such as, "Soul food is one of the big causes of hypertension."[37] The stress, in conjunction with the diet, led the family to believe James was a victim of hypertension.

James was just like many African-Americans—they did not get frequent enough physical examinations. But when Michael read this to James right from an article, James countered by saying, "Hope that article said that most black people can't afford to pay for physical examinations."[38]

But *Good Times* told the African-American community about alternative options. The family educated James, and the public, about clinics that offer physical examinations—for free. In the end, James went and the doctor lightly scolded him, since his visit was long overdue. Luckily, James did not have hypertension, but due to his diet, he did have high cholesterol. Viewers were also strongly advised to eat right. But the most important message that *Good Times* said to the public was to make sure to get annual physical examinations, because health is vital, especially for a person like James, whose family counted on him all the time.

After those first thirteen episodes, *Good Times* lived up to the high expectations that critics had for it. The show focused on relevant topics about poor African-American life, and viewers liked to see that. Those same viewers put *Good Times* in a tie for seventeenth most watched show in America after its first season. And the best was yet to come.

The Epic Sophomore Season

Early in the show's run, Esther Rolle went to Norman Lear, complaining about the lack of issues presented on the show regarding African-American women, attributing it to the lack of African-American women writers on Lear's staff. While *Good Times* did not cover women's issues in depth during the first thirteen episodes, it made up for lost time in the second season, starting in the second season premiere, when Florida felt she needed a little freedom from the monotonous routine of being a housewife.

Previously, the farthest television ever went in showing women's liberation for African-Americans was a one-liner on *All in the Family* and an episode on *Maude*. Archie asked Lionel if "his people" were involved in the feminist movement. Lionel, up to his usual cajoling of Archie, replied, "No, no, not too much, you see, we still working on plain ol' liberation."[39] A year later, an episode of *Maude* aired in which James (then named Henry) tried to force Florida to quit her job.

To start the second season, Florida attended a women's meeting with Willona, and told James she wanted to be an equal, which ultimately confused things more. When James felt threatened by her sudden interest in the feminist movement, Florida told him, "James, I don't want to walk ahead of you, but I don't want to walk behind you either. Honey, I want to walk with ya."[40] The final scene showed that Florida's words were heard, when she sat on the couch with James, picking out a community club to join. Despite it not being the first time independent African-American women were seen on the tube, a television show related the feminist movement to African-American life for the first time in history, something that African-American women could finally relate to. Ten years before, African-Americans were segregated against. Now, *women* of that race were being promoted as equals.

That season, *Good Times* showed the less positive things that happened to women, specifically African-American women. With the advent of the Civil Rights Movement in 1964, women and minorities were being employed in jobs they could have never imagined landing a decade before; and the Equal

Employment Opportunity Commission's demands greatly assisted this. Through *Good Times*, viewers saw how some employers chase minorities and women away because of their race and gender, rather than judging them on their skill level. In this case, James and Florida applied for different jobs at the same location, but the employers decided to kill two birds with one stone. They hired Florida for the job James applied for, leaving James unemployed. That left James fuming, making him vent some anger towards President Ford. "The president said he was gonna bring us all together. None of us knew the meeting place was gonna be the breadline," he thought.[41] But Florida soon learned the pain that James felt every time he was laid off. James explained it clearly to her. She was suffering from the "last hired, first fired blues."[42]

The character of Willona Woods also served as a positive image for the feminist movement. Her character was almost like an African-American version of Carol from *Maude*. She was a sexy woman who was totally in control of her personal steering wheel. She dressed how she wanted; she was single and supported herself working at a fancy boutique; she was one of the few characters in television who was divorced and whose ex was seen on the show; and most of all, she enjoyed all of this.

Sometimes, however, Florida tried to interfere with her status by playing matchmaker, but usually finding someone that did not appeal to Willona. Willona once told her that she did not enjoy the arranged dates, saying, "Where is it written that every woman has got to be married or she's a nobody?" She continued, "A man over thirty who's unmarried — the world calls him a swinger. A woman who's unmarried — they call her an old maid."[43] Characters like Willona helped destroy those stereotypes. Just like Carol, the feminist movement would have been proud of Willona; she was the African-American prototype. To describe Willona in one word, there would be no better choice than "liberated."

While the feminine figures became more prominent during the second season of *Good Times*, so did the major male character, James. Early on, *Good Times* showed just how important James was to the family, when Michael had to write a composition on his hero. First, Michael decided to pick a historical hero such as Crispus Attucks or Jesse Jackson (and when his choices were all men, it led to a mini battle of the sexes). But in the end, Michael chose to write about his father (of course, the women appreciated that).

While James may not have been neither a hero nor a Hollywood superstar, he was the most important figure in Michael's life. Michael recognized that his father was the one who kept him from living in the gutter next to Ned the Wino, and that his father was the one who would sacrifice his life for his family's safety.

Another episode showed how James always trusted and supported his children. At the same time, through the Evans family, *Good Times* took a shot at the jail systems in ghettos, portraying it as a major crisis from several different perspectives. On J.J.'s eighteenth birthday, he got the present of his life, when police officers mistook him as a kid who robbed the liquor store. He was arrested, taken to jail and booked.

J.J. could not leave jail because of the outrageous $500 bail. There were few, if any, people living in the ghetto that could afford to pay that out of their pockets. The courts were so backed up that J.J. would have to stay in jail for two to three weeks, before he could even be tried — indicating just how many criminals loitered around the streets of the ghetto. The hearts of the Evans family and audience were being eaten out because J.J. was suffering for something he did not do. He may have been a buffoon, but not a thief.[44]

Finally, the police apprehended the criminal who committed the crime, but *Good Times* once again tried to highlight the faults of the ghetto law enforcement systems. The criminal had the exact opposite physique compared to J.J.; he was short and fat.

Just as in the first season, *Good Times* focused on the financial predicaments that everyday people living in the ghetto faced. Only this time, it focused on senior citizens, and the human consumption of pet food. It was a growing epidemic. John L. Hess, journalist for *The New York Times*, wrote in his column, "A reader asks for recipes for cooking dog food. The intent was doubtless ironic, but not funny. Many poor people, notably the elderly on small pensions, are reduced to eating pet food, and the way things are going, doubtless they will increase."[45] That was when *Good Times* portrayed the issue on a national scale, showing how it was harder for people even much older than James to scratch and survive. Senior citizens were mercilessly afflicted by the inflation epidemic, and in the ghetto, seniors resorted to desperate, but necessary, scratching. As inflation rose and Social Security did not, elders living in the projects were stuck in the middle with little relief. They could not live by working, because they did not earn enough to survive, and they could not live off their inadequate Social Security. If they received Social Security and worked, their benefit was cut in half. In an educated attempt to protest the dilemma in February 1975, *Good Times* became the centerpiece to publicize a fight against seniors' poverty. A proud neighbor had to quit her job as a singing instructor because it was decimating her Social Security check. She could not afford to get paid to give the singing lessons. Due to what John Amos called "economic deprivation"[46] in a TV Land interview, this woman was forced to eat pet food to survive and keep a roof over her head.

Good Times proved this issue was a true dilemma in the projects by showing a realistic situation filled with public service announcements to fight the problem. For example, Thelma told her family that one-third of pet food sold was consumed by humans. The perspective held by people residing in the projects was revealed when Florida noted, "In the richest country in the world, anyone has to be eating pet food."[47] At the end of the episode, the neighbor decided to abandon her sullen attitude towards the quandary, and planned to rally all the seniors in protest. *Good Times* explained how this was a serious problem in the country. Reporters across the country agreed. Mike Fitzpatrick of *The Chicago Tribune* wrote in response to this issue (as well as others), "The people in Washington should stop worrying about what the Israelis, French, Germans, and Africans think of this country and start worrying about what the people of this country think of their own government."[48] A loud ovation from the live audience filled the studio when the neighbor decided to fight for the problem. The talented actors and actresses of *Good Times* contributed to the ovation they received, and overall, the political significance of the show, not only because the emotions they displayed on their faces were genuine, but also because they reflected the facial expressions of lower socioeconomic class Americans.

Pride was an important theme throughout the course of *Good Times'* run. Every character seen on *Good Times* was proud of their heritage and their life, despite the financial woes that accompanied their living situation. That was important; these characters, because they possessed confidence, could give viewers living in poor places the confidence they needed to succeed.

In one episode, J.J. was distraught after he broke up with a wealthy chick from uptown, because her parents did not approve the relationship, due to J.J.'s financial status. But James defended his family, all the members of his community, and his son when the snooty parents walked into the Evans home. It soon turned into a pep rally, giving all the honest people in that social echelon something to take pride in. When the rich snob parents walked into their home and flatly insulted them, snarling, "The faster we get out of here, the better," James responded with indignation, "Yeah, ain't you all heard, there's niggers in here."[49] James gave viewers a sense of pride by stirring up controversy. Then the father said, "You make it sound like success is a dirty word." James replied, "No, success ain't the dirty word. It's forgetting. Forgetting where you came from."[50] He also showed pride in where he lived. When J.J. wanted to avoid seeing his girlfriend's parents, James explained things to him differently. "This is your home. This is one place you don't break and run from nobody."[51] Finally, when they wanted to buy J.J.'s paintings solely as a business investment, James told them, "Get the hell out of my house."[52] The scene was filled with shouts of "Right on," mixed with hoots, claps and cheers of approval from an energized, intense audience.

Partially because of the pride factor, *Good Times* did better in season two than it did in any other season. Season two was its only season in the top ten, ranking eighth. However, for the Evans children, season two was also action-packed.

Lack of Education in the Projects

At the start of *Good Times*, not a single member of the Evans household had ever earned a high school diploma. The head of the house, James Sr., quit school after sixth grade so he could take a job to support his family. Naturally, Florida and James wanted the best possible education for their children. Despite their dreams and desires, the real setback was not that their children lacked talent and motivation, but that there was no quality education offered in the Chicago projects. And James and Florida had the same problems back when they were in school. Education in the projects was a hand-me-down crisis.

In an environment where there were as many gangs as unemployed men and women, a hard-earned education for every person living in the projects was the only way to lower the crime rates; because education gets jobs, jobs shorten lines at the unemployment office, and crime is lowered when all people in a community can afford to live. *Good Times* was the first television show ever to have an all–African-American cast portraying a family with children, and was the first show to ever discuss the low standards of education that African-American children and teenagers received. Consequently, this was the first sitcom to comment on education in the projects and try to change it to benefit Americans of all colors and classes.

The quality of education, the material learned, and the honesty of the schools were issues that *Good Times* tackled right from the start. The quality of education was very low in the projects, and the schools were full of students who lacked the desire to educate themselves. The main character that the writers of *Good Times* used to demonstrate various themes about education was Michael Evans, played by Ralph Carter. Michael's dream was to become a lawyer, and he was a very outspoken child. In the end, one would hope that he became a justice on the Supreme Court, because he was dedicated to his academics and was devoted to overcoming the obstacles that hindered many in his position.

The fifth episode was the first to criticize education. It did so by showing how schools' textbooks were biased against African-Americans. When Michael told his teacher that George Washington was a white racist because he owned slaves, Michael was suspended from school until he apologized, which he refused to do. Then, Michael's father came home from a hard day at work and threatened to whip an adamant Michael who would not apologize to his teacher. Michael would not capitulate because he possessed a strong conviction that, "He wasn't our president, he was their president."[53] Michael was self-educated about African-American history because he always went to the library to read books on the subject. *Good Times* made the first public service announcement dealing with the education of African-Americans. It said that people like Crispus Attucks, who fought and died in American wars, were not included in American history books. This lack of representation of an entire race was unfair in the eyes of Michael Evans, arousing fresh thought in the minds of viewers.

Good Times also depicted what happened to African-American children in the projects who were not as academically conscientious as Michael. In one episode, J.J. passed into the twelfth grade, although he did not earn it. Later, when James and Florida asked the principal why J.J. passed eleventh grade but did not know a thing, the principal responded, "We lack the facilities and money that schools in more privileged areas have ... [I have] a graduating class of 600. Now, if I don't graduate a high percentage of that group, I wind up looking like I am not doing too good a job. If I don't graduate a high percentage, our budget is cut, and if our budget is cut, our teaching staff suffers, and if our teachers suffer, students' education suffers." Nevertheless, James still had a tough time not telling the principal "what to do with [his] system."[54] Later that same day, James was denied a job because he could not articulate in writing why he was the right man for the job. Because he could not get great jobs due to his rudimentary education, he was upset when J.J. was "given the privilege" to move to the twelfth grade. The theme of this episode was a direct example why education shortens the unemployment lines, and why obtaining an honest education was, is, and will continue to be so vital to success. The episode also showed the unfortunate vicious cycle in the schools of the ghettos. Since the students did not academically progress due to the lack of teachers and budget, they were passed through schools without knowing a thing in order to keep the limited budget and staff the schools had.

One of the reasons African-Americans were viewed as uneducated and sometimes were classified as retarded was the unfair standardized testing, mainly the I.Q. tests. For years, African-American children scored significantly lower than their Caucasian peers on I.Q. tests, and most believed that the reason behind this lack of performance was related to genetics. A study by the University of Pennsylvania was completed in January 1974, disproving the myth and stating, "United States white students score higher on intelligence tests because of environmental factors rather than genetics."[55]

Good Times examined why environmental factors were the reason African-Americans scored poorly on intelligence tests. In this episode during the epic second season, Michael walked out of an I.Q. test without finishing the questions, because to him, "It don't tell you how smart you are, just how white you are."[56] One of the questions was, "A mother and father and two children live in a five-bedroom residence. The mother and father sleep in one bedroom, and each of the two children has a room to himself. How many guest bedrooms are there left?"[57]

The Evans family lived in a small, two-bedroom apartment on the seventeenth floor of a building in the ghetto. Michael and J.J. shared the couch that pulled into a bed in the living room. These children did not understand the concept of a guest bedroom. As a result of these biased tests, "75 percent of the black children in classes for the retarded did not belong there," reported *The New York Times*.[58] Five weeks after this episode aired, a Federal judge in San Francisco banned African-Americans from taking I.Q. tests that did not reflect black life. In one response, *Good Times* summarized the opinions of anyone who believed that I.Q. tests were inaccurate in determining the intelligence of blacks. When Michael's principal threw statistics at Mr. and Mrs. Evans to try to explain why the I.Q. tests were so accurate, Mr. Evans coldly responded, "How you gonna know where I'm at if you ain't been where I've been? Understand where I'm comin' from?"[59]

Some of the topics that were discussed on *Good Times* actually surfaced the field of current events two decades before. *Brown v. Board of Education of Topeka* occurred in the 1950s, and desegregation of schools was put into effect, but the movement was stagnant right up until the start of the 1970s. In 1973, *The Washington Post* reported, "Nearly 20 years after the Supreme Court desegregation decision, 63 per cent of black children still attend predominantly black schools."[60]

As the second season of *Good Times* began in the fall of 1974, so did an extremely tense and violent school year in Roxbury, Massachusetts. It was the biggest racial scandal in the decade, and it had to do with children, rather than adults. Adults used children as ingredients to try to fix something they messed up in the first place. By forcefully mandating integration in schools and buses, these adults desperately tried to speed up a process that had previously seen little progress. A group of colored children were deliberately bussed to an all-white neighborhood in Southern Boston, causing pandemonium throughout the city. The children were being used as guinea pigs. Journalist Mike Fitzpatrick of *The Chicago Tribune* would back that up. "Learning is a distant second to social experiment in schools," he said in 1977.[61] Even on the first day, the belligerence was palpable. Phyllis Ellison, one of the African-American students, recalled her first day. "When we started up the hill you could hear people saying, 'Niggers go home.' There were signs, they had made a sign saying, 'Black people stay out. We don't want any niggers in our school.' And there were people on the corners holding bananas like we were apes, monkeys."[62]

The topic of integration on schools and buses was discussed one month into the school year. To a pre-teen Michael Evans, forced busing was simply "nothing but a bunch of honkie four-wheel jives"; he felt that "black ain't beautiful on a yellow bus."[63] James rebuked Michael for not wanting to go to a much better school since it was integrated. Michael countered, "Why should I go to school with people who don't want to go to school with me?"[64] He did not want to put up with those words of enmity written on signs. According to Ellison, inside, the schools seemed segregated. "In the lunchrooms, the black students sat on one side. The white students sat on the other side.... I mean, we attended the same school, but we really never did anything together."[65] In the end, Michael went to the integrated school to make history and to get past the barricades adults set up long before he was born. A roaring ovation was heard from the studio audience. And the cast performed the episode with the children in Roxbury in the back of their minds. Esther Rolle told *The Christian Science Monitor* in 1974, "I hope we get into all the TV stations in the South — but it's also just as important to get into Roxbury, Massachusetts. It's an erroneous assumption to think that the South needs more enlightenment any more than the North. Prejudice is universal."[66]

The ovation from the studio audience conveyed the message that this episode had an impact on the American people, many of whom were affected by the issue when they were not sitting in their living rooms. Because of affirmative action, children were being "used" by adults, some of whom still preferred to live in the segregated Fifties. The topic was controversial around the country. Now, most of America understands the success of integration, but it was not as clear cut back then. In May of 1974, four months before this episode aired, *The Washington Post* ran an article saying that "academic success for these [African-American] children would increase competition for the better jobs and put even greater strain on our tormented class structure."[67] However, two years prior, the same paper printed an article that asked the question "Is it really worth it?"[68] The Caucasian demographic primarily dominated the face of the news and media, so whites' opinions were the only opinions to which society was exposed. *Good Times* was the only way America fully saw how African-Americans felt about the situation, providing America with a more balanced view on certain issues.

Before the school year ended, the situation in Boston turned deadly, when a black student stabbed a white student. At the time, Ellison was a sophomore in high school. Even by 1976, things were still violent. In one situation, a black man was impaled with a flagpole. The American flag had become a weapon, not something Betsy Ross would have hoped for.

Later in the same season, an episode showed Thelma getting a scholarship to a fancy, integrated school in Michigan. She was excited to go to this school, although a bit anxious about how the white people of the school would perceive her. Once again, the episode dealt with affirmative action; when a white leader of a sorority came to the Evans' house, she tried to get Thelma to join the sorority because it did not yet have an African-American member. As far as Thelma's parents were concerned, she was being used as a "token black" so that the sorority could meet their, as James pithily put it, "coon quota."[69] The leader revealed that there were other groups looking to get Thelma in their sorority, and that she should join her sorority because they raised money for the NAACP. Reality had it that African-American children were being "used" to give the impression that the world adults had messed up was finally desegregating.

Good Times also showed the education opportunities for adults. In one episode, Florida and James went back to school to obtain their high school diplomas, something they made sure all three of their children obtained. In another episode, James graduated from trade school. *Good Times* discussed the advantages of education when James graduated from trade school and instantly found confidence, and a higher paying job.

The living environment in the projects was poor, and all the poverty and crime stemmed from the low level of education. Therefore, any media that tackled the education of the ghetto were socially and culturally significant. *Good Times* tackled the socially relevant issues about education in the projects, but more importantly tackled them from the perspectives of the people living in the projects, rather than the stances of the people debating about the projects. *Good Times* was the most realistic portrayal of education in urban regions in the 1970s. While this issue focused on teenagers inside the classroom, *Good Times* discussed teenage problems outside the classroom in even greater depth.

Teen Problems

Throughout the twentieth century and continuing into the twenty-first century, choices made by teenagers living in the ghetto heavily impacted their futures. By the 1970s, teenagers seemed to be getting worse and worse at making them. A statistic was released by *The Washington Post* saying that, "Crimes by children — those under 18 — have been growing at a higher rate than the juvenile population. According to FBI data, arrests of children for serious crimes — murder, assault, robbery, and rape — have jumped about 200 per cent in the past 15 years..."[70] Another statistic showed the number of teenage births in Chicago, where *Good Times* took place. "More than 11 per cent of the births in Chicago in 1975 were to school-age mothers ... more than 75 per cent of these adolescent mothers were members of racial minorities and lived in the city's poorest areas."[71]

Due to the environment surrounding them, making proper choices was harder than, for example, it was for teens living in a bucolic and religious community on a Midwest farm, where drug abuse and gangs were and are not rampant. On *Good Times*, there were three children, who were all in their teenage years at some point in the series' run. The three children were role models—they led alcohol- and drug-free lives and never put themselves in a position to become parents at a premature age. Even J.J., who many critics felt was a bad influence for children, was never seen drinking or smoking. In one episode though, J.J. proved not to be a virgin, when he suspected he had venereal disease. But he set a positive example for teenagers, by going down to the clinic and getting tested for the sexually transmitted disease (STD). It turned out he was not infected. J.J., like most, was embarrassed to get checked for an STD. "What would my parents think?" was his biggest concern. But *Good Times* answered J.J.'s worry, saying that there was free testing for venereal disease in every city, and parents did not need to come to the clinic. *Good Times* stressed the importance of safe sex. It called the disease an "epidemic," stating that one out of five students will get VD before they graduate high school.[72] The episode also stressed the importance of getting tested for sexually transmitted diseases early, and discussed the symptoms in detail, so viewers would know whether or not to suspect some change in their bodies. These were all things that viewers may not have known, but now, by watching a sitcom, they were educated about it. In 1974, there were an estimated 2.5 million victims of gonorrhea (the most widespread form of VD), but only 800,000 were officially reported.[73] *Good Times* contributed to changing that statistic.

Before Norman Lear television ever hit the small screen, discussions about sex were controversial and considered racy to watch, so if the "magic word" was uttered, there was never any elaboration. Discussion on sexually transmitted diseases was nonexistent. For example, Lucy Ricardo could never say "pregnant," and television in the 1950s and 1960s rarely showed realistic two-parent families. Censors went as far as to insist that the Petrie couple on *The Dick Van Dyke Show* sleep in separate beds. Shows such as *Leave It to Beaver* only presented the pleasant times between a family and in a marriage, ignoring serious issues. When sex was first touched on in *All in the Family*, and then *Maude,* it was viewed through the adult lens, which set the stage for the discussion of teenage sexual issues on *Good Times*. Lear could keep producing new and innovative sitcoms because he could find new ways to discuss old issues.

Teen pregnancy was a huge dilemma in the projects, because, in most cases, it impoverished two generations of people. Because of that, James Evans was very protective of his daughter Thelma, since she was a sexy teen encircled

by a community polluted with hundreds of Casanovas. While his stance with
J.J.'s relationships was man-to-man, James, for the most part, hated every
teenage boy he saw. In the first season, Thelma dated a college student who
wrote a thesis called "Sexual Behavior in the Ghetto." James was already upset
that his teenage daughter was dating a college student. James really became
enraged when he saw what he interpreted as perverted slander. That was until
Florida read that it said, "In homes with a solid family foundation, especially
a strong father figure, the incidence of unwanted pregnancies is almost nonexistent."[74] James was soon on good terms with Thelma's date.

Good Times showed the importance of having a strong father figure to
educate and protect his daughter(s), hopefully keeping them from making
mistakes and getting pregnant. Teenage pregnancy was a major problem in
the United States; in 1972, 30,000 teenage pregnancies were reported.[75] Part
of that was due to carelessness. In 1974, "at least 140,000 adolescent girls in
[New York City] were sexually active and not using effective birth control."[76]

In a 1975 episode, when J.J. brought his girlfriend, Henrietta, over for
dinner, *Good Times* showed the horrific consequences of a lack of effective
birth control. But a secret about her was revealed when she walked into the
house. This pretty girl exposed a rotund stomach. Henrietta was a teenager
who was pregnant due to an encounter from a previous relationship, and
tried to cover her fear by feigning a jovial personality. Thelma was appalled
that someone her age, present in her own home, was expecting a baby, but
she soon learned that the difference between her and Henrietta was in the
amount of time their parents invested with them. Virgin Thelma had firm
but caring parents; Henrietta had two alcoholics who neglected her needs
and problems, because they had enough of their own. Henrietta wanted to
keep the baby to give love to something, which she felt her parents did not
do for her. However, she knew she could not support herself and the baby.
Florida told her that raising the baby would be "pure hell."[77] *Good Times* once
again grabbed the audience's attention about an issue with superb and realistic acting. The facial expressions that the pregnant girl, Florida, and Thelma
carried duplicated those of people who dealt with these crises in the real
world.

Good Times also discussed the early lives of people like Henrietta's parents. According to the usually aware Thelma, the drug most commonly abused
by teenagers was alcohol. Alcohol was the easiest drug for a teen to get his
or her hands on, so it became the most abused. Thelma's Cousin Naomi was
hooked on booze, and had a plentiful supply available, since her father was
also a heavy drinker, and felt it was all right to drink in front of Naomi. Even
at the Evans' house, Naomi managed to sneak a drink of vodka and gin in
the bathroom, while the family, unaware of the problem, wondered why she

spent so much time in there. This episode had a dramatic scene where the definition of an alcoholic was provided to viewers through dynamic acting, rather than a verbal definition. Thelma confronted Naomi by saying that if she was not an alcoholic, she could quit at any time. In the end, Naomi "drank to that," and the camera zoomed in on a distressed Thelma and a drunk, buoyant Naomi.

With all episodes that discussed teen problems, the victim received sympathetic insight from the characters. This forced viewers to see the issue from several angles. *Good Times* sympathetically portrayed a victim who would normally be looked down upon by relatives, friends, and all of society. The Evans family provided warmth and hope to every person who walked through their door with a problem. *Good Times'* portrayal of problems facing poor African-American teenagers showed that it was possible for those in difficult circumstances to "keep their head above water," and those victims could in fact find the help they needed to solve their problems and get their lives back on track.

From side effects to stereotypes, *Good Times* analyzed the entire issue of teenage alcoholism, which according to *The Chicago Tribune*, was "climbing alarmingly."[78] Unlike some of the other issues discussed on Lear sitcoms, this one was not dated. The attraction that Americans felt towards something they could not legally have was present centuries before the 1970s (i.e., the alcohol consumption during Prohibition), and is still present today. Side effects mentioned on *Good Times,* such as a loss of coordination and an exaggerated sense of one's own importance, have not changed three decades later, and never will change, unless of course the human body undergoes some major adaptation. Judging by today's college dorm binge drinking, the common myth that the consumption of alcohol makes one tough and masculine will not fade quickly. *Good Times* dismissed this myth when Naomi passed out seconds after her father stated this myth, and *Good Times* rebuked this statement when the audience booed at the father, who said, "For a while there I was afraid she was on drugs."[79] This statement had the potential to send chills up the spine of any viewer, who at this point felt they wanted to scream at this father. But there were other parents that also believed this misconception. In January 1975, one parent wrote to *The Chicago Tribune* about her son. "Frankly, I was so relieved that my son wasn't on drugs that I almost welcomed his use of alcohol and I never discouraged his sharing a cocktail with me or even drinking wine with dinner."[80] This situation was similar to Naomi's childhood, and that proved to have a serious backlash.

Most diplomatically, *Good Times* showed respect towards the victim herself. Thelma's Christmas wish was that Naomi would get help and get her life back on track. With support like that, just maybe she, along with many other teen victims of alcoholism in America, got help.

The most potent message showing the horrors of drugs occurred in January of 1976, towards the end of the third season. While the nation believed its priorities were focused on inflation, unemployment, and the looming energy crisis, the writers of *Good Times* believed stopping "dope traffic" should have been another priority. In its best attempt to draw attention to this issue, a frustrated James vented, "In 1961, President Kennedy said we'd have a man on the moon by '70 and we did it. Now you can't tell me that a country that can put a man on the moon can't stop dope traffic."[81]

In the episode, J.J. wanted to propose to his girlfriend Diana. Both J.J.'s parents and Diana's parents forbade an engagement between the two. Although the engagement situation may have exaggerated reality a bit (considering both were jobless high school students) the situation created a stressful situation for J.J. and Diana. To close out the first half of the two-part episode, Diana was shown in the bathroom, crying while injecting heroin into her arm. This sweet girl handled stress in the wrong way. The projects were a very stressful place, and some believed drugs were the easiest way out of the everyday pressure.

When Thelma found the drugs in Diana's purse, she told her parents and Diana's parents. Both sets of parents were astonished. Upon discovering a curious phone number along with the needles in her purse, both fathers decided to find the drug supplier. By pretending to order a supply of heroin, they found the delivery man, who to their shock, as well as the audience's, was not a man — but a little boy younger than Michael. This wiseacre said he only delivered the drugs, and that the drugs came from a long line of people. He also said that this chain of drug possessors originated outside of the ghetto. This was another example of the vicious cycle of crime that plagued innocent children living in the projects.

Once again, *Good Times* showed sympathy to the drug abuser. The writers set this up, because before viewers saw her shooting up, they saw a good-hearted teenager. This episode showed that terrible things happen to good people. In the cases discussed on *Good Times*, it gave support to people in situations where they were in desperate need of self-help.

Depression — especially those severely suffering from it in the ghetto — was a topic *Good Times* talked about in its fourth season, when J.J.'s former high school buddy stopped by his house one night, at a party the Evans children threw with Willona's supervision. In high school, he received a free ride because of his basketball skills, but now, due to poor grades, he had been cut from the team. Basketball was this kid's life, and now that it was gone, he decided to overdose on sleeping pills in the Evanses' bathroom.

But the Evans children came to the rescue, unlocking the bathroom door from the outside and performing the necessary actions to sustain their dear friend's life. While cool and collected, they followed the instructions in their family medical book. At the same time, they showed audiences what to do in emergency situations, so they would not have to waste precious minutes looking up what to do. They called the police while J.J. kept the young man alive by keeping him moving. J.J. saved his friend's life, and at the same time, while hitting him in the face to keep him awake, told him, "There's not a damn thing to die for."[82] While he spoke to his friend, he also spoke to victims of depression, young and old. Unfortunately, that demographic was increasing, as the suicide rate for people fifteen to nineteen years old tripled between the late Fifties and the late Seventies. And while suicides among Caucasians were higher than those of African-Americans, the latter group was catching up.[83]

On several different occasions, *Good Times* also discussed the primary problem for male teens surrounded by ghetto culture: gangs. Not only did this problem affect teen males, it affected the entire ghetto community. Because of the massive numbers of killings seen in papers daily, there was a universal reticence in reporting gang crimes for several reasons. *The New York Times* named a few. "Some say the reluctance to report crimes is partly a language problem; others shruggingly say the police do not respond at all, to emergencies. Others cite apathy and perhaps most significantly, a fear of reprisals, particularly by youth gangs that are believed responsible for much of the crime."[84] Because people did not report crimes, the police could not apprehend the criminals. One angry person said, "Right now, the good people have no protection. Only the criminals have protection."[85] Perhaps the most disturbing article started off by saying, "A police sergeant has been charged with failing to respond to a call for assistance during the Feb. 15 [1974] rampage by members of youth gangs at the Jack-in-the-Box fast food restaurant in St. Albans, Queens."[86]

The staggering number of gangs put the entire community into a state of total fear and paranoia. As a result of the ever-increasing number of gangs, businesses such as restaurants plummeted into financial decrepitude. In 1974, *The New York Times* wrote about how the gang epidemic afflicted restaurants in Chinatown, who would only offer service to patrons with familiar faces. "Business is off by up to 30 per cent," they said. "95 per cent of the restaurants in Chinatown have either been robbed or burglarized."[87] One member of the Los Angeles Police Department put it perfectly. "We're caught up in an epidemic of violence, murder has no meaning, killing has become a game, a way of life."[88]

In November of 1974, *Good Times* discussed all of this—the fear, the crimes, the pressure, the lack of authority from police, and more. And the show's timing could not have been more appropriate. In 1974, "juvenile arrests for major offenses—homicide, rape, robbery, aggravated assault, burglary, larceny, and auto theft—have increased 270% in the last 10 years," wrote *The Los Angeles Times.*[89]

The episode began by showing how teenagers were pressured into joining gangs. Peer pressure was shown at an all-new level of terror—not the kind D.A.R.E. programs talk about with children. J.J. was forced at gunpoint to join the gang by gang leader Mad Dog. J.J. did not voluntarily choose. The only thing he chose was his life versus joining the gang, which in the end, could have also cost him his life. Is there a better example of the clichéd "no-win situation"? J.J. felt he could not talk to his parents about it, because, like many, he feared retaliation by the gang. So he joined the gang with much reluctance. When J.J. went out that night, he bumped into his parents walking down the street. After his parents confronted J.J. and the gang, Mad Dog shot J.J., concluding the first of two parts. Not much out of the ordinary happened in the first part; what happened was seen almost every day in the papers: sad, gruesome murders.

The second part was what separated the Evans family from the average person found in the newspapers. It turned out J.J. only suffered a flesh wound, but the real surprise was James' undaunted boldness. James did not care that Mad Dog was armed. He was ready for retaliation, giving his wife an analogy. He took five pretzel sticks, said they were Mad Dog's fingers, and broke them all in half. Florida feared vengeance, protesting with themes from the Bible. James responded, "I'm not gonna kill him with the jawbone of an ass, but I'm gonna bust that ass's jawbone."[90] James was ready to take Mad Dog to court and get him locked up, and maybe rough him up on the side. *Good Times* distinguished itself from other media because it gave advice to be strong, and report these incidents. The situation will not resolve itself if the gang members are not reported. *Good Times* showed a character in James Evans that would go through any obstacle to report the criminal that nearly killed his son.

Second, *Good Times* brought attention to the lethargic law enforcement systems. At the trial, Mad Dog was not put in jail, because there were no vacancies in the prisons. The judge, like society, was frustrated with the system, which led to a line that resonated with the audience, drawing loud applause and cheers. "No vacancies? What the hell are we running—a jail system or a Holiday Inn?" he asked.[91] But *Good Times* dissected the real problem soon after. Because there were no vacancies in jail or reformatories, Mad Dog received probation, putting him back on the streets. In Los Angeles in 1973, "1,250 persons on probation or parole committed a serious act of violence."[92] That was the root of the gang epidemic. Judge William P. Hogobloom, the judge at the Los Angeles County Juvenile Court, told *The Los*

Angeles Times, "We're grossly understaffed and undermanned, in judicial manpower, in prosecutors, public defenders and probation officers. There just aren't enough people to take care of 30,000 cases [the reported number of juvenile crimes in Los Angeles in 1973] if we're going to process them in this very formal manner in the court."[93]

Finally, *Good Times* showed Mad Dog's mother, once again boldly proving the importance of a father figure. Mad Dog's father ran away when he was a young boy, and his way of exhibiting that grief was by joining a gang. Now those thugs were the main male figures in his life. When his mother said she wished her husband was there, Mad Dog replied with tears, "What if he was? He'd be a wino in the gutter.... Where was he?"[94] The scene was a lesson to parents; it is vital to communicate with their children. And teenagers and children watching saw what happens if they use, as Mad Dog put it, his "underprivileged"[95] status, as an excuse to join gangs.

Good Times wanted to impress upon its viewers the need for a strong father figure. Esther Rolle said, "[Lear and the writers] had to work on that one for a year. We didn't want to show the gang without showing the social ills behind it. There are reasons why boys band together. They might be missing some important images in their lives, which was the case with the gang leader [Mad Dog] who shot J.J. He was jealous that J.J. had a father."[96]

However, two years later, James died in a car accident, leaving the family fatherless. At that point, *Good Times* looked at the issue yet again. Only this time, it focused on Michael. Younger teenagers were also physically forced into gangs, so that older members could have them do the dirty tasks, and the penalties would not be as stiff. Michael felt obligated to join after his friend, who refused, received a broken jaw in return.

While Michael hid this from his family, Florida, unaware that Michael was involved in one of the most bellicose gangs, held a meeting with several parents concerned with the gang situation in schools, and how to stop it. One man, Mr. Parker, vividly demonstrated his plan, receiving loud approval from the audience. He took walnuts, using them as a symbol for gang members, then took a book, which represented the parents, and slammed it down on the walnuts with all its force. "The only way to break up a gang is to break up each member," he proclaimed with confidence in his belief.[97] Judge Hogobloom from the Los Angeles County Juvenile Court agreed. "To do otherwise," he said, "would be like saying we're going to cure malaria by putting people who have it in a desert penthouse and if they make it, fine, and if they don't they die. A better way is to go down and drain the swamp and get rid of the goddamn mosquitoes so people won't get malaria."[98]

However, Florida disagreed. "We are concerned parents, not vigilantes ... controlling these kids is up to the parents."[99] Many across the country agreed. The Chinatown restaurant owner said, "If they're underage, their parents have to be held responsible."[100] The Los Angeles Board of Education said, "Parents must be accountable for the actions of their children."[101] But Florida soon learned that method was easier said than done, when she found Michael's gang jacket in the oven, right in front of Mr. Parker's angry eyes.

The latter portion of the episode reached a happy medium between the solutions that Florida and Mr. Parker devised. This was the method that *Good Times* showed to be the most effective. First, though, Michael decided to follow the advice of his late father and get out of the gang, telling them what he thought about them. When Florida figured out that he was going to tell the gang off, she chased after him. Through the character of Florida, *Good Times* was now a positive image for single parent families. Florida, now a widowed mother, knew that it was harder to raise her children without James. "Oh how I wish James was here. There would be no way in the world Michael would be in the gang," she said to herself.[102] However, she did not give up on her children because daddy had died. She took on the responsibility of raising her children the right way, providing strong images in their lives. *Good Times* encouraged the same thing.

Florida may have been against physically asserting herself, but she soon changed her mind, when she witnessed the brutality of juvenile gangs. She was no longer watching from the mezzanine or reading the daily news when she went to rescue Michael. When the gang members tried to steal the wedding ring that James gave to her, she elbowed them. Soon, when Michael tried to defend his mother by beating the bully up, Florida took a baseball bat, held it in the air, and threatened, "I'll break every bone in your body," receiving lavish applause and hoots from the audience.[103]

In the episode, hints of the late James were seen throughout the characters. Michael was a miniature version of James—always ready to say what he felt, no matter what the obstacles. He was a brave child with a dream. Two years before, Florida pleaded with James not to interfere with Mad Dog, but if she could speak to him at this point, she would probably disagree. It was as if she experienced an epiphany. All of these strong images seen on the tube were positive influences for viewers, especially those caught up in the same dilemmas. By seeing characters that asserted themselves, audiences were encouraged to do the same.

However, the episode would have been very different if James had not died. And the reason he had died was also because of the actions of teenagers. John Amos was fired, all because of his feelings about the oldest teenager in the Evans family. That was just how important images were to the actors and actresses on *Good Times*.

The Dy-no-mite Discordance

Early in the first season of *Good Times*, J.J. casually spoke the word "dyna-mite." It was not an exclamation, it did not put an exclamation point on the show, it was not preceded by "kid" or some rhyme, and the audience laughed, but not hysterically. For the writers, it was just one simple word. At that time, they did not understand that one word could make and break their series—in that order.

As the first season progressed, the pronunciation of the word slowly changed. By the beginning of the second season, it gradually evolved into, "Dy-no-mite!" But as the word began to be featured in every episode, at least once, J.J. became the 100 percent guaranteed comedic go-to guy.

By the time the episode aired in which J.J. was shot by a gang, the original stars of the show, Esther Rolle and John Amos, had realized that Walker had sabotaged their stardom. During the taping of the scene where J.J. was shot and his parents were down on the ground with him, Amos admitted to it, improvising, "This'll kill us in the Nielsens if *he* dies!"[104]

Amos and Rolle may have been angry that Walker stole the spotlight. But they could never say he was unprepared. Ja'net DuBois said, "We'd get a script on a Monday, and on a Tuesday, Jimmie would put his script down and

John Amos (left) and Esther Rolle (right) were fed up with the "coon-like" qualities of character J.J. (Jimmie Walker, center). Both left the show at some point because of it.

know every word."[105] Ralph Carter agreed. "We're talking coming in from a long weekend of stand-up comedy work. My man came in and knew his lines."[106]

However, the cast excluding Walker, as well as co-creator Eric Monte, was frustrated because the material began to lag. As shows began to focus on J.J.'s love for women and Kool-Aid, the political resonance of the sitcom began to fade completely. As J.J.'s clothes got brighter, Amos and Rolle's cheeks got redder. J.J. became an icon overnight, as millions bought "Dy-no-mite!" T-shirts; the phrase became part of American jargon. It was the word that everyone wanted to exclaim, but it was not the word James Evans was yelling when getting job rejection after job rejection. On top of that, the cast was angry at the white writers, feeling their depiction of poor African-American life was totally inaccurate, and on some level, offensive. Ja'net DuBois said, "When you have an all-white group of people writing for black people, it's going to be touchy because you don't know me."[107] African-American writer Donald Bogle called J.J.'s character a "coon," saying he was as "unreal as Sunday morning cartoons," and as far as the writers, they "exploited his character for laughs."[108] At the beginning of the series' run, Esther Rolle was confident that the show was funny, but real. "When you manufacture comedy that has no basis in truth, it falls short of being funny," she said right before the show debuted.[109] And now she, and much of the cast, felt the comedy was being manufactured.

So did Eric Monte. Monte was a key figure early on in the war versus the producers. Initially, Monte was the man responsible for the realistic approach taken in *Good Times*. Nobody knew more about this sort of reality than Monte, who grew up in one of the most dangerous ghettos in the country — Cabrini Green in Chicago. He came to Hollywood solely because he was motivated to reconstruct the image of African-Americans on television. He believed the tube was the biggest source of propaganda in the world.[110]

When Mike Evans (who played Lionel Jefferson on *All in the Family*) found him in 1971 and brought him to Hollywood, the two began working on *Good Times*. Before and after the show's debut, Lear and Monte would often be embroiled in arguments. Monte believed Lear and his Jewish writers for *Good Times* (Jack Elinson, Norman Paul, and Allan Mannings) possessed only a stereotypical view of African-American life.[111] Monte was not about to let that stereotypical view be perpetuated for tens of millions of viewers. Monte told *E!* in 2000, "If the show failed, the networks would say black stuff don't sell. And I couldn't let that happen. So I had to make sure *Good Times* was a hit, for there ever to be any hope for anybody else. That was my goal."[112]

Then Lear told Monte about an opportunity for him. Lear knew that producer Steve Krantz needed an African-American writer for a movie he was directing, and Monte left for the opportunity to write *Cooley High* in 1974.

Amos and Rolle were even more frustrated after the departure of Monte, as they were the only ones left to fight the white writers and their stereotypes.

Before the show's third season, Amos sat out for a week of taping because he wanted more money. But throughout the next few months, money was the last of the worries on Amos' mind. He angrily demanded that the show focus more on family values than J.J.'s antics. Ralph Carter said about Amos, "He was very sensitive to the types of scripts that were there. Again, we live in a culture where the son never becomes greater than the father. If that was attempted, it did happen on *Good Times*. And that is taboo in black culture."[113] But it was not as easy as that for Lear. The show was prospering under the lead of J.J., and Lear was in a business situation. He jumped on the J.J. bandwagon, which kept growing and growing.

"J.J.'s empire grew so large that his personal touch was no longer there and he began to delegate responsibility to people who were not as capable," said John Amos during a TV Land documentary in 2004. "And that's when the show began to disintegrate."[114] Lear commented in that same documentary, "What happened with this wonderful cast was that they represented, to their community, the only image that existed on television. In addition to actors, they became social critics of the script that was presented to them. John became impossible, out of what he was feeling. And while I honored what he was feeling, I couldn't honor it in a five-day week when we had to get shows made. So we made the decision to lose the character."[115]

The relationship between Lear and John Amos was "quite abrasive."[116] To kill off James Evans, Lear pulled out a familiar script from his back pocket — the one that killed Archie Bunker. This time though, it actually aired — except James Evans was killed in a car accident in Mississippi, rather than in Buffalo. When Amos was fired, he said, "I wasn't exactly surprised ... but what bothers me is that now there will be no positive black male image on any television show."[117] Not only did it "bother" Amos, but it also bothered the African-American community. The father figure was one of the things that *Good Times* was proud of, separating it from shows such as *That's My Mama*. Kids who did not have an everyday father could look up to James. Eric Monte was originally the one who emphasized the importance of a strong father figure on television. Later, Esther Rolle made sure the series only existed if her television children had a father. That was one stereotype Monte and Rolle wanted to obliterate. *Good Times* had the opportunity to help these young children, and now some felt that it would now be hurting them by bringing back that stereotype. The African-American community's anger turned into rage when one of Lear's associates released a false statement reading, "Norman has just decided that it would be interesting to experiment with what might happen to this kind of family if the father were to leave."[118]

On several occasions during Amos' last season, *Good Times* showed the importance of a father figure for children living in the ghetto. In one instance, James received a job on the Alaska Pipeline paying $500 per week, and he took it in a heartbeat. He did not realize how that would affect his children, until Michael came home with bruises, looking to retaliate against a gang that beat him and his friends up. He then noticed that the children needed a father figure, and substituted his children's well-being for financial well-being.[119]

When Amos left the show, a special two-part episode aired to begin the fall of 1976, the fourth season of *Good Times.* Several hours before the taping, Lear received a death threat. If he showed up to the taping, his life would be in jeopardy. An undaunted Lear went to the taping without bodyguards, and proceeded to warm up the audience as always. Lear went to bed that night safe and sound.[120]

In the episode, it was explained that James had gotten a job in Mississippi, and the family was packing to move there. However, at the going-away party, Florida received a life-altering telegram. "We regret to inform you that your husband, James Evans, was killed in an automo..."[121] Florida began reading the telegram with a smile, and ended speechlessly, with a crying Michael in her arms. The mellow background music faded away. Lear could not believe his eyes. Minutes later, he told the studio audience, including the young, rowdy African-American men in the back row, "As many times as I've seen this show now, it still knocks all the wind out of me."[122]

During the last half hour (which was taped at another time), a party was held in the apartment following James' wake. Throughout the party, Florida was her buoyant self, much to her children's consternation. But in the final scene, Florida cleaned up the mess from the party, saw the roses from the funeral, grabbed a punchbowl, and let loose. Dropping the punchbowl, shattering it into pieces, clenching her fists, she crescendoed, "Damn! Damn! Damn!"[123]

As Florida cried those words, *Good Times* writer Judy Ann Mason also cried. "The show died when James Evans died," she said.[124] From a professional perspective, Ralph Carter agreed it was never the same. "I did not enjoy the work as much as I did when John Amos was there."[125] Jimmie Walker, whose character greatly affected why the producers decided to kill off James, said, "I was waiting for the two-parter to be over so we could get back to the serious, all-out comedy. That was my thing."[126]

The departure of John Amos left an insurmountable void in the cast. Temporarily, Florida and Willona did their best to cover the hole, but then producers acquired two male actors to contribute. The landlord Bookman, also known to Willona as "Buffalo Butt," became a more prevalent character, providing comedy and occasional support. Johnny Brown, formerly of *Rowan and Martin's Laugh-In*, became a cast member in the show's fifth season. Next, Moses Gunn, from the highly popular 1971 film *Shaft*, played Carl Dixon, Florida's new love interest, as well as a role model for the children. Although the ratings may only have dropped two spots from the previous season, it was apparent the show had lost the spark it possessed when James was the head of the house.

But then things went from bad to worse. When Dad died, J.J. sometimes failed to cope under the pressure of being man of the house, by joining dishonest scams (dealing with drugs, prostitution, and gambling) to pay the rent. When Florida found out, she kicked J.J. out until he stopped. Rolle kept receiving scripts like this and began to contemplate following in her former partner's footsteps. She felt that these scripts were degrading towards African-Americans, and she used to be able to veto these plots. Originally, it was her show, her spin-off, until J.J. took over. In 1986, Rolle told *The Washington Post* about her departure, "I insist that you can have humor and good taste, but they never delivered the changes. It was no longer a happy thing. The role of Florida didn't require much digging. There was no depth. And when you start getting knots in your stomach each time you have to go off to work, it's time to quit. Life is too precious."[127] Rolle left the show after the fourth season. In the fourth season finale, Florida said yes to a proposing Carl, and went on a honeymoon that would wind up lasting longer than normal honeymoons. Rolle went into the clouds, leaving the show in the hands of Ja'net DuBois.

Willona the Mother

The show that almost never aired, because there was only one parental figure in the script, now had no biological parents in it. At the start of the 1977–78 season, the Evans family lived all alone, with Willona next door. Ja'net DuBois became the adult star by default, her name now leading the opening credits.

On the show, it was explained that Florida had decided to live in Arizona, where she and new husband Carl had spent their honeymoon. The conditions were best for Carl's health. On the sidelines, this situation angered Rolle, who said, "It's a matter of black pride. A mother just wouldn't do that. It's wrong, terribly wrong."[128]

However, Lear went in an entirely different direction. The beginning of the fifth season brought the presence of yet another J.J. However, this time those famous initials stood for the actress' name — Janet Jackson.

With limited resources, Lear and his team brought a new child to the mix. Jackson, now a pop superstar, was then known to America as Michael

Jackson's sibling from the Jackson 5. Now Janet was about to have a support-ing role in a television show, playing the television daughter of Ja'net.

Jackson's character's impact was instantly going to be very topical. The girl she played, Penny Gordon, would be a victim of child abuse. Jackson was able to show off her dramatic talents at a very young age, when Penny went through a major custody change in a four-part episode opening the fifth sea-son. Willona became Penny's surrogate mother, removing her from her abu-sive past, living with her single mother. Now, *Good Times* consisted of a parentless family in addition to a newly found single parent family — very different from what Eric Monte, John Amos, and Esther Rolle originally con-ceived. However, there were many important messages that arose out of the relationship between Penny and Willona.

Child abuse, the problem that triggered the birth of this relationship, was the most socially relevant topic that *Good Times* discussed from this point on in the series, as it tried to keep the theme of political resonance that it possessed in its early years. Initially, *Good Times* clearly defined "child abuse" by showing it on the screen. *The Los Angeles Times* said in 1975, "Child abuse and neglect cases range from black and blue marks from vigorous spankings to intentional, recurring neglect and abuse, such as the appalling — and trag-ically many — cases when a child has been locked in a closet for weeks with-out proper nourishment and is released only to be beaten, burned, or whipped."[129] That was exactly how *Good Times* portrayed it. From the start of the show, viewers saw the results of child abuse, when Penny's mother burned her with the iron after coming home late, and then, when Willona saw her severely bruised back. Then Penny's mother broke her daughter's arm. Instantly, viewers saw that Penny's situation was far different from when James used to hit his kids as a disciplinary measure. Despite violence being associated more with men than with women, the episode was right on track by showing an abusive mother. In 1977, *The Chicago Tribune* stated that "more mothers than fathers act violently towards their children ... [it is] the only situation in which human females are more violent than males."[130]

The child abuse problem was a growing issue. *The Chicago Tribune* said, "An estimated 3.3 to 3.9 million children have been kicked, bitten, or punched by parents— about half of them in 1975."[131] Even worse, in most homes, the problem was being kept in the closet. "Testimony during Senate hearings in 1974 on child abuse gave conservative estimates that at least one million inci-dents were thought to have occurred that year on a nationwide basis, yet only 60,000 cases were reported," wrote *The Washington Post*.[132] However, *Good Times* attacked those who were reluctant to report cases. In one case (before the adoption), the doctor could not treat Penny's broken arm because her mother would not sign the papers. When Willona tried to explain that it was child abuse, the doctor still refused to treat her because child abuse was hard to actually prove. Willona became angry though, as *Good Times* tried to show why reporting the case was so vital — to save this cute little girl's physical and psychological health. "You better get yourself a heart transplant 'cause, baby, you *need* one," she angrily told the doctor after he refused to treat Penny. Later, she commented, "They're [the doctors and lawyers] sweeping the whole mess under the rug."[133] Willona's message got across to the doctor eventually, when he called later and agreed to help Penny. *Good Times* stressed the vitality in helping the victims. As *The Los Angeles Times* stated in 1977, "Approximately one quarter of those children [the one million victims of child abuse] will be permanently injured for life as a result of being mistreated, according to statistics compiled by Attorney General Evelle J. Younger."[134]

The four-part episode of *Good Times* did not shy away from showing that, either. Penny's mother was the one who showed the psychological damage that past victims experience during adulthood. As a child, she went through the same torture she was putting Penny through. And she did not want to do that either. She loved Penny. *Good Times* actually showed a small amount of sympathy towards the abusive mother, and encouraged her to seek help for her problem.

This portion of the episode discussed the existence of the non-profit organization, Parents Anonymous. The group served the same purpose as Alcoholics Anonymous did for problem drinkers— getting victims the help they need to get their lives back on track, and specifically in this case, potentially saving their children. Thelma pleaded with Penny's mother to attend Parents Anonymous meetings, but she felt that these meetings held the connotation of "crazy." Of course, she was entirely mistaken. Sandi Borowicz of *The Los Angeles Times* wrote about Parents Anonymous, "Parents Anonymous, one of the most widely known self-help child abuse groups, consists of ex-child abusers who are helping abusive parents deal with their problems. The nationwide organization has three Valley chapters as well as other branches citywide."[135] In addition to that, Parents Anonymous also had a 24/7 hotline. On *Good Times*, Thelma described it to Penny's mother as a place where "a lot of people get together with the same problem that you have and they help each other."[136] Many people in Penny's mother's situation were getting help — one center reported that half of the women helped there were single parents.[137] Because of the issue and the obvious emotional and psychological state of Penny's mother, viewers saw that therapy is actually a positive method of treatment. Willona said, "Do yourself a favor. Get some help — you need it badly."[138] Willona showed it as a vital step in her and her daughter's recovery.

However, at the same time, *Good Times* did not let Penny's mother make excuses for her abusive behavior. Even though there was a sympathetic side, the show did not tolerate Penny's mother's behavior. While *Good Times* promoted treatment for mothers who abuse their children as victims, the show did not make Penny's mother sound innocent. *Good Times* stressed that there is absolutely no reason to hurt a child. Penny's mother tried to rationalize, saying that she had an excuse because her parents abused her, and she was a single parent. *Good Times* did not appreciate excuses. Willona responded, "Big deal. I was raised without a father. My mother didn't go upside my head."[139] And the audience was deeply engrossed in the episode, and Willona's motives. Their reactions could be heard, even verbal ones, including "Yeah Willona!"

Minutes later, Penny's mother committed the darkest sin against any child — she abandoned Penny. She ran away from Penny in tears, crying, "She deserves something better than me!"[140] Off she went as she closed the elevator door, leaving Penny's future to Willona's discretion. Willona initially felt obligated to do as the papers were recommending: "children of parents convicted of child abuse [should] be placed in foster homes at the parents' expense."[141] However, Penny begged to live with Willona, and was determined to make that happen. Finally, after taking care of the legal aspects of the situation, Willona gained custody of Penny. Penny spoke the final words of the four-part episode, when she said to Willona, "Oh Mama!"[142] Those words marked the perfect denouement to yet another emotionally trying performance by the cast of *Good Times*.

The ratings from the fifth season proved that, although the J.J. character was extremely popular, *Good Times* could not and did not function as "The J.J. Show." The departures of John Amos and Esther Rolle left a huge lesion in the on-screen chemistry of the show, resulting in a lesion in the ratings. *Good Times* dropped to 58th in the Nielsen ratings, over thirty slots, since the show's direction shifted into a parentless world. [143] But there was one last ray of hope.

Florida Returns

In the fall of 1978, Ja'net DuBois passed the baton back to original series star, Esther Rolle. DuBois did her best to compete in the relay race, but the series lost many viewers after Rolle left. But now she was back.

Rolle agreed to return to *Good Times* under one condition — that the antics of her television son would be toned down, and that Jimmie Walker would finally portray an honest young African-American. That season, J.J. taught art while searching for a full-time job and Florida got a job as a bus driver. But that was not the way the sixth season started.

Not only did Rolle rejoin the cast, but Ben Powers hopped on board also. He played Thelma's boyfriend Keith Anderson, and after his first appearance, Keith and Thelma became engaged. It seemed like all of the Evanses' money problems had been solved. Keith was a top NFL prospect who was negotiating a million dollar deal to play professionally. That was until his wedding ceremony, when Keith tripped over J.J.'s foot, breaking his leg and losing that million dollar opportunity. The entire family moved into the Evans home, once again unable to make it out of the ghetto.

Meanwhile, across the hall, Willona continued to raise Penny to the best of her ability, although there were some rough times. In one case, Penny's friend became pregnant. When a confused Penny asked what was happening to her friend, Willona lied and said she had stomach mumps. Matron Florida cleared the problem up. In another case, Willona dated what seemed to be a very nice guy, until he insisted on throwing a party at her house. Willona did not know that his guest list consisted of prostitutes and drug addicts. However, the whole incident was a scam contrived by Penny's biological mother in an attempt to regain custody of her daughter, by making Willona look completely irresponsible. Needless to say, she lost.

Across the hall, J.J. managed to run into trouble with the local loan shark, Sweet Daddy Williams. J.J. witnessed Sweet Daddy commit a crime, and Sweet Daddy threatened to hurt J.J. if he did not lie in his favor. In the end, J.J. chose honesty over perjury. Several episodes later, Sweet Daddy needed blood, and J.J.'s was the only matching blood type.

However, the Nielsen ratings showed that, by this point, few viewers tuned in to care about the latest struggles of the Evans family. *Good Times* was cancelled after earning pitiful ratings, becoming one of the least watched shows in the CBS schedule during the 1978–79 season. Things were looking glum from the start of the season, and by December, *Good Times* was put on hiatus. Gary Deeb of *The Chicago Tribune* wrote, "[CBS] is putting *Good Times*, a six-year veteran, on the 'injured reserve list.' The faltering comedy series will return in April or May, play out its remaining episodes, and then probably get cancelled."[144] It was cancelled that summer, filling the spot of the 84th most watched show in America.[145] And to think that four years earlier, it was in the top ten. The behind the scenes politics truly hurt one of the most popular shows in the 1970s, and a television classic that could have made it well into the 1980s.

The *Good Times* finale seemed to be an aberration, when looking at the first 132 episodes. In the final episode, fate seemed to be the Evanses' long-lost friend, when J.J. was offered a job as a cartoon artist, Keith's leg healed and he was offered the football contract, Thelma became pregnant, and they all moved into the same apartment complex — out of the ghetto!

During *Good Times'* six years on the air, the show had made a major impact on culture. Jimmie Walker's J.J. became the first African-American teen icon. Never before had the face of an African-American entertainer covered millions of T-shirts, coffee mugs, and many other novelties. But *Good Times* was more important than that. Throughout its run, the show presented dozens of public service announcements, about topics ranging from venereal disease to gun control. *Good Times* showed how both single- and two-parented African-Americans live, by developing realistic parental images like James and Florida Evans, who became role models for those who watched. And despite all that "Dyn-o-mite," *Good Times* was the most realistic taste of poor African-American life ever seen on television at the time, and arguably, in the history of television.

5

The Move on Up

The Jeffersons' George Jefferson thought he knew everything about life—yet he knew almost nothing about it at all. When he was seen on *All in the Family,* he seemed to be an African-American clone of Archie Bunker. Yet unlike Archie, this angered bull did not seem to have any trace of love inside—even going to such offensive lengths as calling Edith Bunker "the honkie's wife" in one episode.[1] However, in 1975, Norman Lear took George Jefferson and placed him, along with his wife and college student son, in a luxurious apartment. Lear stuck this African-American Jefferson family in the center of a white-collar world, and showed how they would react to it. Lear rewarded George for opening a chain of dry-cleaning stores all over the city.

George instantly welcomed himself into the white-collar world, a world in which money was his top priority. Decades before, when he lived in Harlem, George wished for money, something that he could have used to provide the bare necessities of life for his family. Now George had it, and kept praying for more. He wanted every cent he could get his hands on. George was to bank, as child is to candy store. George also wanted to appear wealthy, so he bought an expensive grand piano, bid on useless antiques, and joined an all-white tennis club. To make more money, he opened more cleaning stores and even bought a pair of bicycles as his anniversary gift to his wife—but only to stalk Mr. Whittendale, the mega-wealthy banker who owned the building he lived in, and who rode bikes for recreation.

Many times, it was almost as if George had forgotten his past. Not quite though. He had his wife, Louise, to remind him. Louise refused to become "Mrs. Money." She felt she was born a Harlemite, and would die a Harlemite. Sure, she enjoyed the money and George's success, but she chose not to be the queen and sit on her balcony, enjoying the view of New York City. She refused to look down on her old Harlemite neighbors from her twelfth-story penthouse perch. It took years for Louise to adjust, whereas George adjusted with a snap of his energetic fingers.

George adjusted instantaneously, but not because he wanted to live a white life in a white world. He was as proud of his heritage as it got, incessantly boasting that he climbed the ladder of success with a "black burden."[2] George was the kind of guy that was undeniably proud of his achievements, and would not stop at anything to make that clear. Not all of him was selfish. He pushed his son, making sure he graduated college, so he could photocopy his diploma, and post it in each of his cleaning stores. But more importantly, he knew that his son's climb to success would be facilitated by a college diploma. Just like Archie Bunker, George loved his family. Maybe he was not so evil after all. Maybe, just maybe, he had a bit of sensitivity inside him.

Lionel, George, Louise, & Co.

Before America ever got their first glance at Archie Bunker, they got a quick look at Lionel Jefferson. In the first few minutes of the first episode of *All in the Family,* viewers learned that Lionel was studying to be an electrical engineer, and was doing odd jobs around the community to earn petty cash. When Gloria gave Lionel a dollar for the flowers he delivered, Lionel told her, "Where I get my flowers, this represents a buck profit."[3] Viewers also learned that he loved to play the game of racism with Archie. "Give the people what they want," said Lionel.[4] That was why he pronounced it "electical" engineer around Archie, who felt that African-Americans were not as intelligent as whites like him. Although Archie never realized it, Lionel always had the last laugh. Instantly, viewers liked him. By the end of the first episode, he had already received an ovation from the live studio audience.

Michael Evans was the actor who played Lionel Jefferson. He believed acting was an art of using many faces with skill. For example, he would use a different face when talking to Mike or Gloria and Edith rather than Archie. "You have to use a different face for every person," Evans told *TV Guide* in 1973. "I learned the trick doing door-to-door magazine selling. I became immune to that guy who says he doesn't want any. Strike the right attitude, and all you got to do is tell 'em the price and mumble the rest. Before he knows it, he's bought $250 worth of stuff he doesn't want. Man, that's total selling."[5]

Lear chose Evans for the part after auditioning numerous other actors because, he said, "The kid had the gift of being himself. And that happened to work."[6] Evans remembered the moment when he got the part. "The adrenalin began to rush to my head, I jumped over a fence, tripped and fell on my face. But I recovered. 'This is ridiculous,' I told myself. 'You're an actor. You got to be *cool.*'"[7] Evans was certainly dedicated to his craft. On *All in the Family*, he wished that he appeared in more episodes, since he was still being paid. He told *The Los Angeles Times* in 1975, "The one thing I don't like is to be paid for not working."[8]

As the new episodes kept coming and *All in the Family* gained more and more of a fan base, Lionel became the "fifth Bunker." America laughed harder and harder each time Lionel patronized Archie. In one case, Archie was surprised to see Lionel in a blood bank, since he thought that only white people were eligible to donate blood. Lionel, knowing Archie's view, simply remarked, "Yeah, I sweeps up."[9] It was an innocent game that Lionel loved to play, and America loved to watch him play it.

Four episodes after the two bumped into each other in the blood bank, Archie met Lionel's entire family, as they moved out of the projects and right next door. For the first time, Louise, Lionel's mother, played by Isabel Sanford, appeared. Soon, Louise became the sixth Bunker. But Lear had not been able to find a consummate actor for Louise's husband. In the final episode of the first season, it was explained that Lionel's father refused to step into a white household.

Two more seasons went by, and still the actor for George Jefferson had not been found. Then Lear thought of Sherman Hemsley, whom he had seen in the 1970 Broadway musical *Purlie*. Lear called the performance "particularly exquisite."[10] Now Lear had to find the actor, who, at the time, was working for the U.S. Postal Service. By late 1973, George Jefferson finally stepped into a "honkie household." In a 1982 *TV Guide* interview, Hemsley recalled getting recruited. "I thought they wanted me for *Sanford and Son*. I called. Lady named Sylvia O'Gilvie answered the phone. 'Don't move!' she yelled, like I was a criminal or something. 'We've been looking for you everywhere.' Anyway, they flew me down.... When I needed bread later, Lear loaned me his credit card."[11]

Hemsley was the exact opposite of George Jefferson's short-tempered personality; he was the reserved type. Producer Don Nicholl said, "Sherman is the gentlest actor I've ever met. But when we feed him these very harsh lines, he becomes a feisty bantam rooster."[12] Hemsley's personal fashion tastes were also completely different from his character. A 1975 photo of Hemsley showed him in a tie-dye shirt and jeans, while viewers were used to seeing him in a finely tailored suit. He got along just fine with the cast. Michael Evans said, "It's not like we're real close, but I like him a lot. I know when he needs to talk and when he needs to be left alone. He's a good human being."[13] And the relationship between Isabel Sanford and Hemsley was also normally cordial. There was the occasional exception, though. Anonymously, one cast member (of *The Jeffersons*) told *TV Guide*, "Sure they had a falling-out. Isabel was dieting and when that happens she's mad at everybody. She's entitled. Next day she was OK."[14]

By 1974, Lear decided to grant America's favorite next door neighbors a spin-off; but it was not an ordinary spin-off. It did not show the Jeffersons

A cast photo of *The Jeffersons*, taken in the show's second season. Top row: Franklin Cover, Roxie Roker, Berlinda Tolbert, Damon Evans. Bottom row: Paul Benedict, Isabel Sanford, Sherman Hemsley, Zara Cully. (Photograph provided by Franklin Cover.)

living next door, like they had done for the last four years. Instead, it showed the Jeffersons after they hit it big in George's cleaning business, and this African-American family moved into an apartment that the Bunkers could never afford.

Critics were worried about this show at the start; even pro–Lear critic John J. O'Connor claimed, "Even Archie is an 'appealing' bigot."[15] They were worried how George Jefferson, who, as one critic put it, was "simply irrational and unlikable,"[16] would influence viewers as an African-American man who believed he could conquer the world with his wallet. That same critic said, "While we know that television's version of reality has usually little to do with the real thing, there is a dangerous political message in a program that presents the fears of a black man in America as a simple aberration."[17] But there surely was hope for this show. He also said, "If Lear gets some black input into the writing end of this program, it might move away from the brink of absurdity and develop into a pretty good television program."[18]

Lear's television programs were able to succeed because of the wise utilization of supporting characters. In all of his sitcoms, it seemed that Lear liked to have supporting characters who were the neighbors of the main family—from the Jeffersons on *All in the Family*, to Julio on *Sanford and Son*, to Arthur and Vivian on *Maude*, to Willona on *Good Times*, and now, to Harry Bentley on *The Jeffersons*. In 1978, *TV Guide* described Bentley as "a wide-eyed innocent who works at the United Nations, is completely blind to color differences and even feels that getting the door slammed in his face by a ranting, raving George Jefferson is actually a gesture of love."[19] Bentley was a British scholar. In 1968, Lear saw Paul Benedict in the off–Broadway production of *Little Murders*, and featured him in his 1970 film *Cold Turkey* (which also starred Jean Stapleton). Four years later, Lear contacted him for *The Jeffersons*, but Benedict kept turning him down, even after beating out pure British actors in the audition. His final excuse was that the taping of the pilot was on the same day as a movie commitment.

When Lear heard that, he called the movie director and made him change the day of the shooting.[20] That was how much he wanted Benedict. That also demonstrated the power that Lear had in Hollywood. Then, a flattered Paul Benedict flew to Los Angeles, as Harry Bentley.

Benedict said of his character, "Bentley would help anybody. He cares a great deal. You can put him into any situation—as ludicrous as you can imagine—and there's still a reality for him. Because he's the kind of person who always gets into those situations but passes through them sort of unruffled."[21] Benedict was similar to Bentley in some ways. Marla Gibbs (who played the Jeffersons' maid, Florence) said, "I don't know anybody who has a bad word to say about Paul Benedict."[22]

Bentley was not the only neighbor that the Jeffersons had; therefore, he was not the only person who was on the receiving end of a door slam by George Jefferson. Upstairs lived an interracial couple, Tom and Helen Willis. Tom Willis was played by Franklin Cover, and his television mate was Roxie Roker. The show's success could be partially attributed to the chemistry between Cover and Roker. The two knew each other from years on Broadway — where Lear discovered them both. Roker said about Cover, "If you dig beneath that jovial, backslapping exterior you will find one of the last of the genuine eccentrics."[23] Lear enjoyed their on and off-screen chemistry: "Franklin and Roxie look like they've been married for 20 years."[24] Critics liked them, too. Gary Deeb wrote in his column the day before the show's debut that they were "charming, friendly, and ingratiating. Producer Lear often manages to pick up superb but relatively unknown talent from the New York stage, and he's done it again here."[25]

"I knew the plot generally from the trade paper's description," Roker told *The Washington Post* in 1976. "I was told they wanted a tall — taller than George Jefferson — because I'm supposed to look down on him — elegant East Side lady."[26] But the thing that truly attracted Roker to the part was that it resembled her life. She was an African-American woman married to a white man for many years.

Her partner and true friend Franklin Cover took the role in a heartbeat. Cover recalled in a personal interview, "Norman Lear had seen me on Broadway — [he] called one night in 1974 and told me to get on a plane and I went for a meeting. We talked and I was cast that night. Of course, I had no idea it was a ten-year run."[27] Lear described Cover in 1980 as "a great white polar bear,"[28] because of his blithe disposition on and off the set.

Tom and Helen Willis had a daughter, Jenny Willis, played by Berlinda Tolbert. Jenny was Lionel's girlfriend, and later, wife. And in the first few seasons of *The Jeffersons,* George's mother was an acid-tongued geriatric getting on the nerves of Louise, without even trying. Zara Cully played Mother Jefferson, or Mother J. as she was sometimes called, until her death in 1978.

The set of *The Jeffersons* was very different from sets of other Lear sitcoms. While calamity was everywhere when the cameras rolled, it was quiet behind the scenes. The cast and crew were a family. Director Jack Shea said, "We don't have the kind of ego problems I've had on a number of other shows."[29] Even Carroll O'Connor would visit the set of *The Jeffersons*, say hello to some of his former work buddies, and bask in the warmth of this extended family. Perhaps the serene atmosphere was the one of the reasons *The Jeffersons* was Lear's longest running sitcom.

The Pilot—Dough and Domestics

In 1975, network television looked something like the following picture. It was the era of Norman Lear; *The Jeffersons* was the fifth sitcom Lear put on the air in four years. It was the era of the sitcom; that year, the four existing Lear-produced sitcoms all were amongst the ten most watched programs in America. It was also the era of the African-American sitcom; two of those four had African-American casts. Because the show possessed all three qualities, it was the era of *The Jeffersons*. This new sitcom instantly became a success, ranking fourth in the Nielsen ratings after its first airing, on January 18, 1975.[30] John J. O'Connor said, "The Lear method is ingenious. Every TV producer is preoccupied with the problem of product sampling, getting the audience to tune in just to discover what the basic situation and characters are all about. Mr. Lear simply incorporates a number of samplings into his own shows, which happen to attract the largest audiences in television."[31]

This was Lear's third African-American sitcom in three years. But while the first two, *Sanford and Son* and *Good Times*, focused entirely on poor African-Americans, this one took place on the Upper East Side of Manhattan. African-Americans could amount to anything, just like Caucasians, Lear figured, so why not make them wealthy — much wealthier than their old neighbors, the Bunkers? That scenario attracted a younger audience. During February of 1975, African-American students surveyed at the University of Utah claimed "[they] liked it 'better than *Good Times*,' primarily because it dealt with a black family 'making it' rather than a family enjoying 'not making it.'"[32]

The African-American sitcom was also able to wear away at bigotry, and at the same time, produce stellar ratings. Gary Deeb, writer for *The Chicago Tribune*, had a hypothesis on why African-American sitcoms were so successful. He explained it in a January 1975 article. "Many white people, who have very little social contact with blacks, tune in the black TV shows in a subconscious effort to rid themselves of doubts about their own essential goodness as human beings."[33]

However, unlike *Sanford and Son* and *Good Times*, *The Jeffersons* was able to depict all financial brackets of African-Americans, and how they interacted with one another. From the first minute of the show, viewers saw a poor African-American maid and a nouveau riche couple of the same color interacting. Diane (Pauline Myers), a maid, instantly became friends with Louise. The two got along, since financial status was not important to either of them. Only Diane was under the impression that Louise was also a domestic; she thought Louise's home was the place she cleaned in order to keep a roof over her head.

George cleared that up when he came home, but Diane could not believe it. The only rich families Diane knew were white ones. She did not know any colored wealthy people, and she was intimidated. "You ain't tall enough to be no basketball player," Diane told George, fretting.[34] She assumed that George was a crook, and ran out of the house.

When the Jeffersons went searching for a maid, Louise refused to hire her friend Diane, so she hired a maid named Florence Johnston. But Diane confronted Louise for not hiring her. Then, Florence, who was also Diane's friend, bowed out and let Diane take the job. But not before asking one quick question. Florence, like Diane, was confused that an African-American family was living the high life, so she asked Louise, "Well, how come we overcame and nobody told me?"[35]

As soon as Marla Gibbs, the actress who played Florence, said that, the audience went crazy. It was the last line of the first episode, and one of the most remembered lines from the show's history. It was supposed to be Gibbs' last line on *The Jeffersons*, but because of the audience's reaction, Florence got the job as the maid instead of Diane, even though, on-screen, it was never explained why. Gibbs appeared a few episodes later, and Pauline Myers was never seen again. Gibbs knew that the line got her the job as Florence. In a personal interview, Gibbs said it was "because of the response of the audience at the taping and the viewing audience."[36]

While everything else in the first episode referred to the Jeffersons' wealth, Florence's one-liner put it out in the open for everyone to take in. African-Americans could conquer anything, including the Upper East Side lifestyle. The line that Florence uttered also acknowledged those who were still working as domestics. Gibbs said that viewers laughed because of "the delivery," because of "their [the audiences'] knowledge of the history that it came out of," and "the knowledge for many that they had not overcome."[37] Writer Donald Bogle analyzed the line, saying it "explained the state of her life. It made audiences immediately identify with her."[38] Gibbs delivered the line with sympathy towards those who had not overcome, almost as if she was comforting those in the same boat as Florence. Eight years later, *TV Guide* commented on the audience's response to the line. "[It was] a laugh that acknowledged that Florence, like the medieval Fool of old, spoke the deepest truth and the greatest wisdom of all. We all know full well that the majority of black people are not living in a high rise dream world of mink, Ultrasuede and corporate investments."[39] Joe Garner wrote in his book *Made You Laugh: The Funniest Moments in Radio, Television, Stand-Up, and Movie Comedy*, "A good deal of the show's comedy emanated from them — the arrogant uppity boss who demanded deference from someone he'd *like* to feel superior to, and the employee who refused to let him forget ... whence he came."[40]

The Jeffersons never sided against the poor. In fact, the show demonstrated the equality between rich and poor people. It also showed that money is not proportionate to intelligence. *TV Guide* wrote, "Florence reflects a long and dignified tradition of the servant who is often wiser than her employer."[41] And unlike ex-maid Diane, Florence was not afraid of the Jeffersons, or better yet, she was not afraid of the Jeffersons' paychecks. She would not give her employers permission to subjugate her, just because of money. George felt he could chastise Florence — all because she was not as financially stable, and because she was an employee. (George, addicted to his newly acquired prosperity, had forgotten that his wife had worked as a domestic for many years before he opened cleaning stores across New York City.) Florence was the one who would really put George in place, showing him, as well as the audience, that money does not equate to power. *TV Guide* noticed about Florence, "She has a crusty belligerence that 'don't take no stuff'" off her employers even though they are materially better off than she is."[42] Once, when Lionel was looking for a book that Florence thought was in the kitchen, George told

Florence the maid (Marla Gibbs, center) always got the last laugh over George (Sherman Hemsley, left) and Louise (Isabel Sanford, right).

him it was the only thing Florence had not burned. Florence then suggested it could have been in the bathroom, since "It could be one of the books Mr. Jefferson stands on to reach the sink."[43] If Louise was going to the store, Florence would make her pick up cucumbers so she would not have to go out herself. If the door rang and George was right in front of it, he would often bark at Florence, who was in the kitchen, to answer it. But she refused to let her employer boss her around. Much to his dismay, George would have to take three steps and greet whoever stood outside his door.

George Jefferson was portrayed just like his old foe, Archie Bunker. He was to be laughed *at*, not with — the butt of all the jokes. He was the one Louise and Florence attempted to straighten out, just like Mike, Gloria, and Edith did to Archie. Before the series began, critics such as Joel Dreyfuss of *The Washington Post* were correct — George was "simply irascible and unlikable."[44] But Dreyfuss worried about a "dangerous political message" that *The Jeffersons* was going to broadcast week after week, until viewers got tired of it. However, because the supporting characters would not let George have any power, viewers could learn an important lesson from *The Jeffersons*. And the truth about money was not the only thing viewers learned.

Interracial Issues

Dr. James Coleman, a sociology professor at the University of Chicago during the time of *The Jeffersons*' premiere, suggested alternative solutions for integrating America. He named interracial marriage the primary one, saying it was "the best way to bring integration.... Certainly, many people will oppose mixed marriage, but it is not the business of the third party to oppose a voluntary arrangement between two people."[45] Ultimately, his goal was integration, or free interaction between the white and non-white citizens of America. Coleman also proposed the idea of integrated summer camps for adolescents, arguing that teenagers, both white and non-white, "would learn to know and understand each other better."[46]

The Jeffersons was on the exact same page. Lear decided to make interracial marriage one of the major themes that *The Jeffersons* would tackle, episode after episode. But the acceptance of this lifestyle was not the primary message of *The Jeffersons*; just like Coleman's, its primary message was integration. By viewing harmonious relationships between members of different races, *The Jeffersons* promoted integration, without even telling viewers what it was up to. It did not even matter that the relationship was a marital one; the only thing that mattered was that the relationship was *strong*.

In the pilot episode, Lear decided to introduce — and distinguish — the interracial couple that he weaved into the show. Franklin Cover and Roxie Roker would play the Willises, supporting characters on *The Jeffersons* for all eleven seasons the show aired. And he introduced them with his personal touch — controversy. Twenty minutes into the first episode, Lear's script had the Willises kiss and make up — right on the lips! Lear said, "You can't get any wetter than that."[47]

The usual CBS panic attack occurred before Lear aired the kiss. Producer Jack Shea recalled a moment when, "One day a vice president cornered me. He was shaking. He said you can't let them do that. You can't show an interracial couple kissing."[48] However, the cast was much more optimistic. Cover told *TV Guide* in 1980, "Norman was very active in preparing our first show, and one day he asked me what would happen if we saw Tom and Helen Willis kissing. I said, 'The heavens will open and bolts of lightning will come down. No, actually I don't know what will happen, but I think it's great — let's do it.'"[49] Needless to say, CBS went with Cover's opinion, rather than that of the CBS vice president.

CBS executives had reason to feel butterflies in their stomachs. Seven years before, the white Petula Clark touched the arm of the African-American Harry Belafonte. That sent chills down America's back, emerging into a large controversy. There had been one previous interracial kiss on television, which came in that same year. On *Star Trek*, Captain Kirk and Uhura kissed against their will. Of course, one of the most memorable kisses in television history was the interracial smooch that Sammy Davis, Jr., planted on Archie Bunker's cheek in 1972. But three years later, were viewers ready for more interracial physicalness beyond the comedic gesticulations of Sammy?

After the first episode, viewers said yes. *The Jeffersons* was an instant ratings hit, and viewers seemed to care more about the Willises and less about their color. The kiss did not draw as much controversy as expected; four protest letters were received about the kiss, and one of the four writers later wrote another letter apologizing for her previous comments.[50] After only a half-hour of exposure, the Willises were embraced as two of America's favorite characters, as seen by the cheers from the audience each time they refuted one of George's derogatory comments about their marital status, as well as the high ratings after the first season. (The show was the fourth most watched show in America, not bad for its first season.) Still, various people questioned the validity of the marriage, students at the University of Utah among them. *The Los Angeles Times* reported, "Some white males appeared to be embarrassed by the show's interracial married couple. White females were somewhat in awe. Black males felt interracial marriage should have been left out. Black females responded that the black males felt that way because the show's male was white and his wife was black, rather than the more common opposite situation."[51] However, interracial marriage was not all that alien. In Hawaii, 43 percent of marriages that took place in 1973 were interracial ones.[52]

Those who watched *The Jeffersons* witnessed a positive relationship between people of different races. However, it was not like the show simply took place in a time where race was not important to the public. Arrangements like the one Tom and Helen shared received their share of censure from society. By reflecting these opinions of censure through various characters, and then criticizing these characters' beliefs, *The Jeffersons* always showed how these prejudices were morally wrong.

However, things were even trickier in the Willises' family tree. First, the Willises did not speak to most of their original family members, because, years later, the families were still infuriated by their marriage. On top of that, there was a sibling rivalry between the Willises' two children, Jenny (Berlinda Tolbert) and Alan (Jay Hammer). In the first season finale, Alan (in this episode played by Andrew Rubin) returned from a two-year trip to Paris, only to receive a cold shoulder from sister Jenny, who was jealous that, because Alan's skin color was much lighter than hers, he had many more opportunities. All her life, she had been asking the question, "Why you?"[53] However, she did not know that Alan asked the question, "Who am I?" as he lived his life desperately trying to pass as white and ignore his origin.[54] *The Jeffersons* showed that it is important to be proud of one's heritage. Only by being proud of one's origin, can one achieve full confidence. The elder Willises did possess that full confidence, because they were 110 percent confident about their marriage. In this episode, Helen Willis responded to one of George Jefferson's comments, saying, "I am happy with what I got, 'cause he [husband Tom] is everything you are not."[55]

Roxie Roker had a hand in writing this episode, due to her experience with interracial marriage — she had lived that lifestyle for many years, and sometimes felt the need to revise rather stereotypical and unrealistic scripts. Roker had many objections to the original script for this episode. She returned the script the right back to the producers. Roker told *The Washington Post* in 1976, "Our son who had been abroad returned. He's fair-skinned and able to pass. Our daughter, who's on the show regularly, is dark complexioned. Now the script wanted me to show favoritism to her because she's brown like me. I couldn't. I'm the mother. I wouldn't treat any child that way. More than anything I want the script to make us believable."[56]

Making the characters believable was vital. Images were fragile — the tens of millions of people watching would pick up even the slightest negative image. That was a common worry of many of the actors and actresses on all of the Lear shows. Certainly, on *Good Times*, John Amos and Esther Rolle could have repeated Roker's line verbatim, regarding, "More than anything I want the script to make us believable." However, on *The Jeffersons*, this state of reality was achieved much more quietly. Entertainment magazines were never filled with any backstage drama regarding the show, and there were no massive firings that hurt the show's ratings. Soon, the Willises' racial situation evaporated, and they became a regular married couple, just like they always were.

The Story of Rich African-Americans

The Jeffersons played a monumental role in the way African-Americans were viewed. On the show, African-Americans were portrayed as everyday people with major responsibilities and work loads (owning a growing chain of dry cleaning stores), interests in the arts and theatre (the exquisite paintings hanging on the walls of the Jeffersons' apartment that showed their aesthetic taste), and cognizance of contemporary issues (Louise was well aware of the feminist movement and what it stood for). As *The Jeffersons* continued to air as the years went by, it did not acknowledge the color of the characters as much. Even though race was no longer a central issue, the show did not, of course, ignore the Jeffersons' race altogether. Viewers were exposed to a world where African-Americans were accepted as equal to Caucasians. After each episode, the argument that African-Americans could amount to anything became more and more convincing.

The Jeffersons was able to attain this status despite various cast changes during the series. After the first season, Mike Evans left the show, and was replaced by Damon Evans (no relation), who played Lionel Jefferson until the end of the fourth season. Mike Evans returned to the series in the sixth season (1979–80 season). In that span, Zara Cully, who played Mother Jefferson, died at a very advanced age. During the fifth season, Jay Hammer joined the cast as Jenny's white brother, Alan, for one year. Meanwhile, *The Jeffersons* changed time slots on nine different occasions during Mike Evans' hiatus (September 1975 to September 1979). During that span, the show never ranked higher than twenty-first, a huge gap from fourth in the first season and eighth in the sixth season.

In the seventh season, *The Jeffersons* made advancements off the screen, in addition to the ones they had been making on screen for so long. This time, Isabel Sanford (who played Louise) made the contribution, due to her fine work episode after episode. On September 13, 1981, Sanford made history at the Emmy Awards, winning in the category for Outstanding Lead Actress in a Comedy Series. She was the first African-American woman to earn an Emmy Award, setting the precedent for all African-American actresses. In addition, she was nominated for the award for seven consecutive years while playing Louise Jefferson between 1979 and 1985, the last seven seasons of the sitcom.

Norman Lear (center), celebrating the 200th episode of *The Jeffersons* with stars Sherman Hemsley (left) and Isabel Sanford (right). It was the second of three Norman Lear sitcoms to reach the 200-episode plateau mark.

After Sanford's Emmy victory, *The Jeffersons* maintained their previous ratings, ranking in the top twenty until 1984. During the show's tenth season, it ranked nineteenth in the Nielsen ratings. The eleventh season brought some plots that nobody would have ever expected to happen back when the show began in 1975. Tom Willis and George Jefferson managed a bar together! It was a true testament to the cliché that people do change, and it gave viewers the message that change is, in fact, positive.

But then the cast of *The Jeffersons* underwent some major change. The cast went on hiatus after season eleven without a shadow of a doubt that they would be returning for season twelve. However, CBS had other ideas. Shockingly,

The Jeffersons was cancelled without giving the fans a proper finale. *The Jeffersons* ended with over 250 episodes, and is still the longest running African-American show in television history.

During the final year of *The Jeffersons*, a new show aired on NBC called *The Cosby Show*. It was a direct reflection of the hard work, success, and innovation of *The Jeffersons*, because it was the second television show in history to portray an upper-middle class African-American family. Obviously *The Jeffersons* succeeded, allowing other shows of the same nature to flourish. *The Jeffersons* paved the way for *The Cosby Show*, which received almost no criticism at its start, and was not considered groundbreaking like *The Jeffersons*— the ground had already been broken. Unlike *The Jeffersons*, *The Cosby Show* rarely made reference to their race, and they were looked at more as a family rather than as a black family. The show was able to ignore the factor of race because Lear and *The Jeffersons* had fought that battle for them, back in the 1970s.

The Cosby Show, like *The Jeffersons*, focused on African-Americans in the white-collar world. Cliff Huxtable (Bill Cosby) lived with his wife Clair (Phylicia Rashad) and their five children. Cliff was an obstetrician, and Clair was a successful attorney. The Huxtables lived with the same luxury that the Jeffersons had enjoyed for the previous ten years— although they lived there without having to answer any questions from the public.

The year after *The Jeffersons* was unexpectedly cancelled by CBS, Marla Gibbs was rewarded with her own show over at NBC. It was not a spin-off of *The Jeffersons*. It had Gibbs playing a character wealthier than Florence, but not nearly as wealthy as the Jeffersons or the Huxtables. *227* focused on Mary Jenkins and her neighbors in an apartment complex in Washington, D.C. Once again, because of the work of *The Jeffersons*, it was no longer taboo to see African-Americans on the tube. Ultimately, what had happened by the 1980s was that African-American television programming had become standard fare. These sorts of shows also continued to be moneymakers and big hits for networks, like the African-American sitcoms of the 1970s were. *The Cosby Show*, for example, became the most watched show in America throughout the mid- to late 1980s, ranking atop the Nielsen ratings for five consecutive years. Sound familiar? That was because it tied the record that *All in the Family* set from 1971 to 1976 — five consecutive seasons as the top rated show in America. Meanwhile, although no *Cosby*, *227* ran for five successful seasons (1985–90) on NBC, and like *The Cosby Show* and *The Jeffersons*, found no problem reaching syndication and having DVD sales long after its end.

Just by looking at television history in terms of chronology, the shows with African-American characters that aired before *The Jeffersons* had a much different reception from the ones that aired in the post–*Jeffersons* era. African-Americans seen in the pre–*Jeffersons* era raised eyebrows, while African-Americans seen in the post–*Jeffersons* era caused almost no controversy at all — proving that *The Jeffersons* influenced television history, and the way that viewers saw African-Americans both on and off the screen.

The Move on Down

Gary Deeb of *The Chicago Tribune* wrote on January 12, 1975, "As this story goes to press, all signs point to the likelihood that ABC will make history of sorts later this month by telecasting a comedy series called *The Hot L Baltimore* ... there are no pratfalls, and the humor hinges on more compelling issues than which flavor of ice cream Ozzie will choose for Harriet."[57] While still on a hot streak, Lear aired another situation comedy only one week after the premiere of *The Jeffersons*. The show that he aired could not have differed more from *The Jeffersons*. The Jeffersons and their neighbors were a group of wealthy, settled folks who lived in the upper-class world. The characters of *Hot L Baltimore* were young, poor question marks of society. Everyone on *The Jeffersons* was white-collar. *Hot L Baltimore* detailed the lives and struggles of prostitutes, homosexuals, and an entire assortment of pariahs of society. The characters were poor transients currently residing at the dilapidated Hot l Baltimore, whose façade was so destroyed that the "e" in "hotel" failed to light up.

Lear got the idea for the show from a Lanford Wilson play, and acquired the rights to develop the play into the television series. Lear and Rod Parker (who was also executive producer of *Maude*) developed the play into a half-hour sitcom. Many critics who had originally seen the play felt Lear distorted it, although they did not believe the show was doomed from day one. John J. O'Connor felt, "If ABC or Mr. Lear and company can get a more professional grip on the project, *Hot L Baltimore* could turn into a significant, and no doubt controversial, development for television entertainment."[58]

On January 24, 1975, *Hot L Baltimore* premiered on ABC. That meant a great deal to ABC, who had been hurt by the Lear shows airing on CBS. (Even NBC aired one of his shows.) The dynasty could have been all theirs, had they not relinquished *Those Were the Days* back in the late 1960s. This was the network's opportunity to get back into the Nielsen ratings race.

Hot L Baltimore had a disclaimer similar to the one that preceded the theme song of *All in the Family* for its first six episodes, although much more concise. By this time, America had been forced to accept Lear's controversy. It began with, "The following program deals with mature subject matter. Parental judgment and discretion are advised."[59]

The pilot episode showed one of the prostitutes, Suzy (Jeannie Linero), getting married, since she thought her soon-to-be husband had a role in Hollywood. Her friend April (Conchata Ferrell, better known for her role on *Two and a Half Men*), who was also a prostitute, said, "There's something kind of sweet and romantic about a hooker getting married. Sort of like the U.S. government stamping 'prime' on a side of bad beef."[60] However, Suzy dumped him when she found out her new man was a cigarette lighter salesman. After the first episode, "Even with Baltimore, Jacksonville, and Toledo blacking out the program and 12 more towns delaying it until later at night, *Hot L* beat the *CBS Friday Night Movie* and gave *The Rockford Files* a good run."[61] In the next episode, a client of one of the prostitutes dropped dead while she was stripping, and the hotel transients bickered over how to hide the body.

But *Hot L Baltimore* did not do so well after the pilot. It was airing on ABC, which was not in the same league in ratings as CBS, where Lear's other sitcoms aired. It was also airing on Friday nights at 9 P.M. ET, not the ideal time slot for a series trying to find an audience. There was a slew of complaints about the show. Three weeks in, Ben Stein of *The Wall Street Journal* completely censured the show, calling *Hot L Baltimore* "one of the biggest failures of this or any other season," and giving advice to his readers. "Unless you are a ghoul, fascinated by lifeless things, you should avoid it if at all possible."[62] And on the subject matter characterized as PG, Stein said, "If parents really do give any consideration to the show, they will not watch it themselves, let alone allow their children to see it."[63] But by late February, some critics still thought there was a last ray of hope for the series, when an episode was taped about the homosexual relationship between characters George (Lee Bergere) and Gordon (Henry Calvert). "Perhaps, ironically, *Hot L* shows signs of softening some of its harshness, lowering its formerly grating hysteria level, and settling into a fairly decent comedy series, one that is about people interacting and not about freaks spouting gags."[64] But that sort of comment was outnumbered by the people calling *Hot L Baltimore* the "disaster in Baltimore."[65] *Hot L Baltimore* was cancelled in April, marking Norman Lear's first unsuccessful sitcom. The streak had ended, and ABC was unable to cash in on the Lear empire.

6

The House of Women

To an outsider on the street, *One Day at a Time*'s Ann Romano seemed like the perfect woman. Her appearance exuded poise and confidence. Ann always seemed to say what was on her mind; she spoke clearly and loudly, and gestured to fully convey confidence in what she was saying. Whether telling her superintendent, Schneider, to stop hitting on her, or telling her daughters an answer they did not want to hear, Ann seemed like she was in the driver's seat, with complete control of the gas and brake.

But to people who spent considerable time inside her apartment, like anyone who watched *One Day at a Time*, they knew that Ann Romano was just learning how to drive. Ann was slowly evolving as an independent woman — she certainly always possessed the heart and devotion for it. As a single mother, she had tough decisions to make and did not always know what the correct decision was. She certainly made mistakes along the way, but raised her children, Barbara and Julie, to the best of her ability; most of the time, the actions of her children proved that she was succeeding better than most. Her personal characteristics, such as her devotion towards reaching certain goals, were evident in her children right from the first minutes of the pilot: for example, when Barbara tried out for the all-boy basketball team, and became the only girl to make it. Obstacles were never impasses for anyone in the Romano household. Ann once said to Barbara and Julie, "Stick with me, huh? We'll make it. I promise."[1] While the Romano family stuck together, viewers stuck with the Romano family. The show was in the top twenty in the Nielsen Ratings each of its first eight seasons.

Three to Get Ready

Even before *The Jeffersons* took off in the Nielsen ratings and *Hot L Baltimore* landed at the bottom in January of 1975, Norman Lear had begun to work on a show that he planned to debut at the beginning of the new season, in September of 1975. Like all of Lear's shows, it was controversial, and Lear

148

had to fight many battles with CBS for months to get some of the material in the script to actually be broadcast.

Lear, working closely with *Good Times* writer Allan Mannings, developed a pilot script in December 1974 called *Three to Get Ready*. At first, Mannings proposed the idea of a show focusing on a thirty-eight-year-old single mother living with her sexy eighteen-year-old daughter. Lear changed Mannings' idea around a bit, making it a show centering on a slightly younger woman who had separated from her husband and was searching for her own importance in the world. However, as *The New York Times* writer Richard M. Levine worded it, "[CBS] was not about to let a Norman Lear script about a divorced woman pass with a wink and a nod."[2] Despite network vigilance, CBS vice president Fred Silverman gave Lear and Mannings the nod of approval, since he was looking for a show with an "emerging-woman" theme.[3] So Lear and Mannings wrote a pilot episode, and began making cast selections. At this moment in time, there was never a show centering on a divorced woman struggling to find her personal identity. The closest television had ever come was *Maude*, who had been divorced in the past, but *Maude* took place when Maude was comfortably married to Walter.

In the first draft of the pilot, Lear and Mannings wanted to show the life of Ann Benton, several weeks after she had separated from her husband. While watching the Broadway play *Applesauce*, Bonnie Franklin stood out, because, as Lear put it, "I loved the stride, the purposeful way she moves across a stage."[4] Allan Mannings also remembered Franklin from the made-for-TV movie *The Law*, where she played a role similar to Ann. In 1976, Mannings told *TV Guide* the things that stood out about the character Franklin played. "I was caught by the vulnerable quality. She is not really into women's lib. She embraced its values but did not pick up its banners. Which is really what the show is all about," Mannings said, discussing the same characteristics that Bonnie Franklin brought to the character of Ann a year later.[5] In addition, Franklin was also a divorcee. Once Mannings pointed out Franklin to Lear, Lear called her and said, "Don't take work till you hear from me."[6]

The producers made Ann a nurse, and conceived the character of Dr. Carl Silvers, a love interest for Ann. Ann had a teenage daughter, Julie (Mackenzie Phillips), and an upstairs neighbor, Gael Morris (Marcia Rood). In the first episode, Ann and Carl's first date would be interrupted by the arrival of Ann's former husband Ed, who was picking up Julie for the weekend.

Two major similarities in the pilot episode of *Three to Get Ready* in comparison to Lear's five other sitcoms were that there was lots of yelling, and that the script was juiced with one-liners. That was the way the Lear system operated. In the pilot script, Ed told Ann how she felt about her dating, "You're out here slaving over a hot stove for some jerk you hardly know!"

Ann bit back with, "Would you rather I was back home slaving over a hot stove for a jerk I've known all my life?"[7] However, some of these lines in the pilot were a bit too juicy for CBS censors. Actually, twenty-six of them were.

Ray Cunneff, program practices director at CBS, was only thirty-two years old and his generation was part of the counterculture in the 1960s. However, Cunneff was a deeply religious man with strong views on what should and should not be on television. About his feelings on religion, *The New York Times* gave a perfect example. They said, "On one wall of his office Cunneff had hung a reproduction of Michelangelo's 'The Creation' from the ceiling of the Sistine Chapel, only he had asked an artist friend to retouch God's hand from its original index-finger-extended pose to a thumbs-down position."[8]

Cunneff found twenty-six lines that he wanted deleted, all from a twenty-six minute script. Lear and Mannings had some serious rewriting to do, with a week remaining before the scheduled taping. At the same time, they began to rehearse the pilot with the cast, and ran into problems, since cast members disputed the lines and the characters they were playing. By the middle of the week, the set was quite turbulent. It was time to sit, slow down, and seriously revamp the script. Lear and Mannings met with the cast and they spent an entire day making revisions. By dusk, they had deleted twenty-two of the twenty-six lines initially flagged by Cunneff.

Lear was very adamant about keeping the four remaining lines. Two of them were Julie's accounts of teenage life. In one, she described a boy's behavior at a party, as he was "quick like he tries to sneak up my sweater," and in the other one she used the term "b.a.," an abbreviation for bare ass.[9]

The day of the taping, CBS announced that the episode would not be broadcast on the network if the four lines were not given the axe. Lear still refused to acquiesce. Due to legal issues, Lear was still required to follow through with his commitment to tape the episode. He taped it, with those four lines still in the script, and then after it was over, he did one last thing that was a paradigm of the adamancy that made him remarkably successful as a creator of television shows. *The New York Times* recalled Lear in action. "After the taping, Lear shouted, 'Keep the audio running,' to the sound man in the control booth and ran down to the stage before the audience began filing out. He announced that the network considered the program they had just watched unfit for family viewing and asked if anyone agreed with CBS. Dead silence. 'Does anyone disagree?' Enthusiastic applause. It would be the last sound network officials in New York who reviewed the tape would hear."[10] Once again, Lear went to the greatest extreme to prove his point—America was, in fact, ready to hear what he had to say.

The next step for Lear was editing. Out of the four disputed lines, Lear actually deleted all of them except the sweater line, but for reasons other than censorship. His daughter told him that the "b.a." reference was a long outdated colloquialism, and the other lines did not change the actions of the script.

However, even after Lear and Mannings deleted three of the four lines, CBS still felt the script was weak, and asked Lear to revise the script and shoot it once more. This time, though, Lear got rid of Marcia and Rodd, and added three more cast members. Ann acquired another biological daughter, Barbara, played by Valerie Bertinelli. Ann also acquired a superintendent named Schneider (Pat Harrington, Jr.), who constantly made passes at her. And finally, Ann's divorce attorney, David Kane (Richard Masur), became a close friend of the Romano family, although he always wanted to be more to Ann. Nevertheless, he helped out with many family issues, providing financial and moral support. For the new pilot, the character of Ann also changed. Her last name was now Romano, and she was no longer a nurse. She was now an Avon lady who divorced (no longer separated from, like in the original draft) her husband an entire year before, and had already begun life on her own. The show did not meet the cut-off date to air in September, and was held in reserve to be a midseason replacement.

That September, a series called *Fay* aired on NBC. It had a similar plotline to *One Day at a Time* — a divorced woman moving away with two children (a boy and a girl) and entering the dating world. However, *Fay* was a ratings flop, and was cancelled by the end of the season. Lear, therefore, was not the first to bring struggling divorcees to the small screen. However, he was soon about to be the first to make a show about a struggling divorcee popular.

The start of the 1975–176 season was not memorable for CBS, and the network cancelled several shows. Then, they brought in *One Day at a Time* (the name of the show had changed). The outlook was mostly positive from the start. Ben Stein (who soon after found himself writing for Lear's *Mary Hartman, Mary Hartman* and *All's Fair*) wrote in *The Wall Street Journal*, "[*One Day at a Time*] is a veritable schematic diagram of what a good television comedy should be."[11] John J. O'Connor of *The New York Times*, on the other hand, called the show "ordinary" and "irritatingly superficial and labored." He also commented, "The Lear penchant for loud shouting, for aggressive comedy, is beginning to bulge uncomfortably in the wrong places."[12] But unlike "ordinary" sitcoms, *One Day at a Time*, like the other Lear sitcoms, allowed for personal reflection and impact. Sander Vanocur of *The Washington Post* noted, "We can identify with the characters because they come to us with problems central to the family, whether splintered or intact, black or white. These problems evoke laughter, even if they are not nearly so laughable, at least to those of us with children, when they happen to us."[13]

Putting critics' hype aside, *One Day at a Time* had a promising future as soon as the Nielsen ratings came in from the first episode. The pilot was the eleventh most watched show in America during the week it aired.[14]

The Many Layers of Ann Romano

On December 16, 1975, Norman Lear introduced America to a new type of American family—a family with no men. The holidays of 1975 brought America three girls living in an Indianapolis apartment — a divorced, now single mother, Ann Romano, and her two outgoing teenage children, Barbara and Julie. Of course, women conversations were prevalent in this household. Once, the three women sat together on a bed and talked about Ann going away with a man for the weekend, and if she would "shack up."[15] The bathroom had pink tiles, berry colored rugs to match, and lots of lingerie, textiles, and miscellaneous clothes decorating it. And as if the feminist theme was not blatant enough just by the setting, the characters (especially the independent and unbound Ann) made sure to refer to their womanhood quite frequently. Lear wasted no time introducing the principal theme of *One Day at a Time*, exposing it in the first several minutes.

The storyline of the pilot episode was that Julie wanted to go on a camping trip, with three boys and two other girls. However, Ann objected, and asserted that her opinion was now the only one that counted. "I'm going to have to be both mother and father.... As your mother; I guess I'm going to have to say what I always did. It's up to your father," said Ann. Then Ann received a patronizing, bribing hug from Julie. Ann nevertheless sternly responded, "No way!"[16]

However, despite her attempts, Ann was not able to dismiss the issue. Julie tested Ann's newly acquired assertiveness. By doing this, the writers were able to peel back layers of Ann and show that she was still searching for her own identity in a world that still treated women with inequity. When Julie threatened to go live with her father because of her mother's intransigence, Ann stuck to her decision, giving Julie bus fare for the ride. However, the second that Julie slammed the door, viewers were exposed to the insecurities that lay behind Ann's exterior. "For the first seventeen years of my life my father made the decision and the next seventeen my husband made the decision. The first time in my life, I make a decision, and I blow it," Ann cried.[17] As her tears poured out, she internally questioned whether she made the right decision by going through life serving as both the father and the mother for her children.

For audiences, especially women, Ann Romano was a woman very similar to them — one that put up a strong front, but had qualms. Many believed that was the reason why *One Day at a Time* was a success. Allan Mannings told *TV Guide* in 1976, "Our divorcee is not a chicly-turned-out woman of the world.... Instead she is vulnerable and scared — like a woman stepping off a high diving board and suddenly realizing she doesn't know how to swim."[18] Ann, however, was a positive figure for these women, because she never did give in. She acknowledged that her life journey was a difficult one; for example, when in the pilot she prayed, "God, a lot of people think you're really a woman. If you are, how about rooting for our team?"[19] However, she always strove to make the correct decision. In this case, she finally let Julie go on the coed camping trip, but in the end, Julie did not go because she wanted to respect her mother's initial wish.

Through the character of Ann Romano, *One Day at a Time* promoted the lifestyle of an independent woman. Even though Ann struggled with stabilizing herself, *One Day at a Time* made this lifestyle appealing to its audience, because it showed that Ann was pleased with her new life as an emerging woman. There were many instances where Ann was actually having fun. There was a certain enjoyment that Ann got out of things she had not done in a long time, such as turning down men. Two men were after her at the same time — the "player" superintendent Schneider and her divorce lawyer, David Kane. Ann spent a fair portion of time considering whether or not to start a relationship with David. Although she sometimes kissed him with "her mouth open,"[20] as Barbara phrased it, Ann decided that she wanted to be single, showing Americans that there is nothing wrong with not wanting to be in a relationship. When David proposed to Ann, she declined, kindly telling him, "I don't want to marry anybody right now."[21] When she was not tolerating David's attraction for her, she was saying "No" to her favorite person to reject — the horny superintendent Schneider. When Schneider made a pass at Ann, she shot him down, saying, "Time sure flies when you're striking out." Several moments later, Schneider said about his wife, "I give her all the love that she can handle, but I have so much more love — to give — that I just have to spread it around." Ann, loving her new single status, told him, "Well, go spread it on the lawn."[22] As she was enjoying her comment, she was also saying that being in control is the "cool" thing to do.

The second episode once again focused on the single independent woman, when Ann introduced her children to her new boyfriend, whom she had been seeing for a couple of weeks. Barbara and Julie were worried that their mother got "picked up," so Ann decided to embrace her new life to the optimal level, and have fun with the situation. When Julie scorned her mother, "You got drunk and picked up," Ann remarked, "No, I got picked up, then I got drunk."[23] Of course, she later told her kids that she had been dating him for several weeks, and that they met while she was sober.

However, *One Day at a Time* was not all about fun and games; after all, most Lear sitcoms were not. Ann Romano could not have all the fun she wanted to, especially when it came to having fun with her own children. When Barbara and Julie began spending a lot of time with their father's new girlfriend, Ann became jealous that she could not always have the same relationship with her children. "[I want to] get to do all the fun stuff and be nice all the time ... [but] I can't. I've got to be Annie Romano, the grudge, the villain, the harpy, the shrew," lamented Ann.[24] However, like emerging women do, Ann experienced growth, an epiphany, in a short amount of time. She recognized how she appreciated her own mother's austerity while raising her, and later when she helped Julie solve an issue, she received the same compliment she had just given her mother earlier that day. Julie praised her mother, joking, "I get awful tired of you being right all the time."[25] Like the emerging women watching, Ann was realizing that she had a vital role in the world, and she was slowly beginning to find her personal identity, something she seemed incapable of doing before the divorce.

The evolution of Ann Romano continued in the next episode, when she hit the job world. At the same time, Lear and *One Day at a Time* took a close look at another issue that had not been looked at before its time — sexual harassment in the workplace, from the perspective of the worker being "harassed." After Ann's interview, the company boss asked to discuss the job at Ann's apartment, later that night. When Ann figured out that she was wanted for more than filing papers, she did not let the boss into her home, and the next day, told him, "I do want this job but I want it on the basis of my qualifications not 'cause — ah — you like to look at my legs."[26] When she left the room, she overheard the boss making a pass at another female applicant, using the same exact line that he used on her. In defending all women who underwent this experience, she played a little trick on the boss. In a seductive voice, Ann flirted, "You know when a man puts his hand on a girl's shoulder, but he's really thinking lower?" The intrigued boss replied, "Yes." In response, Ann kicked him in the shin and said, "I'm thinking higher," and walked out of the room like a winner.[27]

Ann was the winner in this case, because she maintained her independence. She did not succumb to the boss' courting, even when people like Schneider told her that there was nothing wrong with harmless flirting. Ann was reliant on her own ability and had enough self-confidence — and professionalism — to not use her body as a tool to get a job. Those were the characteristics of a confident, independent woman, even though the character that exhibited them was still on her way to complete independence. Ann Romano's resilience was a positive example for women watching, something that viewers could easily admire.

Ann Romano (Bonnie Franklin) is in the center of things as always, as she engages in conversation with Superintendent Schneider (Pat Harrington, Jr., left) and attractive daughter Barbara (Valerie Bertinelli, right).

However, Ann still suffered because she declined the job. Two episodes later, she experienced financial difficulty. She was having problems providing for her family, especially with the widespread inflation. Things became even more difficult when Julie kept groaning that she could not attend a private school. David stepped in with an offer to pay Julie's tuition, which would cost $900 per semester. However, Ann, a woman of pride, turned down the money. "One of the biggest problems with my marriage was I felt there had to be more to life than being supported by another person.... If I take your help, I lose my self-respect," she told David.[28]

One Day at a Time succeeded as all of the many facets of Ann Romano appealed to audiences. America enjoyed this woman who was fun and strong, yet very vulnerable in a human way. However, there was another vital component to the success of *One Day at a Time*—sex appeal.

Boys, Bottoms, and Bosoms

In a very succinct manner, a 1976 *TV Guide* article summed up the controversial nature of *One Day at a Time*. "The dialogue is sometimes racy, the new 'liberated' kind that would have been a no-no in the '60s and even now makes the network nervous. A mother talks candidly to her 16-year-old daughter about real stuff—like sex, why she can't go on an overnight camping trip with three boys, and the possible consequences of what can and frequently does go on in sleeping bags, no matter how well zipped."[29] The sexual dialogue of Norman Lear sitcoms had been overlooked by the racial dialogue, but now with a show that did not talk about race, Lear decided to talk more and more about sex, and he used teenage characters to do this. He had three teenage characters on *Good Times*, but once again, they were usually used as vehicles to discuss racial issues burdening America in the 1970s. There was a distinct disparity between the ways the teenagers on *One Day at a Time* were portrayed as opposed to the teenagers on *Good Times*. For *One Day at a Time*, run-of-the-mill teenage problems were right behind women's liberation in terms of consistent intensity of discussion, whereas average teenage problems were talked about on certain episodes of *Good Times*, but certainly not all of them. Lear's portrayal of teenagers dug into territory that had never been seen on television. Lear began discussing his view of teenagers by manipulating the language that characters Barbara and Julie used, and by pinpointing the issues that contemporary teenagers were fretting and fighting over.

In its second episode, physical features became a primal concern of Julie's. When she asked Barbara what her best physical quality was, Barbara responded, "You're sitting on it."[30] Then, several minutes later, Julie responded to meeting her mother's new beau by flaunting her posterior at him.

In the following episode, things got even more controversially comedic. First, as Julie was describing her ex-boyfriend's new girl, who was a cheerleader, Barbara intervened, "With pom-poms out to here," while using her hands to convey the fact that this girl had a robust bust.[31] Later that episode, Julie was stuffing her shirt with tissues, because she felt she was in competition with the other girl. Surely, teenage debates on breast size were controversial, but after all, this was, and is, an issue discussed by teenagers. It certainly must have been a concern of women before 1975, yet Lear was the first to realistically replicate what was uttered by the average teenage female. The average teenage girl was probably more concerned with how boys perceived her rather than learning how to cook and sew.

Lear did not gyp the male actors out of sexy one-liners, though. In fact, Lear gave the character of David a line that could be construed as one of the raciest in the show's history. When the zipper on Ann's dress was not zipped,

David, the man who was infatuated with Ann, said, "Allow me. I mean it's not much, but it's a lot more fun than fooling with my own zipper."[32] A masturbation reference was quite unexpected in the presence of Barbara and Julie, but by 1976, viewers knew to expect the unexpected from Lear sitcoms. Minutes later, when the two children were not in the room, Schneider walked in while David was still trying to zip Ann's dress. Schneider, who saw David as an obstacle in his quest for Ann, retorted, "If all the men in the world were as slow as you we'd never need the pill." David, being the adroit lawyer, defended himself. "You know who could have used the pill," David asked Schneider. Then David responded for him. "Your mother."[33]

By the eighth episode of the series, Lear had put in place the building blocks for the issues he wanted to discuss. Now it was time for storylines to revolve around teenage sex. The first storyline was a rather simple one — a realistic plot that teenage girls faced all over. It was the oldest story in the book — boy wants to have sex with girl while parents are away at night, girl does not think she is ready, boy tries to convince her it will be all right, and girl is faced with a tough decision. However, Lear spun the issue into several different directions. He showed how parents should handle the issue, how the stereotypical boy handles the issue, and how teenage girls could use women's liberation to handle the issue the way they wanted to.

The way Ann handled Julie's thoughts on losing her virginity was something that many parents watching could have picked up on. Ann kept her equanimity and talked to Julie as the teenage girl that she once was. Ann was not a martinet about the issue. She discussed sex with Julie in a compassionate manner, and in response, Julie listened and respected what her mother was telling her. Ann knew that Julie was not ready to have sex, and she quietly told her this. However, even though she kept her cool, Ann had a firm stance about the issue. "Your self-esteem quotient is in the basement," she told Julie.[34] Ann, a newly liberated woman, was trying to pass along the feminist message to her daughter. The essence of Ann's speech was that a woman is the only person who can and should be allowed to determine whether or not to sleep with a man. It is not up to the man; it is up to the woman.

However, there were obstacles for Julie, as her boyfriend Chuck, who was the quarterback on the high school football team, kept pressuring her. Julie said to her mother, "He told me if I don't help him we'll lose the game Saturday."[35] Chuck's purpose in the script was to serve as a stereotypical boy who wanted sex more than he wanted a relationship. That night, Chuck got angry at Julie when she pulled away after he started to kiss areas below her lips. He asked, "Do you realize that at the rate you're going now you could still be a virgin when you're a senior?" Ann's earlier talk worked on both Julie and the audience, which was booing Chuck's question. Julie was also angry, and asked him, "What's wrong with that? I read an article once that said twenty percent of all the freshmen in college are still virgins." Chuck responded, "You mean to stand there and tell me you want to be in the bottom twenty percent.... Only freaks and weirdos don't make love when they feel the urge!"[36]

Julie learned an important lesson that night. As she told her mother, "I found out what being a woman really means."[37] Julie had conquered sexual freedom — the ability for a woman to choose what to do with her body. *One Day at a Time* was not necessarily preaching abstinence in this episode; rather, it was preaching women's liberation, like it did in almost every episode. Julie proudly kept her virginity, declaring, "A woman has to stand up for what she really wants to do, and I didn't want to do it. And if Chuck never calls me again, then he loses."[38] Julie, truly for the first time in the series, asserted her independence, and now teenage girls had a positive role model to look up to. At the same time, the days of the perfect teenager on television were officially over.

A still photo of Mackenzie Phillips, who played Julie, the first teenager on television to worry about the size of her breasts and her virginity.

The Impact of One Day at a Time in the 1970s— and 1990s

One Day at a Time went through a number of major cast changes during its nine-year run. Despite the disruption caused by these changes, the show managed to keep its head above the top twenty mark in the Nielsen ratings much of the time. The most influential cast change for the writers was the firing of Mackenzie Phillips—twice, due to drug addiction. Another major cast change was that the character of David Kane (Richard Masur) was written out after the first season. This opened up even more opportunities for Ann to enter the dating world. Ann would have future boyfriends, and by 1981, she would even have a fiancé, Nick Handris (played by Ron Rifkin). However, Nick was not Ann's fiancé for too long. Nick soon became a tool that the writers used to discuss one of the most powerful public service announcements ever discussed in the history of the series. This topic was a new subject to television, yet it killed 26,000 people the year before, in 1980.[39] However, a television portrayal of one incident was more powerful than a statistic acknowledging 26,000 of these cases, because it deeply altered the lives of characters that America had been caring for almost every week for six years. In 1981, Ann's beloved fiancé, Nick, was killed in a drunken driving accident.

In this episode, America witnessed the unfortunate death of an innocent character that they cared about. But also, the accident crushed the hopes of someone who was finally going to get married after America rooted for her to get married for the previous six years. The fatal consequences of driving while intoxicated were depicted to the fullest level — and by doing that, it embedded in people's minds that drinking and driving is indeed a pretty perilous pair. And in the case of Nick, the episode showed how drunk drivers kill innocent people. The episode's obvious poignancy had the power to appear in people's minds the next time they had a few drinks and pulled their keys out of their pockets. What could be a more powerful mechanism to say, "Drink responsibly," than by showing the most brutal consequences occur to popular, beloved television characters?

Three seasons later, *One Day at a Time* ended, after the first season in which it did not rank in the top twenty in the Nielsen ratings. Originally, the finale was supposed to have a spin-off, in which Schneider moved to California to raise his late brother's children. However, the spin-off never happened, and *One Day at a Time* went off into the sunset — actually, to syndication, as most of the Lear shows did. However, the effects that *One Day at a Time* had on other shows were visible, even before the series ended. Actually, they began a year after the show first aired.

Another show on CBS, *Rhoda* (produced by Grant Tinker, who was known for *The Mary Tyler Moore Show*), used the formula that *One Day at a Time* used to spice up their series. Writers became bored with Rhoda and her husband, so they decided to divorce them. The writers would probably not have made this an option for Rhoda's future had *One Day at a Time* not pioneered the idea — and succeeded with it. Rhoda's divorce became a huge story arc for the *Rhoda* writers—they spent an entire season with Rhoda and her husband separated, trying to make their marriage work. In the end, though, Rhoda's marriage ended up in the same way that Ann's did (although Rhoda did not have any children).

Divorce soon became an issue on television taken for granted; there was neither stigma nor controversy associated with the issue. By the 1990s, the shock value of divorce became worthless, since *One Day at a Time* made it comfortable for Americans to hear that word while watching television. On *Friends*, divorce was used several times as a storyline for characters—but it was used as something that could generate laughs. Because of *One Day at a Time*, the producers of *Friends* had much more freedom when discussing what used to be an extremely sensitive topic for a situation comedy. On *Friends*, the character of Ross went through three divorces during the show's ten-year run. All three divorces resulted from something that was easy to laugh at. Ross' first divorce occurred when his wife realized she was a lesbian; the next divorce occurred shortly after he said his ex-lover's name at the altar; and the final divorce after he, and the girl whose name he had accidentally said at the altar, got drunk in Las Vegas and then got married at a wedding chapel while under the influence.

Friends also took after *One Day at a Time* in terms of language. In fact, there was even more freedom with the dialogue in a *Friends* script. Discussion of sex was not something producers Marta Kauffman and David Crane avoided. And even the masturbation jokes were a bit juicier and even graphic. For example, when the pages of a magazine were stuck together, the character of Joey accused his best friend of pleasuring himself. "Chandler!" he yelled.[40] And if breast sizes were controversial while *One Day at a Time* was on the air, the male characters of *Friends* were once sitting in a coffee house discussing their penis sizes. In another instance, a character was searching for a tape measure, which she found in Chandler's bedroom.

Meanwhile, on the television show *Will and Grace*, the character of Grace was doing more than stuffing her bra with tissue paper, like Julie did. In one episode, Grace brought a hydro bra to impress a date. All was going well until the hydro bra popped and water squirted from her chest! Just by looking at this rather hilarious example, it is easy to see just how many different ways *One Day at a Time* influenced American culture. It allowed women on television to openly discuss themselves, and at the same time, it brought many more opportunities for verbal comedy and physical comedy on contemporary sitcoms.

7

Final Successes and Failures

After the premiere of *The Jeffersons*, Lear had a perfect batting average. He was five for five — with five home runs: *All in the Family*, which was a grand slam, and *Sanford and Son, Maude, Good Times*, and *The Jeffersons*. However, in January 1975, Lear's batting average dropped with the ill-fated series *Hot L Baltimore*, which only lasted several months. It was the first Lear show not to make it a whole season, not to make the top ten in the Nielsen ratings, and not to make syndication.

Well, nobody is perfect.

Then Lear got back on track, with two major successes. The first was *One Day at a Time*, a show that, in the end, ran for as many seasons as *All in the Family* — nine. When he proposed the idea for a new show called *Mary Hartman, Mary Hartman*, all three major networks declined, so Lear made his mark on cable television, as 10 million viewers tuned in to watch after the first week — despite the show airing during odd hours, such as during the day or late at night. His made his second success in a way that no television producer had ever found success in before. By 1976, Lear seemed to be deeply involved in the best of both television worlds.

But his nearly immaculate slate soon got filthy with chalk. *All's Fair* and *The Dumplings* received abysmal ratings, and abysmal ratings from critics. The entertainment world began to wonder if Lear was losing his magic. John J. O'Connor of *The New York Times*, who before 1975 usually wrote paeans about Lear and his shows, was starting to believe Lear's writing was not at its best, and noted it in his columns. "The Lear product has become noticeably strained," he wrote, in an article titled, "Is Norman Lear in a Rut?"[1]

Lear quit while still ahead of the game in 1978, before he could be blamed for ruining his reputation. He was heading to the movies, where partner Bud Yorkin had gone several years back. He left *All in the Family* after eight seasons, at the same time Rob Reiner and Sally Struthers did, and said goodbye to the everyday routine of supervising *Good Times, One Day at a Time*, and *The Jeffersons*.

But Lear would be back three different times in the 1990s. His final try at restoring that old magic came in 1994, with the sitcom *704 Hauser*. It took place in the same spot his first sitcom did — the 704 Hauser Street living room. Lear's legacy had lived throughout an entire generation. *All in the Family* reruns were still being shown during prime-time hours on CBS when *704 Hauser* aired. First viewers saw the Bunkers living there; then they saw a black family living in the same home. Nobody ever covered the generation gap better than Norman Lear.

Highs in Fernwood; Lows in Washington

While Lear had six successful shows running on the air, he had a difficult time trying to find a home for his seventh idea. Compared to previous television programs— even compared to his own six shows— this new program, called *Mary Hartman, Mary Hartman*, was a complete aberration. Lear began discussing it with the public in 1974, when he was getting started with *Good Times*, and *The Jeffersons* had not even aired. He told Arthur Unger of *The Christian Science Monitor* in July of 1974, "I love it and I think if it ever gets to the air it will be as important and different and fun as anything we've ever done. It's called *Mary Hartman, Mary Hartman* and runs on two levels."[2]

So Lear went to CBS with this idea burning in his mind. Lear wanted *Mary Hartman, Mary Hartman* to be a half-hour show airing five times per week. However, although Lear was responsible for making the network tops among its competitors, CBS had other ideas. They wanted it to air once a week, each episode being an hour in duration. Lear was known for threatening to leave CBS if he did not get his way, although in cases such as Maude's abortion and Mike's impotence, CBS always gave in. This time, they did not. Lear proved that those threats were not bluffs.

He went to NBC, who also declined to air the project. Then he went to ABC. Same scenario, different network. Although all three networks turned Lear down, he had one more plan to get *Mary Hartman, Mary Hartman* on the air. On August 23, 1975, Lear invited the presidents of more than one hundred cable stations to Hollywood. Over an expensive dinner, they got a sample of the show, watching the first two episodes. Within four months, eighty-seven of those presidents agreed to buy the series in syndication, and air it starting in 1976. So finally *Mary Hartman, Mary Hartman* was destined to air on what Lear called "the fourth door," meaning the alternative for television programming.[3] But what was in these two episodes that attracted cable stations, but not CBS, NBC, or ABC?

According to a statement that Lear's company released in 1976, the networks did not grab on to the satire-soap-comedy because "the public was not sophisticated enough to understand its many facets."[4] For starters, it seemed as if *Mary Hartman, Mary Hartman* was taped on another planet. The setting took place in the fictional town of Fernwood, Ohio, and the first thing viewers found out was that housewife Mary Hartman's cardinal concern was that there was "waxy yellow buildup" on her kitchen floor.[5] However, her stress about the kitchen floor was replaced by bad news when she found out that several blocks away, murders had taken place: five people, two goats, and eight chickens. In the second episode, Mary described the bizarre setting perfectly, using only one line. "It's just incredible. Fernwood Flasher, mass murders, goats, chickens, and my floor is yellow," she muttered.[6]

Viewers, and networks, were left all alone to figure out what the hell was going on. The death of eight chickens surely perplexed many. In addition to that, the show was not taped in front of a studio audience like Lear's other five shows, meaning there was no laughter or noise in the background. Who knew what was supposed to be funny and what was not supposed to be? That was all up to the people watching.

Every aspect of *Mary Hartman, Mary Hartman* was obscure. Trying to determine its genre could leave one pondering for hours. Did it air once a week? No, five times. Was it a soap opera? Yes. Was it comedy? Yes. Was it satire? Yes. Was there a bit of fantasy? Yes. Could it make a person laugh? Yes. Could it make a person cry? Yes. Could it confuse a person? Always. But most importantly, did people care about these eccentric characters? Certainly.

However, there was one more major aspect that sent the three networks out the revolving door. Was *Mary Hartman, Mary Hartman* controversial? Extremely. What about racy? Even more, as a healthy portion of the first episode took place in the bedroom.

Things that were considered red flag material for mere mention on television were central topics discussed throughout multiple episodes of *Mary Hartman, Mary Hartman*. Impotence was a primary example. About four years earlier, Lear and CBS president Robert Wood had a major feud over whether or not to air a single episode of *All in the Family* focusing on impotence. Lear threatened to axe *All in the Family* from the CBS lineup if he could not present an episode dealing with Mike's spells of impotence. But in *Mary Hartman, Mary Hartman*, impotence was an ongoing struggle for Tom Hartman (played by Greg Mullavey) and his wife Mary, who felt sexually starved as a result. And the intensity of the discussion was much deeper than it was when Mike had the problem. Now, Mary was trying to excite Tom right there in bed, passionately kissing him on the neck and mouth. Mike and Gloria were only seen discussing the issue while standing up, and had to camouflage their language with funny expressions like "stuck in neutral" (Archie's description of the problem). *Mary Hartman, Mary Hartman* did not fear saying "making love," rather than "you know," or "it." However, nothing negative came out of saying things straight — it only benefited those who watched. *Sexual Medicine Today* told its readers in 1976, "*Mary Hartman* is legitimizing talk about sexual problems previously draped in double-entendres, double looks and double talk. The physician can find many of his experiences with patients reflected in *Mary Hartman* — and it can be an instrument that will help him and his patients discuss sexual problems."[7] While Mary told Tom, "There's no law against our making love," *Mary Hartman, Mary Hartman* told America that there is no law against saying "making love."[8] The show obviously took a major step forward in the words "penis" and "vagina" soon becoming entries in the television dictionary.

But then shades of *Maude* were thrown into the picture; it became an issue of male versus female libido. Tom claimed that it was his job to take care of when he and Mary made love, and until he was ready, she would have to wait. Mary, on the other hand, was tired of waiting — she said that it had been five weeks. Tom objected to Mary's pleading, and complained, "Every time I feel like doing something you do it first.... That's not the way it's supposed to be." He told her to "act like a woman" until he was ready to make love to her.[9] Since Mary Hartman was the central character of the show, viewers sympathized with her, and did not appreciate Tom's chauvinism. His chauvinism was ridiculed, and once again, a Norman Lear show portrayed the issues that the feminist movement was trying to point out to America.

Down the block, the Hartmans' neighbors were having a much more exciting time. Loretta, the naïve 22-year old aspiring country singer (Mary Kay Place), was married to a much older man, 43-year old blue-collar worker Charlie Haggers (Graham Jarvis). Their bedroom activity was much more frequent than that of the sexually frustrated Hartmans.

However, "private parts" on *Mary Hartman, Mary Hartman* found a role outside the bedroom. At the end of the first episode, Mary was shocked to receive a call from the police, who had arrested her grandfather for indecent exposure. It turned out that he had flashed a cafeteria lady on a school playground, and this eighty-something year old man, Grandpa Larkin (played by Victor Kilian), became known around the community as the "Fernwood Flasher." While this aspect of the show did not have any major impact on viewers besides comic relief, the eccentric raciness that it represented was far too much for prime-time networks to endorse.

Viewers, who watched it even during odd hours, craved all of these eccentricities. It aired late at night or during the day so that younger children would not see the show, yet mail still poured in from pre-teen children. One ten-year-old wrote, "I like it when you talk about the Flasher and mass murders."[10] *Mary Hartman, Mary Hartman* was the television equivalent of a famous abstract painting. Harry Castleman and Walter J. Podrazik, authors of *Watching TV: Four Decades of American Television*, wrote, "[Lear] went against the conventional programming wisdom ... for the first time, a syndicated program became the most talked about series in television."[11] After the first week that *Mary Hartman, Mary Hartman* aired (it debuted on January 6, 1976), it had reached an audience of approximately ten million viewers — beating out, and scaring, the long-running news programs that served as its competition.[12] By the end of the month, on some stations, the cost of advertising on *Mary Hartman, Mary Hartman* increased twice since the start of the show, and it was boosting the ratings of shows that aired before and after it.[13] *TV Guide* wrote, "Within a month anyone with any claim to being trendy had to be able to discuss the Fernwood Flasher and Loretta's chances of becoming a country-and-western star."[14]

However, during the first month, *Mary Hartman, Mary Hartman* drew much criticism. One appalled viewer told *Soap Opera Digest*, "How in the world can anyone put such a filthy, vulgar show on the air at 3:30 P.M. for grown people to be exposed to all the filthy talk Mary Hartman stands for, to say nothing about the children coming home from school?... This is the reason so many teens are dope addicts, VD carriers, and drunks. My goodness, let's clean this filth up."[15] One day, the Lear offices received a phone call from a vice president at one of the stations, who said, "I've got 75 people marching on my station this afternoon to protest *Mary Hartman*. I love it."[16] Soon though, the fans outnumbered the critics by a landslide, and *Mary Hartman, Mary Hartman* seemed like it would be on for a long time.

But money was a huge factor. T.A.T. Productions (Lear's second company after Tandem, which controlled this show as well as other shows like *The Jeffersons*) was losing money week after week, because of the regular production costs, plus the costs for selling, distributing, and preparing individual copies of the tapes for each network.[17] This forced T.A.T. to renegotiate after the show's twenty-sixth week on the air.[18] In the meantime, producers were on a very low budget. In one episode, a man drowned in a bowl of chicken soup in Mary's kitchen. Producers wanted to have the funeral ceremony in a mortuary, but that was impossible because of the tight budget. They could not even have it in Mary's living room, since that did not yet exist, either. In the end, the funeral was held in the kitchen, oddly enough. Producer Viva Knight said, "A lot of people said the choice was inspired, but they don't know what inspired it."[19]

For the cast and crew, there was mixed reaction to the workload on the set. Writer Ben Stein said about working on *Mary Hartman, Mary Hartman* in his autobiography, "I enjoy it so much I can hardly call it working."[20] However, series star Louise Lasser told *TV Guide* in June 1976, "I'm exhausted.

It's not physical fatigue; I'm emotionally exhausted. The strain is unbelievable. Thank God for makeup."[21] Greg Mullavey used Transcendental Meditation to keep himself calm under the daily stress load.

As the series progressed, Lear had to make some adjustments to his normal work routine. Since episodes had to be produced nearly every day, the show airing five times per week, scripts did not have much time for modification. However, editing was one of the most important things to Lear. One of his writers once told *TV Guide*, "Norman demands eight rewrites on every script. I once asked him if he ever saw a script he could use as is. He told me, no, that the best he could say would be, 'It'll rewrite well.'"[22] Lear's role changed slightly, though, for *Mary Hartman, Mary Hartman*. Lear told *The Washington Post*, "I go over the material. I see that the bus is in good shape, but they [the cast] have to drive the bus."[23]

The wheels on the bus kept on going round and round, but the main driver, Louise Lasser, was running very low on fuel, and it did not help that she had to drive day after day, for long hours at a time. Lasser rarely had a minute to herself, since she, as the main character, was a major part of nearly every scene. For many of these scenes, she only had a few hours to prepare the lines—usually from the time she had her makeup put on to the time the camera began rolling. By 1977, she had enough—it was now taking too much of a toll. She announced she was leaving the show, and after 325 episodes spanning a year and a half, *Mary Hartman, Mary Hartman* ended. Had Lasser stayed aboard, who knew how many episodes could have been produced. But Lear kept some of the characters alive, as the show gave birth to three spinoffs: *Fernwood 2Night* (September–December 1977), *Forever Fernwood* (October 1977–April 1978), and *America 2Night* (April 1978–July 1978).

In addition to influencing the American public, breaking new barriers and contributing to the sexual revolution of the 1970s, *Mary Hartman, Mary Hartman* was a television first because it opened the door for cable television. Show creators were no longer limited to the three networks—they now could take other routes to air their material. Because of *Mary Hartman, Mary Hartman*'s success, cable television became more popular. TV Land, a cable station since 1996, which, at one point, aired *Mary Hartman, Mary Hartman* in reruns, ought to thank the show and Lear for making cable programming popular and worthwhile in the first place. And on a much bigger scale, megahit shows *Sex and the City* and *The Sopranos* did not air on ABC, NBC, or CBS—they aired on cable network HBO. Like Lear while working with cable, the writers of these shows had extreme liberties. For example, the *Sex and the City* vixens often discussed threesomes, oral sex, and anal sex.

Mary Hartman, Mary Hartman and *One Day at a Time* were both huge successes for Lear, but that was the last luck he would come across. Soon, viewers were no longer craving the new tastes Lear was creating. According to ratings, the new Lear shows created after *Mary Hartman, Mary Hartman* "jumped the shark" right from their respective day ones.

A month after *Mary Hartman, Mary Hartman* debuted, Lear tried another show, going back to the same network that currently owned *Sanford and Son*— NBC. *The Dumplings* featured a rather heavy couple that owned a restaurant in New York City. Joe and Angela Dumpling loved to show their affection for one another — no matter where they were, even if it was in their restaurant in front of customers. The show's one-liners consisted of many fat jokes, which did not grab America. Critics submerged the show in contempt from day one across the country. In response to the premiere of *The Dumplings*, critic John J. O'Connor said, "The time may have arrived for the Norman Lear factory to close down and take serious stock of its product. The machine may be overworked."[24] Critics dictated the future of the series— it did not make it past two months.

Lear did not immediately listen to O'Connor. In the summer of 1976, Lear tried again to find the sitcom magic. *All's Fair* was the name of his next project. It was set in Washington, where a 49-year-old conservative (Richard Crenna) and a 22-year-old die-hard liberal (Bernadette Peters) would find love despite age and political beliefs. They were, as the original title of the show said, *Strange Bedfellows.* Overtime, their goal was to show that they

Norman Lear (right) reminiscing with Mike Douglas (left) in 1977.

were not "strange." Lear remembered Peters from a guest appearance on *Maude*, and he liked what he saw. She was cast first. When Crenna originally declined a spot on the show, Lear called him up personally to ask him, "What is this crap you don't want to do it?"[25] Lear, the master of persuasion, convinced Crenna to join Peters on *All's Fair*.

However, casting was not Lear's biggest challenge. The writing was. He had to be able to accurately portray a confident conservative on television. Lear had nobody to model this conservative character after. That was until he called on Ben Stein.

Stein was a man of many worlds. First, he was a speechwriter for Richard Nixon and Gerald Ford. Next, he was the man who ripped apart Lear's *Hot L Baltimore* in *The Wall Street Journal* in 1975. He was also a writer for *Mary Hartman, Mary Hartman*. Lear wanted to model the character after his conservative buddy, Stein. Lear told *The Washington Post* in 1976, "If we are going to put a conservative on the screen, there's an obligation that we deliver him intelligently."[26] Stein was happy to fulfill this opportunity because he felt "it might stop people from thinking that conservatives are gangsters."[27]

However, it did not matter. *All's Fair* did not find an audience, and was off the air after one season, being cancelled in the spring of 1977. While *All's Fair* was on the air, Lear tried to find new success twice, but failed both times, with *The Nancy Walker Show* and *All That Glitters*. One year later, in the spring of 1978, Lear stepped down from television.

But he would be back.

Lear in the 1990s

Carroll O'Connor, the man who was Archie Bunker throughout the 1970s, was now a Mississippi detective on the hit drama *In the Heat of the Night*. Meanwhile, Sally Struthers was on a world hunger crusade, while Rob Reiner was a prolific writer and director, a venture he had begun on the set of *All in the Family*.

Redd Foxx went through bankruptcy and then returned to the sitcom universe, starring on *The Royal Family*. However, he died from a heart attack on the set, just like the ones his manipulative character of Fred Sanford used to feign way back when. As a result, *The Royal Family* was cancelled several episodes later. At Foxx's funeral, old buddy and co-star Demond Wilson was conspicuous by his absence. He, the man who reportedly chased Lear around the set with a pistol, had become a minister and had lost touch with one of his old drug buddies.

Bea Arthur and Rue McClanahan were co-starring on another hit series, *The Golden Girls*. The series ended the same way *Maude* ended—when Bea Arthur decided to leave the show.

Dy-no-mite mania had certainly faded as Jimmie Walker became an alien to the small screen. But Janet Jackson was on her way to becoming one of the most renowned pop superstars in the world.

The Jeffersons returned briefly — as Isabel Sanford and Sherman Hemsley, along with Marla Gibbs, reprised their old roles for several laugh-filled episodes of *The Fresh Prince of Bel-Air*, including the show's series finale. In one case, when George did not want to buy a house, Florence chirped, "That's because he's cheap!" receiving one last ovation.[28] Hemsley had just finished a successful series called *Amen*, and Gibbs had finished *227*.

But one of the biggest surprises in the early 1990s television could be summarized by the following line from *The Wall Street Journal* on May 28, 1991. "This week, Norman Lear returns to the sofa where he belongs, with a new sitcom."[29]

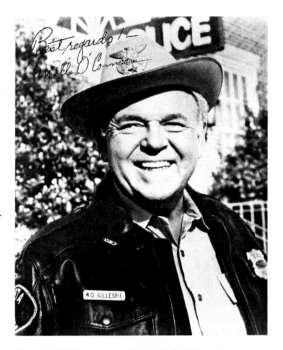

Carroll O'Connor as Chief Bill Gillespie on the hit 1990s drama, *In the Heat of the Night*. After his extensive experiences while working on and off the set with Norman Lear, O'Connor produced, wrote, and starred in this show, which lasted eight seasons.

Lear was about to unveil his latest creation, modeled after his new life. He was no longer married to Frances; they divorced in 1988. Now he was married to a woman twenty-five years his junior. The two main characters on *Sunday Dinner* were Ben Benedict (Robert Loggia), a man in his fifties, who recently had become engaged to thirty-year-old T.T. Fagori (Teri Hatcher, now known for *Desperate Housewives*).

Of course, Lear's show would be edgy. *Sunday Dinner*'s controversy rested in the fact that it condemned lack of spirituality, and promoted religion. Lear told reporters in 1991, "The subtext for the '90s for me is the spiritual emptiness. The American people have an unmet spiritual need. I think we all need to talk again and remind ourselves of the inner need. I want *Sunday Dinner* to provoke people to talk about those issues — mortality, eternity, morality, God. What's it all about? What are we doing here?"[30]

Sunday Dinner received backlash from critics even before the first airing. The American Family Association, led by Reverend Donald Wildmon, was the primary naysayer. He was disgusted with how, for example, T.T. referred to God by the title of "Chief," and labeled Lear as anti–Christian. Lear responded, "The religious right is after me. They [American Family Association] insist on dealing with God in only one way. [*Sunday Dinner's*] leading woman doesn't know if God is a man or a woman or what. They [Wildmon and his people] couldn't tolerate that."[31]

However, the debate was short-lived, as *Sunday Dinner* got off to an abysmal start, ending up off the air after six episodes. Perhaps viewers did not seem to be interested in watching religion in a sitcom.

Lear's longest-running sitcom in the 1990s came next, although it only spanned twenty-one episodes. Lear teamed up with old partner Rod Parker (from *Maude*) and Marta Kauffman and David Crane (later known for their mega-success *Friends*) to produce the show *The Powers That Be.*

Perhaps the most significant change from the 1970s to the 1990s was the relationship between John Amos and Lear. By this point, the two men had put their turbulent past relationship behind them, and had begun to work together once again, on Lear's final sitcom to date, *704 Hauser.*

Lear turned back the clock ever further, back to 1971, right in the Bunker home. That would be the setting for *704 Hauser* — although now there was one major change. One night, after his accountant questioned him for still paying rent on the *All in the Family* set, Lear had a dream about a new family living there. It was not Archie or any of his relatives. Even more shocking, the home was inhabited by African-Americans! What would Archie say? Lear said in 1994, "I have no guess. I don't think a lot about Archie."[32] *The New York Times* journalist Sam Roberts predicted, "[Archie Bunker] might be peppering neighbors in some Florida retirement community today with wistful memories of the good old days and lamentations about a hometown gone to hell."[33]

However, Amos' character, Ernest "Ernie" Cumberbatch, had the same racial beliefs that Archie possessed, only in the opposite direction. He portrayed the reciprocal of Archie, always complaining about how he was cheated out of opportunities. The show was also not afraid to curse. "Ain't that a bitch!" slurred Ernest in one situation.[34] Twenty years before, Lear was the first person ever to write that swear word into a television script, when Maude called Walter a son of a bitch. Certain aspects of the show that Lear originally brought to television were incorporated into the scripts.

704 Hauser also brought in a representative of youth to counter the older generation's belief system, like *All in the Family* did with the character of Mike Stivic. Yet again, the arguments were opposite. The older generation was the liberal one, still searching for freedom, while the young adult, Goodie (T.E. Russell), called himself a "conservative." Lear said in 1994, "Twenty years ago, I don't ever remember a black conservative-vs.-liberal argument. When you mix the conservative viewpoint and race, it is not Republican vs. Democrat and it is far more than ultra-conservative versus radical liberal."[35] However, Goodie certainly was not a bigot. *704 Hauser* incorporated themes from *The Jeffersons* into the character of Goodie Cumberbatch. He was dating a white Jewish woman, much to his father's dismay.

Amos' character of Ernest carried some characteristics similar to his James Evans role — pride in what he had accomplished in his life. He and his family were in the same financial bracket as Archie Bunker — getting by with somewhat minimal breathing room. And Ernest was proud of that.

In the first episode, Joey Stivic stopped by to see the house that he once lived in. However, even he could not lure viewers to turn on CBS. The show was a ratings failure, spanning only five episodes.

On May 9, 1994, after the final episode of *704 Hauser*, fans would never again see another new episode of a Norman Lear–produced sitcom. The man who brought America to America back in 1971 was officially done with television twenty-three years later. He changed the face of television forever — from the language barriers to the broadening of subject matter on television. At the same time, he made a true impact on the American public, for example, giving women the courage to fight for their rights through his show *Maude*, or helping people to solve their sexual problems through *Mary Hartman, Mary Hartman*, or even getting somebody to stop using racial epithets through *All in the Family*, *Sanford and Son*, and *The Jeffersons*.

Norman Lear is arguably the most successful television producer in history; while the ratings of his 1990s shows may not have measured up to his earlier successes, he was the first person to have five different television shows in the top ten in the Nielsen ratings at one time. Meanwhile, he changed television vocabulary forever, and rewrote television's book of etiquette. He gave new meaning to the definition of *sitcom*, showing that there can be more than simple laughs from Lucy getting a trophy stuck on her head. Lucille Ball questioned what Lear was doing back in 1971, and while she holds a dignified place in the world of television acting, Lear is her equivalent in the world of television producing. Norman Lear is the best of the best, because he, like Lucy, did what no one else has ever done on television.

Chapter Notes

Chapter 1

1. "Two's a Crowd," *All in the Family*, originally broadcast 12 February 1978, CBS.
2. Lear quoted in Donna McCrohan, *Archie, Edith, Mike, and Gloria: The Tumultuous History of All in the Family* (New York: Workman Publishing, 1987), 48.
3. Lear quoted in Martin Kasindorf, "Archie & Maude & Fred & Norman & Alan," *The New York Times*, 24 June 1973, 226.
4. Rooney quoted in Gerard Jones, *Honey, I'm Home! Sitcoms: Selling the American Dream* (New York: Grove Weidenfeld, 1992), 204.
5. Lear quoted in *E! True Hollywood Story: All in the Family*, originally broadcast 2000, E!
6. Lear quoted in Arnold Hano, "The man under the hard hat," *TV Guide*, 20 November 1971, 29–34.
7. Lear quoted in McCrohan, op. cit., 123.
8. Lear quoted in Dwight Whitney, "For the Dingbat, These are the Days," *TV Guide*, 27 May 1972, 21–26.
9. Stapleton quoted in Whitney, Ibid., 21–26.
10. Stapleton quoted in McCrohan, op. cit., 16–17.
11. Frances Lear quoted in Geoffrey Cowan, *See No Evil: The Backstage Battle Over Sex and Violence in Television* (New York: Simon and Schuster, 1979), 23.
12. Wood quoted in Harry Castleman, Walter J. Podrazik, *Watching TV: Four Decades of American Television* (New York: McGraw-Hill Book Company, 1982), 226.
13. Wood quoted in Castleman, Ibid., 191.
14. Alison Gwynn, *The 100 Greatest TV Shows of All Time* (New York: Time, Inc., 1998), 13.
15. Reiner quoted in Mark Laswell, *TV Guide: Fifty Years of Television* (New York: Crown Publishers, 2002), 19.
16. Struthers quoted in Jeanie Kasindorf, "It's Better Than a Studio Tour," *TV Guide*, 14 December 1974, 24–26.
17. Struthers quoted in *E! True Hollywood Story: All in the Family*, op. cit.
18. Brown quoted in Jones, op. cit., 205.
19. John Beaufort, "Viewing Things," *The Christian Science Monitor*, 15 August 1970, 12.
20. John J. O'Connor, "At One Time You Couldn't Say 'W.C.,'" *The New York Times*, 15 October 1972, E9.
21. Smith quoted in *E! True Hollywood Story: All in the Family*, op. cit.
22. Martin Kasindorf, op. cit.
23. Lear quoted in Cowan, op. cit., 26.
24. Schneider quoted in Cowan, Ibid., 39.
25. "Meet the Bunkers," *All in the Family*, originally broadcast 12 January 1971, CBS.
26. Reiner quoted in Garner, *Made You Laugh: The Funniest Moments in Radio, Television, Stand-Up, and Movie Comedy* (Kansas City: Andrews McMeel Publishing, 2004), 42.
27. Carroll O'Connor, "I Regret Nothing Except My Own Anger," *TV Guide*, 22 September 1979, 28–30.
28. Leonard Gross, "Do Bigots Miss the Message?" *TV Guide*, 8 November 1975, 14–18.
29. Ibid., 14–18.
30. Stapleton quoted in McCrohan, op. cit., 1987.
31. "Meet the Bunkers," op. cit.
32. Bennett Harrison, William Spring, Thomas Victorisz, "Crisis of the unemployed — in much of the inner city, 60 percent don't earn enough for a decent standard of living," *The New York Times*, 5 November 1972, SM42.
33. "Meet the Bunkers," op. cit.
34. Ibid.
35. Ibid.
36. Betty Garrett, *Betty Garrett and Other Songs: A Life on Stage and Screen* (New York: Madison Books, 1998), 234.
37. "Meet the Bunkers," op. cit.
38. "Oh, My Aching Back," *All in the Family*, originally broadcast 26 January 1971, CBS.
39. Arnold Hano, "Why Archie Is So Lovable," *The Chicago Tribune*, 12 March 1972, A1.

40. David Frum, *How We Got Here: The 70's* (New York: Basic Books, 2000), 20.

41. Ibid., 157.

42. Harry Castleman, Walter J. Podrazik, *Watching TV: Four Decades of American Television* (New York: McGraw-Hill Book Company, 1982), 226–27.

43. David Marc, *Comic Visions: Television Comedy & American Culture* (Oxford: Blackwell Publishers, Ltd., 1997), 150.

44. Lear quoted in Cowan, op. cit., 27.

45. Fred Ferretti, "TV: Are Racism and Bigotry Funny?" *The New York Times*, 12 January 1971, 70.

46. Clarence Petersen, "CBS Debuts Courageous New Comedy," *The Chicago Tribune*, 12 January 1971, A9.

47. Cecil Smith, "Bigotry Used as a Laughing Matter," *The Los Angeles Times*, 12 January 1971, G12.

48. William C. Woods, "*All in the Family*: Review," *The Washington Post*, 13 January 1971: B3.

49. Donna McCrohan, *op. cit*, 34.

50. Fred Ferretti, op. cit.

51. Jack Gould, "Can Bigotry Be Laughed Away? It's Worth a Try," *The New York Times*, 21 February 1971, D15.

52. Harrington quoted in Norman Lear, "Laughing While We Face Our Prejudices," *The New York Times*, 11 April 1971, D22.

53. Ibid., D22.

54. Ibid., D22.

55. Bucklew quoted in "Letters," *TV Guide*, 6 February 1972, 22–24.

56. "Display Ad 52 — No Title," *The New York Times*, 26 January 1971, 66.

57. Ibid.

58. Anthony quoted in "Letters," *TV Guide*, 27 May 1972, A4.

59. "Writing the President," *All in the Family*, originally broadcast 19 January 1971, CBS.

60. Lawrence K. Altman, "Use of Commercial Blood Donors Increases With Shortage in U.S," *The New York Times*, 5 September 1970, 1.

61. "Archie Gives Blood," *All in the Family*, originally broadcast 2 February 1971, CBS.

62. George H. Favre, "U.S. homosexuals assert 'rights'; Thousands march; Appeal to hidden group; Wide range noted; Conference sags election ironroads claimed," *The Christian Science Monitor*, 5 August 1970, 4.

63. "Judging Books by Covers," *All in the Family*, originally broadcast 9 February 1971, CBS.

64. David Frum, op. cit., 207.

65. Jane E. Brody, "More Homosexuals Aided to Become Heterosexual," *The New York Times*, 28 February 1971, 1.

66. Edward Ranzal, "Homosexuals Bill Protecting Rights is Killed by Council: Homosexuals Bill Killed in Council," *The New York Times*, 28 January 1972, 1.

67. Lear quoted in Aljean Harmetz, "Maude Didn't Leave 'em All Laughing," *The New York Times*, 10 December 1972, D3.

68. Merv Griffin, *Merv* (New York: Simon and Schuster, 2003), 83.

69. Carson quoted in George Gent, "Scott and Lee Grant Get Best-Acting Emmys," *The New York Times*, 10 May 1971, 67.

70. George Gent, "*All in the Family* Takes First Place in Nielsen Ratings," *The New York Times*, 25 May 1971, 79.

71. Goldberg quoted in *E! True Hollywood Story: All in the Family*, op. cit.

72. Reiner quoted in McCrohan, op. cit., 35–36.

73. Lear quoted in Gent, "*All in the Family* Takes First Place in Nielsen Ratings," op. cit.

74. West quoted in McCrohan, op. cit., 118–19.

75. "Gloria Poses in the Nude," *All in the Family*," originally broadcast 25 September 1971, CBS.

76. Lawrence Laurent, "Archie Bunker has two kinds of viewers," *The Washington Post*, 19 December 1971, 193.

77. O'Connor quoted in Hano, op. cit.

78. Lear quoted in Spencer Marsh, *God, Man, and Archie Bunker* (New York: Harper & How Publishers, 1975), xii.

79. Bennett quoted in Marsh, Ibid., xii.

80. Laura Z. Hobson, "As I Listened to Archie Say 'Hebe'..." *The New York Times*, 12 September 1971: D1.

81. Norman Lear, "As I Read How Laura Saw Archie..." *The Los Angeles Times*, 10 October 1971, D17.

82. "Mike's Problem," *All in the Family*, originally broadcast 20 November 1971, CBS.

83. Wood quoted in Cowan, op. cit., 30.

84. Lear quoted in Cowan, Ibid., 30.

85. Lawrence Laurent.

86. Donna McCrohan, op. cit., 36.

87. Arnold Hano, "Can Archie Bunker Give Bigotry a Bad Name?" *The New York Times*, 12 March 1972, SM32.

88. "Sammy's Visit," *All in the Family*, originally broadcast 19 February 1972, CBS.

89. Donna McCrohan, op. cit., 35–36.

90. "Sammy's Visit," op. cit.

91. Ibid.

92. Ibid.

93. Lear quoted in *100 Most Memorable Moments*, originally broadcast 2004, TV Land.

94. Stephen Battaglio, "100 Most Memorable TV Moments," *TV Guide*, 5 December 2004, 39.

95. Larry W. Jones quoted in *100 Most Memorable Moments*, originally broadcast 2004, TV Land.

96. Quincy Jones quoted in *100 Most Memorable Moments*, originally broadcast 2004, TV Land.

97. Davis quoted in McCrohan, op. cit., 118–19.

98. Cecil Smith, "Bigotry Used as a Laughing Matter," op. cit.

99. McGovern quoted in Courtney R. Sheldon, "McGovern faces tough Nixon fight," *The Christian Science Monitor*, 1 August 1972, 1.

100. Nixon administration quoted in Sheldon, Ibid., 1.

101. Michael C. Jensen, "Young Millionaires Are Big Contributors to McGovern," *The New York Times*, 23 August 1972, 29.

102. David Frum, op. cit., 284.

103. "Mike Comes Into Money," *All in the Family*, originally broadcast 4 November 1972, CBS.

104. Nicholas Von Hoffman, "The Compromising Convention," *The Chicago Tribune*, 17 July 1972, 22.

105. "We're Having a Heat Wave," *All in the Family*, originally broadcast 15 September 1973, CBS.

106. Rich quoted in John Carmody, "Maude," *The Washington Post*, 11 September 1973, B1.

107. "We're Having a Heat Wave," op. cit.

108. Kitman quoted in McCrohan, op. cit., 188.

109. Harry B. Ellis, "Food prices slow their upward climb," *The Christian Science Monitor*, 22 May 1974, 1.

110. Burns quoted in Paul E. Steiger, "Consumers Urged to Battle Inflation," *The Los Angeles Times*, 27 May 1974, A1.

111. "The Cost of Everything — UP," *The Chicago Tribune*, 1 January 1975, E16.

112. Hal Trooger, "Drop Escalator Clauses," *The Chicago Tribune*, 25 June 1974, 10.

113. "The Bunkers and Inflation (1)," *All in the Family*, originally broadcast 14 September 1974, CBS.

114. "The Bunkers and Inflation (4)," *All in the Family*, originally broadcast 5 October 1974, CBS.

115. "The Cost of Everything — UP," op. cit.

116. John Conyers, Jr., "Jobless Numbers," *The New York Times*, 1 January 1976, 15.

117. Ibid., 15.

118. Ibid., 15.

119. Marilyn Bender, "Job Discrimination, 10 Years Later," *The New York Times*, 10 November 1974, 187.

120. Ibid., 187.

121. "Meet the Bunkers," op. cit.

122. Lear quoted in Arthur Unger, "Are Those Network Series Improving?" *The Christian Science Monitor*, 7 October 1974, 14.

123. Josh Ozersky, *Archie Bunker's America: TV In an Era of Change, 1968–1978* (Carbondale: Southern Illinois University Press, 2003), 72.

124. Betty Garrett, op. cit., 236.

125. Kenneth Turan, "Norman Lear's Washington," *The Washington Post*, 19 September 1976, 355.

126. Carroll O'Connor, op. cit.

127. Stapleton quoted in Joseph N. Bell, "*All in the Family*," *The Christian Science Monitor*, 29 January 1974, F1.

128. O'Connor quoted in Dwight Whitney, "An American Institution Rolls On," *TV Guide*, 2 January 1979, 14–18.

129. O'Connor quoted in Bill Davidson, "The Uprising in Lear's Kingdom," *TV Guide*, 13 April 1974, 12–17.

130. Ibid., 12–17.

131. Lear quoted in Arthur Unger, "Behind the Hits," *The Christian Science Monitor*, 25 July 1974, 13.

132. Dwight Whitney, "An American Institution Rolls On," op. cit.

133. Martin Kasindorf, op. cit.

134. Carroll O'Connor, op. cit.

135. Lafferty quoted in *E! True Hollywood Story: All in the Family*, op. cit.

136. Tarloff quoted in Davidson, op. cit.

137. Dwight Whitney, "An American Institution Rolls On," op. cit.

138. Carroll O'Connor, op. cit.

139. O'Connor quoted in *E! True Hollywood Story: All in the Family*, op. cit.

140. Lear quoted in *E! True Hollywood Story: All in the Family*, op. cit.

141. Carroll O'Connor, op. cit.

142. Ibid., 28–30.

143. Ibid., 28–30.

144. Dwight Whitney, "An American Institution Rolls On," op. cit.

145. Lear quoted in Cowan, op. cit., 41–42.

146. Lear quoted in Cowan, Ibid., 40.

147. Ibid., 186.

148. Ibid., 125.

149. Arthur Unger, "Norman Lear," *The Christian Science Monitor*, 10 November 1976, 20.

150. Lear quoted in Unger, Ibid., 20.

151. O'Connor quoted in Cowan, op. cit., 179.

152. Lear quoted in Unger, "Norman Lear," op. cit.

153. "Edith Has Jury Duty," *All in the Family*, originally broadcast 9 March 1971, CBS.

154. David Marc, op. cit., 150.

155. Stapleton quoted in Whitney, "For the Dingbat, These Are the Days," op. cit.

156. Lear quoted in Cowan, op. cit., 24.

157. "Hot Watch," *All in the Family*, originally broadcast 17 February 1973, CBS.
158. "Edith's Problem," *All in the Family*, originally broadcast 8 January 1972, CBS.
159. "Archie's Helping Hand," *All in the Family*, originally broadcast 19 October 1974, CBS.
160. "Edith's Night Out," *All in the* Family, originally broadcast 8 March 1976, CBS.
161. "Archie's Brief Encounter (3)," *All in the Family*," originally broadcast 29 September 1976, CBS.
162. Stapleton quoted in McCrohan, op. cit., 135.
163. "Edith's 50th Birthday," *All in the Family*, originally broadcast 16 October 1977, CBS.
164. Dukes quoted in *E! True Hollywood Story: All in the Family*, op. cit.
165. Dukes quoted in McCrohan, op. cit., 135.
166. "Edith's 50th Birthday," op. cit.
167. Betty Liddick, "Focusing on the Reasons for Rape," *The Los Angeles Times*, 1 December 1977, M1.
168. Donna McCrohan, op. cit., 74.
169. Lear quoted in Tom Shales, "Tonight: Edith Bunker's Ordeal," *The Washington Post*, 16 October 1977, 117.
170. Cecil Smith, "Television Review: The Rape of Edith Bunker," *The Los Angeles Times*, 13 October 1977, OC_A1.
171. Cecil Smith, "Is Edith the Queen or Pawn of TV?" *The Los Angeles Times*, 21 October 1977, K35.
172. Dukes quoted in Elanor Blau, "How David Dukes Solved a Problem in Playing 'Bent'?" *The New York Times*, 13 December 1979, C17.
173. Ibid., C17.
174. Dukes quoted in McCrohan, op. cit., 75.
175. "The Best of *All in the Family* (1)," *All in the Family*, originally broadcast 21 December 1974, CBS.
176. Lear quoted in *All in the Family 20th Anniversary Special*, originally broadcast 1991, CBS.
177. O'Connor quoted in Whitney, "An American Institution Rolls On," op. cit.
178. Geoffrey Cowan, op. cit., 303.
179. Donna McCrohan, op. cit., 164.
180. Lear quoted in Whitney, "An American Institution Rolls On," op. cit.
181. Horn quoted in Whitney, Ibid., 14–18.
182. "California, Here We Are (1)," *All in the Family*, originally broadcast 1 December 1978, CBS.
183. Carroll O'Connor, op. cit.
184. Dwight Whitney, "Why Archie Survives," *TV Guide*, 8 August 1981, 28–30.
185. Tom Shales, "Dingbat's Demise: Life

After Edith Bunker," *The Washington Post*, 1 November 1980, A1.
186. Stapleton quoted in *E! True Hollywood Story: All in the Family*, op. cit.
187. Brisebois quoted in McCrohan, op. cit., 186.
188. Betty Garrett, op. cit., 235.
189. O'Connor quoted in Whitney, "Why Archie Survives," op. cit.
190. Lachman quoted in Whitney, Ibid., 28–30.
191. Lachman quoted in Ibid., 28–30.
192. O'Connor quoted in Kenneth Turan, "Archie, Edith, Mike, and Gloria: A *Family* Journal," *TV Guide*, 3 September 1983, 32–36.
193. Kay Gardella, "He's golden as Archie: O'Connor now a TV institution," *The Chicago Tribune*, 12 September 1982, H5.
194. Ibid., H5.
195. Struthers quoted in Bob Wisenhart, "Sally Struthers Comes Full Circle," *The Los Angeles Times*, 25 June 1982, G23.
196. Ibid., G23.
197. "The First Day," *Gloria*, originally broadcast 26 September 1982, CBS.
198. Lou Richards, personal interview, August 2005.
199. "The First Day," op. cit.
200. Lou Richards, op. cit.
201. O'Connor quoted in Gardella, op. cit.
202. Lou Richards, op. cit.
203. Horn quoted in Carroll O'Connor, "What It Meant to Be Archie," *TV Guide*, 3 September 1983, 26–31.
204. Lear quoted in O'Connor, Ibid., 26–31.
205. Lear quoted in O'Connor, Ibid., 26–31.
206. Lear quoted in O'Connor, Ibid., 26–31.
207. Lear quoted in Kenneth Turan, "Archie, Edith, Mike, and Gloria: A *Family* Journal," op. cit.
208. Brisebois quoted in McCrohan, op. cit., 175.
209. O'Connor quoted in Frank J. Prial, "CBS-TV Is Dropping Archie Bunker," *The New York Times*, 12 May 1983, C24.
210. Haynes Johnson, "Why Pull the Plug On Our Blue-Collar Political Philosopher?" *The Washington Post*, 15 May 1983, A1.
211. Howard Rosenberg, "Tribute to TV's Favorite Bigot," *The Los Angeles Times*, 18 May 1983, G1.

Chapter 2

1. Mark Laswell, *TV Guide: Fifty Years of Television* (New York: Crown Publishers, 2002), 255.
2. "Greatest Show in Watts," *Sanford and Son*, originally broadcast 16 January 1976, NBC.

3. "Fred Sanford Has a Baby," *Sanford and Son*, originally broadcast 23 January 1976, NBC.

4. David Brody et al., *America's History: Volume 2, Since 1865* (New York: Worth Publishers, 1993), A23.

5. Bruce J. Schulman, *The Seventies: The Great Shift in American Culture, Society, and Politics* (Cambridge: Da Capo Press, 2001), 85.

6. Kuhn quoted in Schulman, Ibid., 85–86.

7. Kuhn quoted in Jane Hall, "Old, Bold, and Angry," *TV Guide*, 21 June 1975, 3–5.

8. Leroy Aarons, "'63 Civil Rights Tide Shows to Trickle," *The Washington Post*, 29 August 1973: A1.

9. Foxx quoted in Judith L. Kessler, "*Sanford and Son*: Change in Comedy?" *The Washington Post*, 29 August 1973, B1.

10. "Crossed Swords," *Sanford and Son*, originally broadcast 28 January 1972, CBS.

11. "Here Comes the Bride, Here Goes the Bride," *Sanford and Son*, originally broadcast 28 January 1972, CBS.

12. Tom Shales, "TV: A Massive Spring Facelift?" *The Washington Post*, 9 January 1972, G1.

13. Lear quoted in Kessler, op. cit.

14. Ruben quoted in Kessler, Ibid., B1.

15. Josh Ozersky, *Archie Bunker's America: TV in an Era of Change, 1968–1978* (Carbondale, Southern Illinois University Press, 2003), 73.

16. Paul Gardner, "The Quick Redd Foxx Jumps Into a New Kettle of Fish," *The New York Times*, 6 February 1972, D19.

17. "Crossed Swords," op. cit.

18. Foxx quoted in Kessler, op. cit.

19. Wilson quoted in Kessler, Ibid., B1.

20. Wilson quoted in Gardner, op. cit.

21. "Crossed Swords," op. cit.

22. "Happy Birthday, Pop," *Sanford and Son*, originally broadcast 21 January 1972, NBC.

23. Gerard Jones, *Honey, I'm Home! Sitcoms: Selling the American Dream* (New York: Grove Weidenfeld, 1992), 216.

24. Ibid., 217.

25. "We Were Robbed," *Sanford and Son*, originally broadcast 18 February 1972, NBC.

26. David Frum, *How We Got Here: The '70s* (New York: Basic Books, 2000), 16.

27. "The Puerto Ricans Are Coming!" *Sanford and Son*, originally broadcast 10 November 1972, NBC.

28. Ibid.

29. Edward C. Burks, "Middle-Class Whites Still Leaving City," *The New York Times*, 29 May 1972, 1.

30. "The Puerto Ricans Are Coming!" op. cit.

31. "A Visit From Lena Horne," *Sanford and Son*, originally broadcast 10 November 1972, NBC.

32. Betty Garrett, *Betty Garrett and Other Songs: A Life On Stage and Screen* (New York: Madison Books, 1998), 251.

33. Ibid., 251.

34. Yorkin quoted in Bill Davidson, "The Uprising in Lear's Kingdom," *TV Guide*, 13 April 1974, 12–17.

35. Foxx quoted in Joel Dreyfuss, "Television Controversy: Covering the Black Experience," *The Washington Post*, 1 September 1974, K1.

36. Foxx quoted in www.roctober.com/roctober/greatness/foxx.html

37. Foxx quoted in Michael O'Daniel, "Everything a Performer Could Ask For," *TV Guide*, 14 February 1976, 18–20.

38. Foxx quoted in Louie Robinson, *Ebony*, June 1974.

39. Yorkin quoted in Bill Davidson, "Trouble in Paradise," *TV Guide*, 6 April 1974, 4–8.

40. Yorkin quoted in Davidson, Ibid., 4–8.

41. Foxx quoted in Robinson, op. cit.

42. Billy Ingram, *TV Party* (Los Angeles: Bonus Books, 2002), 250.

43. Robinson, Louie, op. cit.

44. Michael O'Daniel, op. cit.

45. Foxx quoted in Robinson, op. cit.

46. Albin Krebs, "Giscard Endorsed by Servan-Schreiber," *The New York Times*, 15 May 1974, 51.

47. Terrance W. McGarry, "A Star-Studded Day in Superior Court," *The Washington Post*, 24 June 1974, B12.

48. A.H. Wieler, "News of the Screen," *The New York Times*, 22 September 1974, 55.

49. "The Sanford Arms," *Sanford and Son*, originally broadcast 3 October 1975, NBC.

50. Foxx quoted in Larry Kart, "Comedy," *The Chicago Tribune*, 23 January 1983, D24.

51. J. Fred MacDonald, *Blacks and White TV: Afro-Americans in Television Since 1948* (Chicago: Nelson-Hall Publishers, 1988), 186.

52. Arthur Unger, "Worth noting on TV," *The Christian Science Monitor*, 16 January 1986, 27.

53. John Carmody, "The TV Column," *The Washington Post*, 22 January 1986, C8.

Chapter 3

1. "Cousin Maude's Visit," *All in the Family*, originally broadcast 11 December 1971, CBS.

2. Judy Stone, "She Gave Archie His First Comeuppance," *The New York Times*, 19 November 1972, D17.

3. "Cousin Maude's Visit," op. cit.

4. "Maude," *All in the Family*, originally broadcast 11 March 1972, CBS.

5. "Maude Meets Florida," *Maude*, originally broadcast 26 September 1972, CBS.
6. Lear quoted in Flatley, "Gene, for Heaven's Sake, Help Me!!" *TV Guide*, 18 November 1972, 28–32.
7. Ibid., 28–32.
8. Arthur quoted in Flatley, Ibid., 28–32.
9. Arthur quoted in Flatley, Ibid., 28–32.
10. Arthur quoted in Richard Warren Lewis, "There Is No One Else Like Me," *TV Guide*, 24 April 1976, 18–22.
11. Lear quoted in Tom Donnelly, "Mirth and Maude," *The New York Times*, 5 December 1972, B1.
12. "Cousin Maude's Visit," op. cit.
13. Ibid.
14. Ibid.
15. Judy Stone, op. cit.
16. Lear quoted in *TV Land Moguls*, originally broadcast 2004, TV Land.
17. Parker quoted in Bill Davidson, "The Uprising in Lear's Kingdom," *TV Guide*, 13 April 1974, 12–17.
18. Arthur quoted in Davidson, Ibid., 12–17.
19. Arthur quoted in Kirk Honeycutt, "We Ran Out of Controversy," *The New York Times*, 16 April 1978, 103.
20. www.famous.adoption.com/famous-/lear-frances.html
21. Martin Kasindorf, "Archie & Maude & Fred & Norman & Alan," *The New York Times*, 24 June 1973, 226.
22. Lear quoted in Kasindorf, Ibid., 226.
23. Josh Ozersky, *Archie Bunker's America: TV in an Era of Change, 1968–1978* (Carbondale: Southern Illinois University Press, 2003), 79.
24. Parker quoted in Lewis, op. cit.
25. "Maude Meets Florida," op. cit.
26. Al Stump, "Steady Work for a Former Floater," *TV Guide*, 16 June 1973, 26–31.
27. Bill Davidson, "Trouble in Paradise," *TV Guide*, 6 April 1974, 4–8.
28. Lear quoted in Stump, op. cit.
29. Lear quoted in Stump, op. cit.
30. Bill Macy, personal interview, January 2005.
31. Lear quoted in Kasindorf, op. cit.
32. Rolle quoted in John Riley, "Esther Rolle the Fishin' Pole," *TV Guide*, 29 June 1974, 16–18.
33. Ibid., 16–18.
34. Rolle quoted in Riley, Ibid., 16–18.
35. Rolle quoted in Vera Servi, "Florida's now on her own," *The Chicago Tribune*, 3 February 1974, 59.
36. Arthur quoted in Riley, op. cit.
37. Rolle quoted in Servi, op. cit.
38. Rue McClanahan, personal interview, December 2004.

39. Lear quoted in "He Has Become a Household Face," *TV Guide*, 12 January 1974, 12–18.
40. Arthur quoted in "He Has Become a Household Face," Ibid., 12–18.
41. Arthur quoted in Honeycutt, op. cit.
42. Arthur quoted in Honeycutt, Ibid., 103.
43. Lear quoted in Lawrence Laurent, "Controversial Comedies Win High Ratings," *The Washington Post*, 4 February 1973, TVC9.
44. "Edith Flips Her Wig," *All in the Family*, originally broadcast 21 October 1972, CBS.
45. "Maude's Problem," *Maude*, originally broadcast 12 September 1972, CBS.
46. Ibid.
47. Ibid.
48. Ibid.
49. Rue McClanahan, op. cit.
50. "Maude's Problem," op. cit.
51. John J. O'Connor, "TV: *Maude*, a Comedy, Will Make Debut Tonight," *The New York Times*, 12 September 1972, 90.
52. "Edith's cousin," *The Christian Science Monitor*, 9 September 1972, 6.
53. Lawrence Laurent, "*Maude* is the flip side of Archie Bunker," *The Washington Post*, 8 October 1972, TC5.
54. Susan Harris, personal interview, September 2005.
55. Ibid.
56. Lear quoted in Aljean Harmetz, "Maude Didn't Leave 'em All Laughing," *The New York Times*, 10 December 1972, D3.
57. Lear quoted in Harmetz, Ibid., D3.
58. Rue McClanahan, op. cit.
59. Anonymous, "Abortion: A Gynecologist Explains His Tangled Thoughts," *The Chicago Tribune*, 1 November 1972, B3.
60. "Maude's Dilemma (1)," *Maude*, originally broadcast 12 November 1972, CBS.
61. Ibid.
62. Ibid.
63. Susan Harris, op. cit.
64. "Maude's Dilemma," op. cit.
65. Ibid.
66. Aljean Harmetz, op. cit.
67. Fielding quoted in "NOW Suit Over *Maude* Abortion Shows Denied," *The Los Angeles Times*, 25 November 1972, A3.
68. Ibid., A3.
69. Aljean Harmetz, op. cit.
70. Les Brown, "Wood, C.B.S.-TV Head, Defends 'Mature' Shows," *The New York Times*, 16 October 1973, 87.
71. Lear quoted in Harmetz, op. cit.
72. Peter Gorner, "Exploring a Phenomenon: Is Vasectomy Truly Safe?" *The Chicago Tribune*, 15 November 1972, B1.
73. Ibid., B1.
74. "Maude's Dilemma (2)," *Maude*, originally broadcast 19 November 1972, CBS.

75. "Maude's Dilemma (1)," op. cit.
76. Carol Gieger, "Maude's Abortion Was No Joke," *The New York Times*, 24 December 1972, D8.
77. "Maude's Dilemma (1)," op. cit.
78. Aljean Harmetz, op. cit.
79. Cecil Smith, "Maude's Abortion Evokes Protests," *The Los Angeles Times*, 29 November 1972, D25.
80. Joyce quoted in "CBS Accused of 'Betrayal,'" *The Los Angeles Times*, 1 December 1972, D28.
81. Cecil Smith, op. cit.
82. Arthur quoted in Lewis, op. cit.
83. Jane Rosenzweig, "Can TV Improve Us?" *The American Prospect*, 1 July 1999, vol. 10 no. 45.
84. Arthur quoted in Honeycutt, op. cit.
85. Brown, Les. "Wood, C.B.S.-TV Head, Defends 'Mature' Shows." *op. cit.*
86. *"All in the Family* Leads Nielsen Again." *The Los Angeles Times.* 8 November 1972: D22.
87. "Yorkin-Lear Shows Top TV Ratings." *The Los Angeles Times.* 13 December 1972: C32.
88. Honeycutt, Kirk. "We Ran Out of Controversy." *The New York Times.* 16 April 1978: 103.
89. Les Brown, op. cit.
90. Aljean Harmetz, op. cit.
91. John Carmody, "The Problem Drinkers' Problems," *The Washington Post*, 6 January 1973, E7.
92. Jack Houston, "100,000 more each year," *The Chicago Tribune*, 20 March 1974, C11.
93. Ibid., C11.
94. Buxton quoted in "Free Program," *The Los Angeles Times*, 7 January 1973, SG3.
95. Lear quoted in John Carmody, "*Maude*," *The Washington Post*, 11 September 1973, B1.
96. "Walter's Problem (1)," *Maude*, originally broadcast 11 September 1973, CBS.
97. Ibid.
98. Ibid.
99. "Walter's Problem (2)," *Maude*, originally broadcast 18 September 1973, CBS.
100. Ibid.
101. Bill Macy, op. cit.
102. Jack Houston, op. cit.
103. Raymond J. Vince, "Drugs and alcohol," *The Chicago Tribune*, 30 January 1973, 8.
104. John Carmody, "The Problem Drinkers' Problems," op. cit.
105. Bill Macy, op. cit.
106. Ibid.
107. Lear quoted in Lawrence Laurent, "Controversial comedies win high ratings," op. cit.
108. "Maude Meets Florida," op. cit.
109. Ibid.
110. Donald Bogle, *Prime Time Blues: African Americans on Network Television* (New York: Farrar, Straus, and Giroux, 2001), 198.
111. Rolle quoted in Riley, op. cit.
112. Rolle quoted in Arthur Unger, "Esther Rolle: 'We laugh at ourselves,'" *The Christian Science Monitor*, 7 February 1974, 18.
113. "Florida's Problem," *Maude*, originally broadcast 13 February 1973, CBS.
114. Ibid.
115. "Maude's Reunion," *Maude*, originally broadcast 28 November 1972, CBS.
116. Urie Bronfenbrenner, "The Calamitous Decline of the American Family," *The Washington Post*, 2 January 1977, 65.
117. "The Emergence of Vivian," *Maude*, originally broadcast 3 February 1975, CBS.
118. "The Kiss," *Maude*, originally broadcast 16 September 1974, CBS.
119. Rue McClanahan, op. cit.
120. "The Grass Story," *Maude*, originally broadcast 5 December 1972, CBS.
121. E. James Sills, "No, For Medical, Social Good," *The Los Angeles Times*, 2 November 1972, B7.
122. Robert Ashford, "Should Californians Decriminalize Marijuana Use?" *The Los Angeles Times*, 2 November 1972, B7.
123. "The Grass Story," op. cit.
124. Ibid.
125. Ibid.
126. Ibid.
127. Ibid.
128. William H. Chafe, *The Paradox of Change: American Women in the 20th Century* (Oxford: Oxford University Press, 1991), 211.
129. "Consenting Adults," *Maude*, originally broadcast 15 September 1975, CBS.
130. "The Split," *Maude*, originally broadcast 8 September 1975, CBS.
131. William H. Chafe, op. cit., 216.
132. Arthur quoted in Lewis, op. cit.
133. "The Election," *Maude*, originally broadcast 6 October 1975, CBS.
134. Rue McClanahan, op. cit.
135. "The Emergence of Vivian," op. cit.
136. Rue McClanahan, op. cit.
137. "Maude's Facelift (1)," *Maude*, originally broadcast 2 October 1973, CBS.
138. Rue McClanahan, op. cit.
139. "Maude's Facelift (1)," op. cit.
140. Ibid.
141. Rue McClanahan, op. cit.
142. Cecil Smith, "Florida Moves to Chicago via CBS," *The Los Angeles Times*, 8 February 1974, E25.
143. J. Fred MacDonald, *Blacks and White TV: Afro-Americans in Television Since 1948* (Chicago: Nelson-Hall Publishers, 1983), 183.

144. Arthur quoted in Honeycutt, op. cit.
145. Marlene Cimons, "Women Candidates See Feminism as Aid," *The Los Angeles Times*, 6 November 1972, OC_B1.
146. Herring quoted in Cimons, Ibid., OC_B1.
147. Arthur quoted in Honeycutt, op. cit.
148. Quayle quoted in Tim Brooks, Earle Marsh, *The Complete Directory to Prime Time Network and Cable TV Shows, 1946-Present (Eighth Edition)* (New York: Ballantine Books, 2003), 810.

Chapter 4

1. "Florida's Protest," *Good Times*, originally broadcast 25 November 1975, CBS.
2. "The TV Commercial," *Good Times*, originally broadcast 26 April 1974, CBS.
3. Evans quoted in Cecil Smith, "*The Jeffersons*: it's another in the long line of Lear series," *The Los Angeles Times*, 19 January 1975, M1.
4. Martin Kasindorf, "Archie and Maude and Fred and Norman and Alan," *The New York Times*, 24 June 1973, 226.
5. http://homestead.com/shb/rolle.com
6. Rolle quoted in John Riley, "Esther Rolle the Fishin' Pole," *TV Guide*, 29 June 1974, 16–18.
7. Cecil Smith, "Florida Moves to Chicago via CBS," *The Los Angeles Times*, 8 February 1974, E25.
8. Walker quoted in Rowland Barber, "No Time for Jivin,'" *TV Guide*, 20 December 1974, 28–32.
9. Evans quoted in Smith, op. cit., 8 February 1974, E25.
10. Carter quoted in *E! True Hollywood Story: Good Times*, originally broadcast 2000, E!.
11. Rolle quoted in Riley, op. cit.
12. Arthur Unger, "Black Family Portrait," *The Christian Science Monitor*, 7 February 1974, 18.
13. "*Good Times* is a third generation series," *The Washington Post*, 3 February 1974, TC7.
14. Lear quoted in Tom Shales, "*Good Times* Is Coming and It's All in the Family," *The Washington Post*, 8 February 1974, B1.
15. Tom Shales, "*Good Times*: A Rich and Natural Comedy," *The Washington Post*, 16 September 1975, B1.
16. Arthur Unger, op. cit.
17. Rolle quoted in Vera Servi, "Florida's now on her own," *The Chicago Tribune*, 3 February 1974, 59.
18. J. Fred MacDonald, *Blacks and White*

TV: Afro-Americans in Television Since 1948 (Chicago: Nelson-Hall Publishers, 1988), 186.
19. Urie Bronfenbrenner, "The Calamitous Decline of the American Family," *The Washington Post*, 2 January 1977, 65.
20. Rolle quoted in Arthur Unger, "Esther Rolle: We laugh at ourselves," *The Christian Science Monitor*, 7 February 1974, 18.
21. Geoffrey Cowan, *See No Evil: The Backstage Battle Over Sex and Violence in Television* (New York: Simon and Schuster, 1979), 227.
22. Rolle quoted in Unger, op. cit., 7 February 1974, 18.
23. Sandra Haggerty, "TV: The World in Fantasy," *The Los Angeles Times*, 14 February 1975, C7.
24. Urie Bronfenbrenner, op. cit.
25. Rolle quoted in Unger, op. cit., 7 February 1974, 18.
26. Paul Gardner, "The Quick Redd Foxx Jumps Into a New Kettle of Fish," *The New York Times*, 6 February 1972, D19.
27. Leroy Aarons, "'63 Civil Rights Tide Shows to Trickle," *The Washington Post*, 29 August 1973, A1.
28. "Too Old Blues," *Good Times*, originally broadcast 8 February 1974, CBS.
29. Rolle quoted in Servi, op. cit.
30. Bennett Harrison, William Spring, Thomas Victorisz, "Crisis of the unemployed — in much of the inner city, 60 percent don't earn enough for a decent standard of living," *The New York Times*, 5 November 1972, SM42.
31. "Getting Up the Rent," *Good Times*, originally broadcast 22 February 1974, CBS.
32. "The TV Commercial," *Good Times*, originally broadcast 26 April 1974, CBS.
33. David Frum, *How We Got Here: The 70's* (New York: Basic Books, 2000), 16.
34. "The Visitor," *Good Times*, originally broadcast 5 April 1974, CBS.
35. Ibid.
36. "The Checkup," *Good Times*, originally broadcast 3 May 1974, CBS.
37. Ibid.
38. Ibid.
39. "Gloria Discovers Women's Lib," *All in the Family*, originally broadcast 23 March 1971, CBS.
40. "Florida Flips," *Good Times*, originally broadcast 10 September 1974, CBS.
41. "Florida's Big Gig," *Good Times*, originally broadcast 31 December 1974, CBS.
42. Ibid.
43. "The Matchmaker," *Good Times*, originally broadcast 26 November 1974, CBS.
44. "J.J. Becomes a Man," *Good Times*, originally broadcast 24 September 1974, CBS.
45. John L. Hess, "The Macaroni and

Cheese Are What's Wrong," *The New York Times*, 12 January 1974, 39.

46. Amos quoted in *TV Land Moguls*, originally broadcast 2004, TV Land.

47. "The Dinner Party," *Good Times*, originally broadcast 11 February 1975, CBS.

48. Mike Fitzpatrick, "Has something gone wrong?" *The Chicago Tribune*, 29 September 1977, B2.

49. "The Debutante Ball," *Good Times*, originally broadcast 4 February 1975, CBS.

50. Ibid.

51. Ibid.

52. Ibid.

53. "Michael Gets Suspended," *Good Times*, originally broadcast 8 March 1974, CBS.

54. "Junior the Senior," *Good Times*, originally broadcast 29 March 1974, CBS.

55. George Goodman Jr., "I.Q. Scores Linked to Environment," *The New York Times*, 22 January 1974, 16.

56. "The I.Q. Test," *Good Times*, originally broadcast 22 October 1974, CBS.

57. Ibid.

58. "California Judge Extends Ruling Against I.Q. Tests," *The New York Times*, 29 November 1974, 53.

59. "The I.Q. Test," op. cit.

60. Leroy Aarons, op. cit.

61. Mike Fitzpatrick, op. cit.

62. Ellison quoted in David Brody et al., *America's History: Volume 2, Since 1865* (New York: Worth Publishers, 1993), 998–99.

63. "Crosstown Buses Run All Day, Doodah, Doodah," *Good Times*, originally broadcast 1 October 1974, CBS.

64. Ibid.

65. David Brody, op. cit.

66. Rolle quoted in Unger, "Esther Rolle: We laugh at ourselves," op. cit., 7 February 1974, 18.

67. Nicholas von Hoffman, "Brown vs. ': Not as Clear as Black and White," *The Washington Post*, 17 May 1974, D1.

68. Joseph Alsop, "Is It Really Worth It?" *The Washington Post*, 11 February 1972, A25.

69. "Thelma's Scholarship," *Good Times*, originally broadcast 11 March 1975, CBS.

70. Urie Bronfenbrenner, op. cit.

71. "Health board data cited: 11 percent of '75 births to girls under age 18: Reporter," *The Chicago Tribune*, 29 April 1977, B10.

72. "J.J. in Trouble," *Good Times*, originally broadcast 3 February 1976, CBS.

73. "Venereal Disease Rise Called Alarming by the U.N.," *The Los Angeles Times*, 16 November 1974, 2.

74. "Sex and the Evans Family," *Good Times*, originally broadcast 15 March 1974, CBS.

75. Elanor Blau, "Birth-Control Drive Fo-

cuses on Teen-Agers," *The New York Times*, 23 July 1974, 39.

76. Ibid., 39.

77. "My Girl Henrietta," *Good Times*, originally broadcast 25 February 1975, CBS.

78. Joyce Brothers, "Why is teen getting drunk?" *The Chicago Tribune*, 7 January 1975, B4.

79. "Sometimes There's No Bottom in the Bottle," *Good Times*, originally broadcast 10 December 1974, CBS.

80. W.H. quoted in Brothers, op. cit.

81. "J.J.'s Fiancée (2)," *Good Times*, originally broadcast 13 January 1976, CBS.

82. "A Friend in Need," *Good Times*, originally broadcast 2 February 1977, CBS.

83. Urie Bronfenbrenner, op. cit.

84. Frank Ching, "Street Crime Casts a Poll of Fear Over Chinatown," *The New York Times*, 19 January 1974, 16.

85. Ibid., 16.

86. Barbara Campbell, "Police Sergeant Charged With Failing to Respond During Youths' Rampage," *The Los Angeles Times*, 23 February 1974, 35.

87. Tsang quoted in Ching, op. cit.

88. DeLeon quoted in Bill Hazlett, "Juvenile Gangs: Violence and Fatal Assaults on Increase," *The Los Angeles Times*, 14 April 1974, A1.

89. Ibid., A1.

90. "The Gang (2)," *Good Times*, originally broadcast 19 November 1974, CBS.

91. Ibid.

92. "New Approach Needed: Revise Juvenile Court System, Jurist Urges," *The Los Angeles Times*, 14 April 1974, A1.

93. Hogobloom quoted in "New Approach Needed," Ibid., A1.

94. "The Gang (2)," op. cit.

95. Ibid.

96. Rolle quoted in Jacqueline Trescott, "Images and *Good Times*," *The Washington Post*, 5 April 1975, D1.

97. "Michael the Warlord," *Good Times*, originally broadcast 13 October 1976, CBS.

98. Hogobloom quoted in "New Approach Needed," op. cit.

99. "Michael the Warlord," op. cit.

100. Tseng quoted in Hazlett, op. cit.

101. Bardos quoted in John Kendall, "What Will Stop Violence? Bardos Asks," *The Los Angeles Times*, 24 January 1974, B1.

102. "Michael the Warlord," op. cit.

103. Ibid.

104. Amos quoted in Barber, op. cit.

105. DuBois quoted in *E! True Hollywood Story: Good Times*, op. cit.

106. Carter quoted in *E! True Hollywood Story: Good Times*, Ibid.

107. DuBois quoted in *E! True Hollywood Story: Good Times*, Ibid.

108. Donald Bogle, *Prime Time Blues: African Americans on Network Television* (New York: Farrar, Straus, and Giroux, 2001), 201–02.

109. Rolle quoted in Unger, op. cit., 7 February 1974, 18.

110. http://www.jimiizrael.com/ji/2005/0406/11.56.04/index.html#more

111. http://awpublisher.com/heroes.html

112. Monte quoted in *E! True Hollywood Story: Good Times*, op. cit.

113. Carter quoted in *E! True Hollywood Story: Good Times*, Ibid.

114. Amos quoted in *TV Land Moguls*, op. cit.

115. Lear quoted in *TV Land Moguls*, Ibid.

116. Joan Ryan, "Amos: Bad Times," *The Washington Post*, 4 May 1976, B10.

117. Amos quoted in Ryan, Ibid., B10.

118. Geoffrey Cowan, op. cit., 227.

119. "A Real Cool Job," *Good Times*, originally broadcast 9 September 1975, CBS.

120. Geoffrey Cowan, op. cit., 227.

121. "The Big Move (1)," *Good Times*, originally broadcast 22 September 1976, CBS.

122. Lear quoted in Cowan, op. cit., 228.

123. "The Big Move (2)," *Good Times*, originally broadcast 29 September 1976, CBS.

124. Mason quoted in *E! True Hollywood Story: Good Times*, op. cit.

125. Carter quoted in *E! True Hollywood Story: Good Times*, Ibid.

126. Walker quoted in *100 Most Memorable Moments*, originally broadcast 2004, TV Land.

127. Rolle quoted in David Richards, "The Latest Stage of Esther Rolle," *The Washington Post*, 11 November 1986, B1.

128. Rolle quoted in Gerard Jones, *"Honey, I'm Home!" Sitcoms: Selling the American Dream* (New York: Grove Weidenfeld, 1992), 219.

129. Sandi Borowicz, "The Tragic Problem of Child Abuse: We Can Help!" *The Los Angeles Times*, 12 November 1977, N10.

130. Joan Beck, "School for violence — it's home," *The Chicago Tribune*, 14 March 1977, C2.

131. Ibid., C2.

132. Maggie Locke, "Experts believe only a few of total child abuse cases are reported," *The Washington Post*, 24 March 1977, D_C_12.

133. "The Evans Get Involved (2)," *Good Times*, originally broadcast 21 September 1977, CBS.

134. Sandi Borowicz, op. cit.

135. Ibid., N10.

136. "The Evans Get Involved (3)," *Good Times*, originally broadcast 28 September 1977, CBS.

137. Joan Cook, "Bergen Taking Steps to Curb Child Abuse," *The New York Times*, 8 June 1977, 75.

138. "The Evans Get Involved (3)," op. cit.

139. Ibid.

140. Ibid.

141. "Court Suggests Foster Homes for Abused Children," *The Washington Post*, 2 January 1977, 34.

142. "The Evans Get Involved (3)," op. cit.

143. J. Fred MacDonald, op. cit., 183.

144. Gary Deeb, "Tempo: Comedy is king — at least in the CBS midseason programming shuffle," *The Chicago Tribune*, 7 December 1978, A14.

145. J. Fred MacDonald, op. cit., 183.

Chapter 5

1. "The Bunkers and Inflation (3)," *All in the Family*, originally broadcast September 28, 1974, CBS.

2. "George's Family Tree," *The Jeffersons*, originally broadcast 25 January 1975, CBS.

3. "Meet the Bunkers," *All in the Family*, originally broadcast 12 January 1971, CBS.

4. Ibid.

5. Evans quoted in Dwight Whitney, "The Boy Next Door — to the Bunkers," *TV Guide*, 2 June 1973, 28–32.

6. Lear quoted in Whitney, Ibid., 28–32. .

7. Evans quoted in Whitney, Ibid., 28–32.

8. Evans quoted in Cecil Smith, "*The Jeffersons*: it's another in the long line of Lear series," *The Los Angeles Times*, 19 January 1975, M1.

9. "Archie Gives Blood," *All in the Family*, originally broadcast 2 February 1971, CBS.

10. Lear quoted in Dick Hobson, "Up from the Ghetto," *TV Guide*, 21 June 1975, 20–22.

11. Hemsley quoted in Dwight Whitney, "Sherman Hemsley: Don't Ask How He Lives or What He Believes In," *TV Guide*, 6 February 1982, 30–35.

12. Nicholl quoted in Hobson, op. cit.

13. Evans quoted in Dwight Whitney, op. cit., 6 February 1982, 30–35.

14. Anonymous quoted in Whitney, Ibid., 30–35.

15. John J. O'Connor, "TV: Lear's *The Jeffersons*," *The New York Times*, 17 January 1975, 67.

16. Joel Dreyfuss, "All in the (Black) Family," *The Washington Post*, 18 January 1975, B1.

17. Ibid., B1.

18. Ibid., B1.

19. Dick Russell, "Fortunately, there was a doctor in the house," *TV Guide*, 5 August 1978, 24–29.

20. Ibid., 24–29.

21. Benedict quoted in Russell, Ibid., 24–29.

22. Gibbs quoted in Russell, Ibid., 24–29.

23. Roker quoted in Bill O'Hallaren, "It could have been the kiss of death," *TV Guide*, 17 May 1980, 23–26.

24. Lear quoted in O'Hallaren, Ibid., 24–29.

25. Gary Deeb, "Now *The Jeffersons* battle Nielsens, not the Bunkers," *The Chicago Tribune*, 17 January 1975, B13.

26. Roker quoted in Jacqueline Trescott, "Roxie Roker: Movin' on Up," *The Washington Post*, 3 March 1976, E1.

27. Franklin Cover, personal interview, August 2004.

28. Lear quoted in O'Hallaren, op. cit.

29. Shea quoted in Russell, op. cit.

30. John Carmody, "*Jeffersons*: High in the Nielsens," *The Washington Post*, 22 January 1975, B7.

31. John J. O'Connor, op. cit.

32. Sandra Haggerty, "TV: the World in Fantasy," *The Los Angeles Times*, 14 February 1975, C7.

33. Gary Deeb, op. cit.

34. "A Friend in Need," *The Jeffersons*, originally broadcast 18 January 1975, CBS.

35. Ibid.

36. Marla Gibbs, personal interview, January 2005.

37. Ibid.

38. Donald Bogle, *Prime Time Blues: African-Americans on Network Television* (New York: Farrar, Straus, and Giroux, 2001), 215.

39. Mary Helen Washington, "As their blackness disappears, so does their character," *TV Guide*, 30 July 1983, 4–9.

40. Joe Garner, *Made You Laugh: The Funniest Moments in Radio, Television, Stand-Up, and Movie Comedy* (Kansas City: Andrews McMeel Publishing, 2004), 45.

41. Mary Helen Washington, op. cit.

42. Ibid., 4–9.

43. "Marathon Men," *The Jeffersons*, originally broadcast 2 November 1980, CBS.

44. Joel Dreyfuss, op. cit.

45. Luis Overbea, "U.S. busing advocate reverses stand," *The Christian Science Monitor*, 16 July 1975, 6.

46. Ibid., 6.

47. Lear quoted in *TV Land Moguls*, originally broadcast 2004, TV Land.

48. Shea quoted in O'Hallaren, op. cit.

49. Cover quoted in O'Hallaren, op. cit.

50. Bill O'Hallaren, op. cit.

51. Sandra Haggerty, op. cit.

52. "43 percent of Marriages Interracial in Hawaii," *The Washington Post*, 14 February 1975, C7.

53. "Jenny's Low," *The Jeffersons*, originally broadcast 12 April 1975, CBS.

54. Ibid.

55. Ibid.

56. Jacqueline Trescott, op. cit.

57. Gary Deeb, "The midseason TV shuffle," *The Chicago Tribune*, 12 January 1975, H4.

58. John J. O'Connor, "*Hot l Baltimore* Signs ABC Register at 9," *The New York Times*, 24 January 1975, 63.

59. "Suzy's Wedding," *Hot L Baltimore*, originally broadcast 28 January 1975, ABC.

60. "Suzy's Wedding," op. cit.

61. Gary Deeb, "CBS and NBC breathe easier as the midseason shuffle pulls ratings," *The Chicago Tribune*, 31 January 1975, B14.

62. Benjamin Stein, "Disaster in Baltimore," *The Wall Street Journal*, 13 February 1975, 16.

63. Ibid., 16.

64. Tom Shales, "*Hot L*: When Less Is More," *The Washington Post*, 21 February 1975, B15.

65. Benjamin Stein, op. cit.

Chapter 6

1. "Ann's Decision," *One Day at a Time*, originally broadcast 16 December 1975, CBS.

2. Richard M. Levine, "As the TV World Turns," *The New York Times*, 14 December 1975, SM6.

3. Ibid., SM6.

4. Lear quoted in Dwight Whitney, "Portrait of an Overachiever," *TV Guide*, 24–30 July 1976, 33–35.

5. Mannings quoted in Whitney, Ibid., 33–35.

6. Franklin quoted in Whitney, Ibid., 33–35.

7. Richard M. Levine, op. cit.

8. Ibid., SM6.

9. Ibid., SM6.

10. Ibid., SM6.

11. Benjamin Stein, "Another Divorcee and Her Problems," *The Wall Street Journal*, 12 December 1975, 14.

12. John J. O'Connor, "TV: *One Day at a Time*," *The New York Times*, 16 December 1975, 79.

13. Sander Vanocur, "Lear's 'One Day': Another 'Sure' Winner," *The Washington Post*, 16 December 1975, C1.

14. "Ratings dominated by CBS," *The Chicago Tribune*, 25 December 1975, E11.

15. "Chicago Rendezvous," *One Day at a Time*, originally broadcast 23 December 1975, CBS.

16. "Ann's Decision," op. cit.

17. Ibid.

18. Mannings quoted in Whitney, op. cit.
19. "Ann's Decision," op. cit.
20. "David Loves Ann," *One Day at a Time*, originally broadcast 13 January 1976, CBS.
21. Ibid.
22. "Ann's Decision," op. cit.
23. "Chicago Rendezvous," op. cit.
24. "Jealousy," *One Day at a Time*, originally broadcast 30 December 1975, CBS.
25. Ibid.
26. "How To Succeed Without Trying," *One Day at a Time*, originally broadcast 6 January 1976, CBS.
27. Ibid.
28. "Julie's Best Friend," *One Day at a Time*, originally broadcast 20 January 1976, CBS.
29. Dwight Whitney, op. cit.
30. "Chicago Rendezvous," op. cit.
31. "Jealousy," op. cit.
32. "Super Blues," *One Day at a Time*, originally broadcast 27 January 1976, CBS.
33. Ibid.
34. "All the Way," *One Day at a Time*, originally broadcast 10 February 1976, CBS.
35. Ibid.
36. Ibid.
37. Ibid.
38. Ibid.
39. Joseph D. Whitaker, "A National Outrage," *The Washington Post*, 22 March 1981, A1.
40. "The One Where Ross Got High," *Friends*, originally broadcast 11 November 1999, NBC.

Chapter 7

1. John J. O'Connor, "Is Norman Lear in a Rut?" *The New York Times*, 21 March 1976, 79.
2. Lear quoted in Arthur Unger, "Behind the hits," *The Christian Science Monitor*, 25 July 1974, 13.
3. Lear quoted in Lawrence Laurent, "Laugh or cry, it's still *Mary Hartman*," *The Washington Post*, 4 January 1976, 137.
4. Lear quoted in John J. O'Connor, "TV: Lear's *Mary Hartman*, Interesting Innovation," *The New York Times*, 6 January 1976, 38.
5. "Episode 001," *Mary Hartman, Mary Hartman*, originally broadcast 6 January 1976.
6. "Episode 002," *Mary Hartman, Mary Hartman*, originally broadcast 7 January 1976.
7. *Sexual Medicine Today* quoted in Bill O'Hallaren, "A Cute Tomato, A Couple of Slices of Baloney, Some Sour Grapes, A Few Nuts," *TV Guide*, 19 June 1976, 16–19.
8. "Episode 001," op. cit.
9. Ibid.
10. Bill O'Hallaren, op. cit.
11. Harry Castleman, Walter J. Podrazik, *Watching TV: Four Decades of American Television* (New York: McGraw-Hill Book Company, 1982), 277.
12. Les Brown, "*Mary Hartman* Series Is Doing Well," *The New York Times*, 30 January 1976, 64.
13. Ibid., 64.
14. Bill O'Hallaren, op. cit.
15. *Soap Opera Digest* quoted in Donna McCrohan, *Archie, Edith, Mike, and Gloria: The Tumultuous History of All in the Family* (New York: Workman Publishing, 1987), 147.
16. Bill O'Hallaren, op. cit.
17. Les Brown, op. cit.
18. Bill O'Hallaren, op. cit.
19. Knight quoted in O'Hallaren, Ibid., 16–19.
20. Benjamin Stein, *Dreemz* (New York: Harper & Row, Publishers, 1978), 75.
21. Lasser quoted in O'Hallaren, op. cit.
22. Bill Davidson, "Trouble in Paradise," *TV Guide*, 6 April 1974, 4–8.
23. Lear quoted in Laurent, op. cit.
24. John J. O'Connor, "TV Review: *Dumplings*, the Story of Fat, Loving Couple," *The New York Times*, 29 January 1976, 72.
25. Crenna quoted in Kenneth Turan, "Norman Lear's Washington," *The Washington Post*, 19 September 1976, 355.
26. Lear quoted in Turan, Ibid., 355.
27. Stein quoted in Turan, Ibid., 355.
28. "I, Done (2)," *The Fresh Prince of Bel-Air*, originally broadcast 20 May 1996, NBC.
29. Robert Goldberg, "New Fare from Norman Lear," *The Wall Street Journal*, 28 May 1991, A20.
30. Lear quoted in Joanne Ostrow, "*All in the Family* Creator Ready With New Controversy," *The Denver Post*, 24 May 1991, 1E.
31. Lear quoted in Ostrow, Ibid., 1E.
32. Lear quoted in Sam Roberts, "The Cranky Spirit of Archie Bunker Haunts This House," *The New York Times*, 19 December 1993, H33.
33. Ibid., H33.
34. "Ernie Live On Tape," *704 Hauser*, originally broadcast 25 April 1994, CBS.
35. Lear quoted in Ostrow, op. cit.

Bibliography

Books

Bogle, Donald. *Prime Time Blues: African Americans on Network Television*. New York: Farrar, Straus, and Giroux, 2001.

Brody, David et al. *America's History: Volume 2, Since 1865*. Worth Publishers: New York, 1993.

Brooks, Tim. Marsh, Earle. *The Complete Directory to Prime Time Network and Cable TV Shows, 1946-Present (8th edition)*. New York: Ballantine Books, 2003.

Cantor, Paul A. *Gilligan Unbound: Pop Culture in the Age of Globalization*. Lanham: Rowman & Littlefield Publishers, Inc., 2003.

Castleman, Harry. Podrazik, Walter J. *Watching TV: Four Decades of American Television*. New York: McGraw-Hill Book Company, 1982.

Chafe, William H. *The Paradox of Change: American Women in the 20th Century*. Oxford: Oxford University Press, 1991.

Cole, Elizabeth R. Press, Andrea L. *Speaking of Abortion: Television and Authority in the Lives of Women*. Chicago: The University of Chicago Press, 1999.

Cowan, Geoffrey. *See No Evil: The Backstage Battle Over Sex and Violence in Television*. New York: Simon and Schuster, 1979.

Frum, David. *How We Got Here: The '70s: The Decade That Brought You Modern Life — For Better or Worse*. New York: Basic Books, 2000.

Garner, Joe. *Made You Laugh: The Funniest Moments in Radio, Television, Stand-Up, and Movie Comedy*. Kansas City: Andrews McMeel Publishing, 2004.

Garrett, Betty. *Betty Garrett and Other Songs: A Life on Stage and Screen*. New York: Madison Books, 1998.

Griffin, Merv. *Merv*. New York: Simon and Schuster, 2003.

Gwinn, Alison. *Entertainment Weekly: The 100 Greatest TV Shows of All Time*. New York: Time, Inc., 1998.

Ingram, Billy. *TV Party: Television's Untold Tales*. Los Angeles: Bonus Books, 2002.

Jones, Gerard. *Honey, I'm Home! Sitcoms: Selling the American Dream*. New York: Grove Weidenfeld, 1992.

Laswell, Mark. *TV Guide: Fifty Years of Television*. New York: Crown Publishers, 2002.

MacDonald, J. Fred. *Blacks and White TV: Afro-Americans in Television Since 1948*. Chicago: Nelson-Hall Publishers, 1988.

_____. *One Nation Under Television: The Rise and Decline of Network TV*. New York: Pantheon Books, 1990.

Marc, David. *Comic Visions: Television Comedy & American Culture*. Oxford: Blackwell Publishers, Ltd., 1997.

Marsh, Spencer. *God, Man, and Archie Bunker*. New York: Harper & Row, Publishers, 1975.

McCrohan, Donna. *Archie, Edith, Mike, & Gloria: The Tumultuous History of All in the Family*. New York: Workman Publishing, 1987.

Ozersky, Josh. *Archie Bunker's America: TV in an Era of Change — 1968–1978*. Carbondale: Southern Illinois University Press, 2003.

Schulman, Bruce J. *The Seventies: The Great Shift in American Culture, Soci-*

ety, and Politics. Cambridge: Da Capo Press, 2001.

Smith, Sally Bedell. *In All His Glory: The Life of William S. Paley.* New York: Simon and Schuster, 1990.

Stein, Benjamin. *Dreemz.* New York: Harper & Row, Publishers, 1978.

Taylor, Ella. *Prime Time Families: Television Culture in Postwar America.* Berkeley: University of California Press, 1989.

Wellman, David T. *Portraits of White Racism.* Cambridge, Cambridge University Press, 1977.

Newspaper Articles

Aarons, Leroy. "'63 Civil Rights Tide Shows to Trickle." *The Washington Post.* 26 Aug 1973: A1.

"Abortion: A Gynecologist Explains His Tangled Thoughts." *The Chicago Tribune.* 1 Nov 1972: B3.

"Actor Celebrates 60th Anniversary." *The Los Angeles Times.* 23 Oct 1962: C8.

Adler, Dick. "He's the Bigot Next Door." *The New York Times.* 13 Jun 1971: D19.
_____. "Lear Kingdom: II." *The Los Angeles Times.* 23 Jan 1975: H1.

"*All in the Family* Leads Nielsen Again." *The Los Angeles Times.* 8 Nov 1972: D22.

Alpert, Don. "Yorkin and Lear Had It Made When Sinatra Blew the 'Horn.'" *The Los Angeles Times.* 7 Jul 1963: 139.

Alsop, Joseph. "Is It Really Worth It?" *The Washington Post.* 11 Feb 1972: A25.

Altman, Lawrence K. "Use of Commercial Blood Donors Increases With Shortage in U.S." *The New York Times.* 5 Sept 1970: 1.

Ames, Walter. "NBC Local Colorcast Demonstration Will NOT Be Seen on Home Sets." *The Los Angeles Times.* 27 Oct 1953: 24.
_____. "Reserve of Writers Belies Zany Antics of Martin and Lewis." *The Los Angeles Times.* 20 Jan 1952: D6.

"Another Suit At NBC." *The Washington Post.* 26 Mar 1976: B10.

Ashford, Robert. "Should Californians Decriminalize Marijuana Use?" *The Los Angeles Times.* 2 Nov 1972: B7.

Beaufort, John. "Viewing things: Britishisms." *The Christian Science Monitor.* 15 Aug 1970: 12.

Beck, Joan. "School for violence—it's home." *The Chicago Tribune.* 14 Mar 1977: C2.

Bedell, Sally. "Lear Plans to Be Full-Time Producer." *The New York Times.* 19 Apr 1983: C19.

Bell, Joseph N. "John Rich, the man behind ... *All in the Family.*" *The Christian Science Monitor.* 29 Jan 1974: F1.

Bender, Marylin. "Job Discrimination, 10 Years Later." *The New York Times.* 10 Nov 1974: 187.

Berkvist, Robert. "Anybody Here Seen Old Archie B?" *The New York Times.* 2 Jul 1972: D11.

Blau, Eleanor. "Birth-Control Drive Focuses on Teen-Agers." *The New York Times.* 23 Jul 1974: 39.
_____. "How David Dukes Solved a Problem in Playing *Bent.*" *The New York Times.* 13 Dec 1979: C17.

Blume, Mary. "French Cooperating on Bud Yorkin Film." *The Los Angeles Times.* 2 Aug 1968: G8.

Bookey, Ted. "Archie, Laura, Norman." *The New York Times.* 7 Nov 1971: D17.

Borowicz, Sandi. "The Tragic Problem of Child Abuse: We Can Help!" *The Los Angeles Times.* 12 Nov 1977: N10.

Brody, Jane E. "More Homosexuals Aided to Become Heterosexual." *The New York Times.* 28 Feb 1971: 1.

Bronfenbrenner, Urie. "The Calamitous Decline of the American Family." *The Washington Post.* 2 Jan 1977: 65.

Brothers, Joyce. "Why is teen getting drunk?" *The Chicago Tribune.* 7 Jan 1975: B4.

Brown, Les. "CBS Is Switching Some Programs." *The New York Times.* 5 Nov 1975: 87.
_____. "Lithium Use in *Maude,* Medical Issue." *The New York Times.* 22 Jan 1976: 52.
_____. "*Mary Hartman* Series Is Doing Well." *The New York Times.* 30 Jan 1976: 64.

_____. "Notes: *All in the Family* Is Up-rooted Again." *The New York Times.* 18 Apr 1976: 75.

_____. "Wood, C.B.S.-TV Head, Defends 'Mature' Shows." *The New York Times.* 16 Oct 1973: 87.

Buck, Jerry. "*All in the Family* affects other comedians." *The Washington Post.* 12 Sept 1971: 223.

Bunce, Alan. "TV: new 1972 series." *The Christian Science Monitor.* 19 Jan 1972: 6.

Burks, Edward C. "Middle-Class Whites Still Leaving City." *The New York Times.* 29 May 1973: 1.

"Busing — Facts and Fiction." *The New York Times.* 25 Feb 1972: 38.

"California Judge Extends Ruling Against I.Q. Tests." *The New York Times.* 29 Nov 1974: 53.

Campbell, Barbara. "Police Sergeant Charged With Failing to Respond During Youths' Rampage." *The New York Times.* 23 Feb 1974: 35.

"Candidates' Busing Views." *The New York Times.* 23 Feb 1972: 20.

Carmody, John. "All in the CPB Family." *The Washington Post.* 20 Jan 1976: C4.

_____. "*Jeffersons*: High in the Nielsens." *The Washington Post.* 22 Jan 1975: B7.

_____. "*Maude.*" *The Washington Post.* 11 Sept 1973: B1.

_____. "The Problem Drinkers' Problems." *The Washington Post.* 6 Jan 1973: E7.

_____. "The TV Column." *The Washington Post.* 22 Jan 1986: C8.

"CBS Accused of 'Betrayal.'" *The Los Angeles Times.* 1 Dec 1972: D28.

"C.B.S. Comes Out on Top In Second Nielsen Report." *The New York Times.* 5 Oct 1971: 83.

Champlin, Charles. "A Renaissance of Film Originals?" *The Los Angeles Times.* 28 Apr 1967: E16.

Ching, Frank. "Street Crime Casts a Poll of Fear Over Chinatown." *The New York Times.* 19 Jan 1974: 16.

Cimons, Marlene. "Women Candidates See Feminism As Aid." *The Los Angeles Times.* 6 Nov 1972: OC_B1.

Conyers Jr., John. "Jobless Numbers." *The New York Times.* 1 Jan 1976: 17.

Cook, Joan. "Bergen Takings Steps to Curb Child Abuse." *The New York Times.* 8 Jun 1977: 75.

"Court Suggests Foster Homes For Abused Children." *The Washington Post.* 2 Jan 1977: 34.

Deeb, Gary. "CBS and NBC breathe easier as the midseason shuffle pulls ratings." *The Chicago Tribune.* 31 Jan 1975: B14.

_____. "The Midseason TV shuffle." *The Chicago Tribune.* 12 Jan 1975: H4.

_____. "Now the Jeffersons battle Nielsens, not the Bunkers." *The Chicago Tribune.* 17 Jan 1975: B13.

"Display Ad 52 — No Title." *The New York Times.* 26 Jan 1971: 66.

"Display Ad 59 — No Title." *The New York Times.* 14 May 1971: 84.

Donnelly, Tom. "Mirth and Maude." *The Washington Post.* 5 Dec 1972: B1.

_____. "Norman Lear and His Funny Breakthrough Factory." *The Washington Post.* 23 Feb 1975: 125.

_____. "On Toppling Taboos in Tandem." *The Washington Post.* 9 Mar 1973: B1.

_____. "These Soaps Don't Wash." *The Washington Post.* 24 Jan 1976: 133.

Dreyfuss, Joel. "All in the (Black) Family." *The Washington Post.* 18 Jan 1975: B1.

_____. "Television Controversy: Covering the Black Experience." *The Washington Post.* 1 Sept 1974: K1.

"Edith's cousin." *The Christian Science Monitor.* 9 Sept 1972: 6.

Elderkin, Phil. "Change of pace: *All in the Family.*" *The Christian Science Monitor.* 3 Dec 1971: 20.

Ellis, Harry B. "Food prices slow their upward climb." *The Christian Science Monitor.* 22 May 1974: 1.

Favre, George H. "US homosexuals assert 'rights.'" *The Christian Science Monitor.* 5 Aug 1970: 4.

Feldman, Donald P. "Maude's Abortion." *The New York Times.* 24 Dec 1972: D13.

Ferretti, Fred. "TV: Are Racism and Bigotry Funny?" *The New York Times.* 12 Jan 1971: 70.

"43% of Marriages Interracial in Hawaii." *The Washington Post.* 21 Jan 1975: A7.

Fitzpatrick, Mike. "Has something gone wrong?" *The Chicago Tribune.* 29 Sept 1977: B2.

Fraser, C. Gerald. "Spinoff." *The New York Times.* 26 Sept 1982: G6.

Gardella, Kay. "He's golden as Archie: O'Connor now a TV institution." *The Chicago Tribune.* 12 Sept 1982: H5.

Gardener, Paul. "The Quick Redd Foxx Jumps Into a New Kettle of Fish." *The New York Times.* 6 Feb 1972: D19.

Gaver, Jack. "Jacks-of-All-Trades Hit Jackpot on Television." *The Los Angeles Times.* 29 Apr 1955: 34.

Gent, George. *"All in the Family* Takes First Place In Nielsen Ratings." *The New York Times.* 25 May 1971: 79.

_____. "C.B.S. Gives Reasoner Show to Morley Safer, London Chief." *The New York Times.* 18 Nov 1970: 95.

_____. "Scott and Lee Grant Get Best-Acting Emmys." *The New York Times.* 10 May 1971: 67.

Gieger, Carol. "Maude's Abortion Was No Joke." *The New York Times.* 24 Dec 1972: D8.

Gilliam, Dorothy. "The Racial Trap In Black Sit-Coms." *The Washington Post.* 14 May 1978: A1.

Goldberg, Robert. "New Fare from Norman Lear." *The Wall Street Journal.* 28 May 1991: A20.

"Good Times is a third generation series." *The Washington Post.* 3 Feb 1974: TC7.

Goodman Jr., George. "I.Q. Scores Linked To Environment." *The New York Times.* 22 Jan 1974: 16.

Gorner, Peter. "Exploring a Phenomenon." *The Chicago Tribune.* 15 Nov 1972: B1.

Gould, Jack. "Can Bigotry Be Laughed Away? It's Worth a Try." *The New York Times.* 21 Feb 1971: D15.

_____. "TV: *Fonda and Family.*" *The New York Times.* 7 Feb 1962: 56.

Gysel, Dean. "ABC to Make Bold Move." *The Los Angeles Times.* 15 Aug 1968: E29.

Haggerty, Sandra. "TV: The World in Fantasy." *The Los Angeles Times.* 14 Feb 1975: C7.

Hall, Carla. "Marla Gibbs, Maid for TV." *The Washington Post.* 30 Oct 1978: A1.

Hano, Arnold. "Can Archie Bunker Give Bigotry a Bad Name?" *The New York Times.* 12 Mar 1972: SM32.

_____. "Why Archie Is So Lovable." *The Chicago Tribune.* 12 Mar 1972: A1.

Harmetz, Aljean. "Lean Plans 8 to 10 Films a Year From His New Embassy Studio." *The New York Times.* 20 Jan 1982: C19.

_____. "Maude Didn't Leave 'em All Laughing." *The New York Times.* 10 Dec 1972: D3.

Harmetz, Aljean. "Norman Lear Returning to Sitcom Land." *The New York Times.* 31 Jan 1984: C18.

Harrison, Bennett. Spring, William. Vietorisz, Thomas. "Crisis of the *under*employed — In much of the inner city 60% don't earn enough for a decent standard of living." *The New York Times.* 5 Nov 1972: SM42.

Hartigan, Patti. "Lear's looking for revival." *The Boston Globe.* 31 May 1991: NOPGCIT.

Hazlett, Bill. "Juvenile Gangs: Violence and Fatal Assaults on Increase." *The Los Angeles Times.* 14 Apr 1974: A1.

"Health board data cited: 11% of '75 births to girls under age 18." *The Chicago Tribune.* 29 Apr 1977: B10.

Henniger, Daniel. "Norman Lear Goes Latino." *The Wall Street Journal.* 7 Mar 1984: 28.

Hess, John L. "The Macaroni and Cheese Are What's Wrong." *The New York Times.* 12 Jan 1974: 39.

Hobson, Christopher Z. "Letter to the Editor 4 — No Title." *The New York Times.* 7 Nov 1971: D17.

Hobson, Laura Z. "As I Listened to Archie Say 'Hebe' ..." *The New York Times.* 12 Sept 1971: D1.

Honeycutt, Kirk. "We Ran Out of Controversy." *The New York Times.* 16 Apr 1978: 103.

Hopper, Hedda. "Comedy Writers Sign for Two Films." *The Chicago Tribune.* 6 Dec 1962: C15.

_____. "Darin Considered for Movie Lead." *The Los Angeles Times.* 15 Apr 1961: A6.

_____. "Looking at Hollywood: Dean

Martin, Lana Turner to Do *Who's Got Action?*" *The Chicago Tribune.* 31 Aug 1961: B8.

_____. "Van Dyke to Star in Divorce Story." *The Los Angeles Times.* 10 Mar 1965: D11.

_____. "Yorkin and Lear Buy Travel Company." *The Los Angeles Times.* 9 Mar 1961: B10.

Houston, Jack. "100,000 more each year: Ranks of alcoholism grow." *The Chicago Tribune.* 20 Mar 1974: C11.

Jensen, Michael C. "Young Millionaires Are Big Contributors to McGovern." *The New York Times.* 23 Aug 1972: 29.

Johnson, Haynes. "Why Pull the Plug On Our Blue-Collar Political Philosopher?" *The Washington Post.* 15 May 1983: A1.

Kart, Larry. "Comedy." *The Chicago Tribune.* 23 Jan 1983: D24.

Kasindorf, Martin. "Archie and Maude and Fred and Norman and Alan." *The New York Times.* 24 Jun 1973: 226.

Kendall, John. "What Will Stop Violence? Board Asks." *The Los Angeles Times.* 24 Jan 1974: B1.

Kessler, Judith L. "*Sanford and Son*: Change in Comedy." *The Washington Post.* 14 Jan 1972: B1.

Kirby, David. "Sitcom City." *The New York Times.* 26 Oct 1997: CY3.

Klein, Frederick C. "Giving Up: To Many Ghetto Blacks A Steady Job Becomes Only a Distant Hope." *The Wall Street Journal.* 15 Nov 1976: 1.

Krebs, Albin. "Giscard Endorsed by Servan-Schreiber." *The New York Times.* 15 May 1974: 51.

Kriegsman, Alan M. "Yeah, Funny — But Revolutionary?" *The Washington Post.* 15 Jan 1972: D5.

Landro, Laura. "Coca-Cola to Expand Its Entertainment Line." *The Wall Street Journal.* 12 Jul 1985: 6.

Laurent, Lawrence. "Archie Bunker has two kinds of viewers." *The Washington Post.* 19 Dec 1971: 193.

_____. "Controversial comedies win high ratings." *The Washington Post.* 4 Feb 1973: TVC9.

_____. "Laugh or cry, it's still *Mary Hart-*

man." *The Washington Post.* 4 Jan 1976: 137.

_____. "*Maude* is the flip side of Archie Bunker." *The Washington Post.* 8 Oct 1972: TC5.

_____. "Redd Foxx gets out of the blue to play a funny junk dealer in *Sanford and Son.*" *The Washington Post.* 6 Feb 1972: TC5.

_____. "A 'second banana' gets a shot at stardom." *The Washington Post.* 2 Jun 1974: TC5.

Lavin, Cheryl. "She's basking in her own *Gloria.*" *The Chicago Tribune.* 3 Oct 1982: J1.

Lear, Norman. "As I Read How Laura Saw Archie..." *The New York Times.* 10 Oct 1971: D17.

_____. "Laughing While We Face Our Prejudices." *The New York Times.* 11 Apr 1971: D22.

Levine, Richard M. "As The TV World Turns." *The New York Times.* 14 Dec 1975: SM6.

Lichtenstein, Grace. "C.B.S. Head to Speak Out on TV's Rights." *The New York Times.* 26 Sept 1973: 82.

"A Limited Appeal for Black Shows." *The New York Times.* 29 Dec 1998: A12.

Locke, Maggie. "Experts believe only a few of total child abuse cases are reported." *The Washington Post.* 24 Mar 1977: D_C_12.

Lordner, George. "Dingbats, Teach-Ins: Taking on Phase II." *The Washington Post.* 18 Feb 1972: C10.

MacGregor, James. "ABC Ratings — Parity Plan Seen on Target; Network No. 2 in Third TV-Season Week." *The Wall Street Journal.* 12 Oct 1971: 4.

Mannes, Marya. "Whose Right to What Life?" *The New York Times.* 22 Nov 1972: 35.

Marron, Sheila. "Not For Laughs." *The New York Times.* 24 Dec 1972: D8.

Martin, Betty. "Movie Call Sheet: Actress Jean Stapleton Signed for Film Role." *The Los Angeles Times.* 7 Jul 1969: C14.

Martin, Judith. "A Sudsy Satire, A Dose of Reality." *The Washington Post.* 8 Jan 1976: G1.

McCabe, Bruce. "The return of Norman Lear." *The Boston Globe*. 2 Jun 1991: NOPGCIT.

McGarry, Terrance W. "A Star-Studded Day in Superior Court." *The Washington Post*. 24 Jun 1974: B12.

Morgan, Thomas. "Norman Lear Starts Off Museum Lecture Series." *The New York Times*. 16 Jun 1986: C16.

Moss, Robert F. "The Shrinking Life Span of the Black Sitcom." *The New York Times*. 25 Feb 2001: AR19.

"New Approach Needed: Revise Juvenile Court System, Jurist Urges." *The Los Angeles Times*. 14 Apr 1974: A1.

"NOW Suit Over *Maude* Abortion Shows Denied." *The Los Angeles Times*. 25 Nov 1972: A3.

O'Basta, Mrs. James. "Violence against children." *The Chicago Tribune*. 9 May 1977: C2.

"O'Connor isn't like Archie but he kind of likes the guy." *The Washington Post*. 12 Sept 1971: 225.

O'Connor, John J. "At One Time You Couldn't Say 'W.C.'" *The New York Times*. 15 Oct 1972: E9.

_____. "In Archie Bunker's Old House, a New Family Spins Jokes." *The New York Times*. 11 Apr 1994: C18.

_____. "Norman Lear's Comedy On Life in Washington." *The New York Times*. 6 Mar 1992: C32.

_____. "These Little Pressure Groups Went to Market — With a Club." *The New York Times*. 2 Sept 1973: 97.

_____. "TV: Bad Times Hit *Good Times*." *The New York Times*. 23 Mar 1977: 80.

_____. "TV: Lear's *Jeffersons*." *The New York Times*. 17 Jan 1975: 67.

_____. "TV: Lear's *Mary Hartman*, Interesting Innovation." *The New York Times*. 6 Jan 1976: 38.

_____. "TV: *Maude*, a Comedy, Will Make Debut Tonight." *The New York Times*. 12 Sept 1972: 90.

_____. "TV: *One Day at a Time*." *The New York Times*. 16 Dec 1975: 79.

_____. "TV Review: DeLuise, Diana Rigg Star in New Shows." *The New York Times*. 11 Sept 1973: 91.

_____. "TV Review: *Dumplings*, the Story of Fat, Loving Couple." *The New York Times*. 29 Jan 1976: 72.

_____. "TV Review: *Hot L Baltimore* Signs ABC Register at 9." *The New York Times*. 24 Jan 1975: 63.

_____. "TV: Shockley vs. Innis." *The New York Times*. 13 Dec 1973: 95.

_____. "TV View: Is Norman Lear in a Rut?" *The New York Times*. 21 Mar 1976: 79.

_____. "The Year Archie Bunker Came In and Lawrence Welk Went Out." *The New York Times*. 2 Jan 1972: D13.

_____. "Yesterday's Taboos Are Taken for Granted Now." *The New York Times*. 7 Nov 1982: 107.

Ostrow, Joanne. "*All in the Family* creator ready with new controversy." *The Denver Post*. 24 May 1991: 1E.

Overbea, Luis. "U.S. busing advocate reverses stand." *The Christian Science Monitor*. 16 Jul 1975: 6.

Petersen, Clarence. "CBS Debuts Courageous New Comedy." *The Chicago Tribune*. 12 Jan 1971: A9.

Prial, Frank J. "CBS-TV Is Dropping Archie Bunker." *The New York Times*. 12 May 1983: C24.

Pullen, Emma. "Youth Violence, Crime Increasing Sharply." *The Los Angeles Times*. 20 Mar 1977: B1.

Ranzal, Edward. "Homosexuals Bill Protecting Rights Is Killed by Council: Homosexuals Bill Killed in Council." *The New York Times*. 28 Jan 1972: 1.

Raskin, A.H. "Unemployment: 6 Pct. Is Only the Tip of the Iceberg." *The New York Times*. 25 Jun 1972: E4.

Raspberry, William. "Black Students and the Zero Sum Game." *The Washington Post*. 30 Sept 1974: A27.

_____. "Putting Standardized Tests to the Test." *The Washington Post*. 12 Jun 1974: A29.

_____. "Question of Momentum." *The Washington Post*. 3 Mar 1972: A27.

"Ratings dominated by CBS." *The Chicago Tribune*. 25 Dec 1975: E11.

Richards, David. "The Latest Stage of Esther Rolle." *The Washington Post*. 11 Nov 1986: B1.

"Rival for *All in the Family*." *The Washington Post.* 21 Dec 1971: C5.

Roberts, Sam. "The Cranky Spirit of Archie Bunker Haunts This House." *The New York Times.* 19 Dec 1993: H33.

Rosenberg, Howard. "Tribute To TV's Favorite Bigot." *The Los Angeles Times.* 18 May 1983: G1.

"Roxie Roker, 66, Who Broke Barrier on TV's *Jeffersons*." *The New York Times.* 6 Dec 1995: B17.

Ryan, Joan. "Amos: Bad Times." *The Washington Post.* 4 May 1976: B10.

"Sale by Lear of Coke Shares." *The New York Times.* 6 Jul 1985: 29.

Scheuer, Philip K. "New *Horn* Blown by Lear and Yorkin." *The Los Angeles Times.* 9 Oct 1962: C9.

Servi, Vera. "Florida's now on her own." *The Chicago Tribune.* 3 Feb 1974: 59.

Shales, Tom. "Dingbat's Demise: Life After Edith Bunker." *The Washington Post.* 1 Nov 1980: A1.

_____. "*The Dumplings*: Shrill Overkill.'" *The Washington Post.* 28 Jan 1976: C10.

_____. "*Good Times*: A Rich And Natural Comedy." *The Washington Post.* 16 Sept 1975: B1.

_____. "*Good Times* Is Coming And It's All in the Family." *The Washington Post.* 8 Feb 1974: B1.

_____. "*Hot L*: When Less Is More." *The Washington Post.* 21 Feb 1975: B15.

_____. "Perfectly Lear." *The Washington Post.* 4 Mar 1984: A1.

_____. "Tonight: Edith Bunker's Ordeal." *The Washington Post.* 16 Oct 1977: 117.

_____. "TV: A Massive Spring Facelift?" *The Washington Post.* 9 Jan 1972: G1.

Sheldon, Courtney R. "McGovern faces tough Nixon fight." *The Christian Science Monitor.* 1 Aug 1972: 1.

Sills, E. James. "No, For Medical, Social Good." *The Los Angeles Times.* 2 Nov 1972: B7.

Smith, Cecil. "An Award for the Award Show." *The Los Angeles Times.* 28 Mar 1960: A12.

_____. "Bigotry Used as a Laughing Matter." *The Los Angeles Times.* 12 Jan 1971: G12.

_____. "Divorce as the Children See It." *The Los Angeles Times.* 19 Jan 1976: E14.

_____. "Is Edith Queen or Pawn of TV?" *The Los Angeles Times.* 21 Oct 1977: K35.

_____. "*The Jeffersons*: it's another in the long line of Lear series." *The Los Angeles Times.* 19 Jan 1975: M1.

_____. "Kaye Show Reflects Yorkin-Lear Magic." *The Los Angeles Times.* 7 Nov 1961: A11.

_____. "Maude's Abortion Evokes Protests." *The Los Angeles Times.* 29 Nov 1972: D25.

_____. "A Really Good *Good Times*." *The Los Angeles Times.* 30 Dec 1975: F11.

_____. "Television Review: The Rape of Edith Bunker." *The Los Angeles Times.* 13 Oct 1977: OC_A1.

Smith, Sally Bedell. "Lear Fears Loss for Viewers If TV Networks Gain Power." *The New York Times.* 22 Sept 1983: C16.

Steiger, Paul E. "Consumers urged to Battle Inflation." *The Los Angeles Times.* 27 May 1974: A1.

Stein, Benjamin. "Another Divorcee and Her Problems." *The Wall Street Journal.* 12 Dec 1975: 14.

_____. "Disaster in Baltimore." *The Wall Street Journal.* 13 Feb 1975: 16.

Stern, Michael. "Real Factory Pay Here in 1974 Cut 5.1% by Inflation and Taxes." *The New York Times.* 1 Jan 1975: 40.

Stone, Judy. "She Gave Archie His First Comeuppance." *The New York Times.* 19 Nov 1972: D17.

_____. "What's It Like Being the Wife of a Bigot?" *The New York Times.* 29 Aug 1971: D13.

"Stood Up — Again." *The Washington Post.* 9 May 1974: B3.

Sweeney, Joan. "State May Expand Plan on Illegitimate Children." *The Los Angeles Times.* 1 Nov 1972: D8A.

"Tandem Sets New Schedule." *The Los Angeles Times.* 6 Jan 1966: E12.

"The cost of everything — UP." *The Chicago Tribune.* 1 Jan 1975: E16.

Trescott, Jacqueline, "For Frances Lear, Life Is Not All in the Family." *The Washington Post.* 13 Mar 1976: B1.

_____. "Images and *Good Times*." *The Washington Post.* 5 Apr 1975: D1.

_____. "Roxie Roker: Movin' On Up." *The Washington Post.* 3 Mar 1976: E1.

Trooger, Hal. "Drop Escalator Clauses." *The Chicago Tribune.* 25 Jun 1974: 10.

Turan, Kenneth. "Norman Lear's Washington." *The Washington Post.* 19 Sept 1976: 355.

"TV and Censorship." *The Washington Post.* 9 Feb 1972: D9.

"22 Youths Arrested in Bronx Gang Raid." *The New York Times.* 12 Jan 1974: 36.

Unger, Arthur. "Are those network series improving?" *The Christian Science Monitor.* 7 Oct 1974: 14.

_____. "Behind the hits: Norman Lear, producer of caustic, top-rated series." *The Christian Science Monitor.* 25 Jul 1974: 13.

_____. "Black family portrait." *The Christian Science Monitor.* 7 Feb 1974: 18.

_____. "Distorted values with a few easy laughs." *The Christian Science Monitor.* 3 Dec 1975: 39.

_____. "Esther Rolle: 'We laugh at ourselves.'" *The Christian Science Monitor.* 7 Feb 1974: 18.

_____. "Is Norman Lear's new series his 'morality crisis'?" *The Christian Science Monitor.* 22 Dec 1975: 26.

_____. "Meet 'George Jefferson.'" *The Christian Science Monitor.* 23 Apr 1975: 25.

_____. "Network-ratings king CBS adds only four series." *The Christian Science Monitor.* 24 Jan 1975: 13.

_____. "Norman Lear: A producer views the family-hour ruling." *The Christian Science Monitor.* 10 Nov 1976: 20.

_____. "Norman Lear entry features rotund couple." *The Christian Science Monitor.* 26 Jan 1976: 22.

_____. "TV looks at child abuse." *The Christian Science Monitor.* 3 Oct 1977: 23.

_____. "TV's 'new' season starts tonight." *The Christian Science Monitor.* 11 Jan 1974: 14.

_____. "Worth noting on TV." *The Christian Science Monitor.* 16 Jan 1986: 27.

Uviller, Rena K. "Child-Abuse and Snooping." *The New York Times.* 20 Apr 1977: 21.

Van Buren, Abigail. "Working Wives Do Double Time." *The Los Angeles Times.* 27 Jan 1977: F6.

Vanocur, Sander. "Foxxy ABC Is Gathering Stars." *The Washington Post.* 9 Apr 1976: 29.

_____. "Lear's *One Day*: Another 'Sure' Winner." *The Washington Post.* 16 Dec 1975: C1.

_____. "Not Your Basic Soft Soap." *The Washington Post.* 4 Jan 1976: 133.

_____. "Strange Bedfellows." *The Washington Post.* 22 Feb 1976: 113.

Vecsey, George. "Many Nassau Elderly Find Only Isolation in Suburbia." *The New York Times.* 4 Dec 1973: 95.

Vince, Raymond J. "Drugs and alcohol." *The Chicago Tribune.* 30 Jan 1973: 8.

Voight, Mrs. Bonnie. "Not Real." *The New York Times.* 24 Dec 1972: D8.

Von Hoffman, Nicholas. "*Brown vs.*: Not as Clear as Black and White." *The Washington Post.* 17 May 1974: D1.

_____. "The Compromising Convention." *The Chicago Tribune.* 17 Jul 1972: 22.

Wall Street Journal Staff Reporter. "CBS to Add Comedy By Norman Lear to Prime-Time Slot." *The Wall Street Journal.* 5 Nov 1975: 12.

Weiler, A.H. "News of the Screen." *The New York Times.* 22 Sept 1974: 55.

_____. "No Gap Like the Generation Gap." *The New York Times.* 6 Jul 1969: D11.

Whitaker, Joseph D. "A National Outrage." *The Washington Post.* 22 Mar 1981: A1.

Wood, Daniel B. "A Voice of Decency in TV." *The Christian Science Monitor.* 29 Dec 1989: 10.

Woods, William C. "*All in the Family*." *The Washington Post.* 13 Jan 1971: B3.

Zolotow, Maurice. "The Great Martin-Lewis Feud." *The Washington Post.* 20 Jun 1954: AW7.

Television Shows

All in the Family
All's Fair
Archie Bunker's Place

The Beverly Hillbillies
Commander in Chief
The Cosby Show
Desperate Housewives
The Dick Van Dyke Show
The Dumplings
The Fresh Prince of Bel-Air
Friends
Gloria
The Golden Girls
Good Times
Green Acres
Hot L Baltimore
I Dream of Jeannie
The Jeffersons
Julia
The Martin and Lewis Show
Mary Hartman, Mary Hartman
Maude
Murphy Brown
One Day at a Time
Sanford
Sanford and Son
704 Hauser
Soap
thirtysomething
Three's Company
Till Death Us Do Part
227
Will and Grace

Personal Interviews

Franklin Cover
Marla Gibbs
Susan Harris
Rue McClanahan
Bill Macy
Lou Richards

Websites

http://awpublisher.com/heroes.html
http://www.homestead.com/shb/rolle.ht
ml
http://www.jimiizrael.com/ji/2005/04/06
/11.56.04/index.html#more
www.famous.adoption.com/famous/lear-
frances.html
www.roctober.com/roctober/greatness/fo
xx.html

Magazines and Journals

Barber, Rowland. "No Time for Jivin.'"
    TV Guide. 14–20 Dec 1974: 28–32.
Barber, Rowland. "Through Queens with
    Pad and Pencil." *TV Guide.* 30 Aug–5
    Sept 1975: 16–21.
Davidson, Bill. "Trouble in Paradise
    (First of Two Parts)." *TV Guide.* 6–12
    Apr 1974: 4–8.
_____. "The Uprising in Lear's Kingdom
    (Second of Two Parts)." *TV Guide.*
    13–19 Apr 1974: 12–17.
Flatley, Guy. "Gene, for heaven's sake,
    help me!" *TV Guide.* 18–24 Nov 1972:
    28–32.
Gill, Brendan. "The 'Loudmouthed Creep
    ... Will Be Joining Rhett Butler and
    Huckleberry Finn.'" *TV Guide.* 3–9
    Sept 1983: 38–40.
Greenfield, Jeff. "Situation Comedies: Are
    They Getting Better — or Worse?" *TV
    Guide.* 24–30 May 1980: 4–8.
Gross, Leonard. "Do The Bigots Miss the
    Message?" *TV Guide.* 8–14 Nov 1975:
    14–18.
Hall, Jane. "Old, Bold and Angry." *TV
    Guide.* 21–27 Jun 1975: 3–5.
Hano, Arnold. "The man under the hard
    hat." *TV Guide.* 20–26 Nov 1971: 29–34.
"He Has Become a Household Face." *TV
    Guide.* 12–18 Jan 1974: 21–26.
Hobson, Dick. "Up From the Ghetto." *TV
    Guide.* 21–27 Jun 1975: 20–22.
"It's 5:30 in Studio 41 ..." *TV Guide.* 15–21
    Jun 1974: 14–16.
Kasindorf, Jeanie. "It's Better Than a Stu-
    dio Tour." *TV Guide.* 14–20 Dec 1974:
    24–26.
"Letters." *TV Guide.* 6–12 Feb 1971:
    22–24.
Lewis, Richard Warren. "There Is No One
    Else Like Me!" *TV Guide.* 24–30 Apr
    1976: 18–22.
O'Connor, Carroll. "I Regret Nothing Ex-
    cept My Own Anger." *TV Guide.* 22–28
    Sept 1979: 26–30.
_____. "What It Meant to Be Archie." *TV
    Guide.* 3–9 Sept 1983: 26–31.
O'Daniel, Michael. "Everything a Per-
    former Could Ask For." *TV Guide.*
    14–20 Feb 1976, 18–20.

O'Hallaren, Bill. "A Cute Tomato, A Couple of Slices of Baloney, Some Sour Grapes, A Few Nuts..." *TV Guide.* 19–25 Jun 1976: 16–19.

_____. "It could have been the kiss of death." *TV Guide.* 17–23 May 1980: 23–26.

"100 Most Memorable TV Moments." *TV Guide.* 5–11 December 2004: 31–48.

Raddatz, Leslie. "George Bernard Shaw Loved Hermione ... Maddeley." *TV Guide.* 29 Mar–4 Apr 1975: 10–12.

Riley, John. "Esther Rolle the Fishin' Pole." *TV Guide.* 29 Jun–5 Jul 1974: 16–18.

Robinson, Louie. *Ebony.* June 1974.

Rosenzweig, Jane. "Can TV Improve Us?" *The American Prospect* vol. 10 no. 45, 1 Jul–1 Aug 1999.

Russell, Dick. "Fortunately, there was a doctor in the house." *TV Guide.* 5–11 Aug 1978: 24–29.

Stump, Al. "Steady Work for a Former Floater." *TV Guide.* 16–22 Jun 1973: 26–31.

Turan, Kenneth. "Archie and Edith and Meathead and Gloria: A *Family* Journal." *TV Guide.* 3–9 Sept 1983: 32–36.

Washington, Mary Helen. "As their blackness disappears, so does their character." *TV Guide.* 30 Jul–5 Aug 1983: 4–9.

Whitney, Dwight. "An American institution rolls on." *TV Guide.* 6–12 Jan 1979: 14–18.

_____. "The Boy Next Door — to the Bunkers." *TV Guide.* 2–8 Jun 1973: 28–32.

_____. "For the Dingbat, *These* Are the Days." *TV Guide.* 27 May–2 Jun 1972: 21–26.

_____. "Portrait of an Overachiever." *TV Guide.* 24–30 Jul 1976: 33–35.

_____. "Sherman Hemsley: Don't ask how he lives or what he believes in." *TV Guide:* 6–12 Feb 1982: 30–35.

_____. "Why Archie Survives." *TV Guide.* 8–14 Aug 1981: 28–30.

Documentaries

All in the Family 20th Anniversary Special. 1991. CBS.

E! True Hollywood Story: All in the Family. 2000. E!

E! True Hollywood Story: Good Times. 2000. E!

100 Most Memorable Moments. 2004. TV Land.

Prime Time Politics. 2004. TV Land.

TV Land Moguls. 2004. TV Land.

Index